Sam Harris

Critical Responses

In This Series

In Preparation

Sam Harris

Critical Responses

EDITED BY

SANDRA WOIEN

OPEN UNIVERSE
Chicago

Volume 2 in the series, Critical Responses®, edited by Sandra Woien

To find out more about Open Universe and Carus Books, visit our website at www.carusbooks.com.

Printed and bound in the United States of America. Printed on acid-free paper.

Sam Harris: Critical Responses

ISBN: 978-1-63770-024-2

This book is also available as an e-book (978-1-63770-025-9).

Library of Congress Control Number 2021941781

To Joe

Contents

Contents

Contents

Acknowledgments

Many thanks to David Ramsay Steele for making this book possible and for his reliable and astute guidance.

Fred Feldman warrants my warmest appreciation. He has taught me much about well-being throughout the years, and now in retirement, he still generously shared his insights and provided helpful criticism of my chapter. I am also grateful to Shawn Klein and Saoirse Mooney for taking the time to share their comments.

I am especially grateful to Professor Dan Wallace. Before this volume, I had no contact with him, but in a pinch, I reached out. It was a wise decision, for he was generous in sharing his wealth of expertise.

All the contributors also deserve appreciation. This book wouldn't be possible without you, so thank you for contributing and for being a pleasure to work with throughout this process.

Why Sam Harris Matters

STEPHEN R.C. HICKS

Sam Harris has carved out, justifiably, a place in the first rank of our public intellectuals.

He is most well-known for his loose association with Christopher Hitchens, Daniel Dennett, and Richard Dawkins to mount a powerful critique against contemporary manifestations of religion. The New Atheists took on repackaged and, in some cases, evolved forms of religious belief and argued they were false, immoral, and out of place in modern scientific and progressive reality.

Yet Harris's real significance is broader than that important-but-narrow front in the culture wars. His work covers core issues in morality, free will, the nature of consciousness, religious history, psychedelics, artificial intelligence, and the implications of all of those for social theory and politics. He is a comprehensive thinker.

But comprehensive thinkers were largely out of fashion during the twentieth century, for deeply philosophical reasons. The idea of making an intellectual system—or of crossing major disciplinary boundaries—or, for specialist thinkers, of forthrightly applying one's narrow technical knowledge and methods to broader issues—that idea was largely dismissed as outmoded or pretentious.

Such was the state of affairs that by the middle of the twentieth century C.P. Snow's famous Two Cultures thesis took the world by storm. Intellectual culture, Snow argued, was dysfunctionally split into two opposing camps—roughly the scientists and the art-and-literature types. Scientists studied the natural world, prized rigor, and were optimistically progressive. By contrast, the art-and-literature types explored messy people, espoused non-rational and even irrational practices, and were cynically pessimistic.

The turf was divided into two opposing domains, each with its own methods and conclusions—and disdainful of the other. *You scientists,* the artsy types would say accusingly, *are merely white-coated drones who feel safe in your labs but have apparently never read a poem or had wild sex. Try living for a change.* And the advocates for science would retort, *You artists are mostly unwashed bohemians on drugs half the time, throwing paint at a canvas and trying to screw anything that moves. Try growing up.*

More seriously, though, the diagnosis did point to a problem for intellectual life. Each sub-culture had evolved away from the other to the point that, say, a scientist could think himself (or, increasingly, herself) highly educated even though he or she had no knowledge of Goethe and Dostoevsky, the French Revolution, and Post-Impressionism. Or a humanist could be considered PhD-worthy without having the least insight into calculus, genetics, or thermodynamics.

It wasn't just that reality is complex and intellectuals need to have specialties. It was that each side of the divide thought the gulf was *in principle* unbridgeable—and that the other side was *irrelevant* to grasping the truly significant issues.

Fast-forward to the end of the twentieth century, when a young Sam Harris was traveling the world and then returning to university to finish his formal education.

Much of the arts and humanities had descended further in vacuous postmodernism and associated nihilisms, though the sciences had continued their impressive progress. Yet there was widespread recognition of a vacuum to be filled. The two-cultures dynamic had stalled, the two camps were not talking to each other—and the impasse was unimpressive to a new generation of thinkers with more comprehensive ambition and a willingness to make a fresh start.

This new generation was forming a Third Culture, to use science journalist John Brockman's label for it. The emerging view was that humanistic questions *need* scientific insight to be understood and resolved more fully, and that science is itself a *deeply* humanist enterprise, by and for passionate and fully engaged human beings.

This was not an entirely new phenomenon. It was a twenty-first century reinvigoration of the Renaissance and Enlightenment conception of the arts and the sciences as integrated. Think of the universal ambition and the integrated scope of Leonardo da Vinci's projects. Think of Michelangelo's humanistic-ideal art works made possible in significant part only by his detailed empirical anatomical studies. Or think of Francis Bacon's "Knowledge is power"—the power to unveil all of nature's secrets and to apply them to the full range of human aspirations.

But who is best positioned to build the bridge, cross it, and fill the vacuum of the Two Cultures? As it is the scientists who actually have the most real-world focus and the proven track record of solving problems and improving the human condition, we should expect it will be scientifically trained thinkers who, disproportionately, make up the Third Culture. Hence the trend inaugurated late in the twentieth century by science-rooted intellectuals such as Stephen Jay Gould, E.O. Wilson, Carl Sagan, and Douglas Hofstadter *forthrightly* applying their insights and methods beyond their disciplinary confines.

Sam Harris's scholarly base is in the biological sciences, with a PhD in neuroscience. That combines with his undergraduate degree in philosophy and his travels to the far East to experience first-hand its traditions of religion. That positions him with the knowledge-set and the skill-set with which—aided by a considerable dose of chutzpah—to launch his comprehensive intellectual project.

Whether Harris's particular positions on the big issues are correct is not the key point here. His significance is in his project of explaining (or explaining away, sometimes) the whole shebang by applying the best of science and scientific method to those humanistic questions. That is the future-oriented commitment relevant to all genuine intellectuals.

This volume of essays, then, is well-timed. It is also a well-selected range of lively and qualified thinkers who have taken up those aspects of Harris's ideas most worthy of further exploration. I commend editor Sandra Woien, a wide-ranging philosopher in her own right, for her fine work in producing this volume. It's also a strong successor to her *Jordan Peterson: Critical Responses* (2022), focused on another scientifically trained thinker with Third Culture aspirations. I recommend both volumes for careful reading.

The Sam Harris Phenomenon

As a young upstart, Sam Harris popped up on the public radar with his book *The End of Faith* (2004). Aptly dubbed as one of the "New Atheists," he quickly gained prominence for his daring attack on the Abrahamic religions, especially Islam.

Then, he focused his energies exclusively on Christianity in his *Letter to a Christian Nation* (2007). His no-holds-barred approach to religion placed him squarely on the board as a fierce critic of religion and a public intellectual who could not be ignored.

Harris, along with Richard Dawkins, Daniel Dennett, and Christopher Hitchens, due to their criticisms of religion were collectively deemed the "Four Horsemen." This apt moniker was a play on the Bible story. The Four Horsemen of the Apocalypse are among the most dramatic images in the Bible. Described by the apostle John in Revelation 6:1–8, the Four Horsemen are graphic symbols for the destruction that will come to the Earth during the end times. Yet during his attacks on religion, which at times were quite strident, Harris bemoaned how religion holds a monopoly on the ethical and spiritual dimensions—a hold he wants, and eventually tries, to break.

His next book, *The Moral Landscape: How Science Can Determine Human Values* (2010), advances his agenda. Now, not only is religion untenable, but it is also futile; it is unnecessary for making plausible ethical claims. Harris, from a purely secular, and in his opinion, scientific, point of view, defends moral objectivity and a consequentialist framework for judging right actions from wrong ones. In this book he asserts that moral claims are simply facts about "the well-being of conscious creatures" and that answers to moral questions lie in science—not in religion or philosophy.

Harris's next major hit came in 2014, *Waking Up: A Guide to Spirituality without Religion*. In it, he pushes his agenda a step further by a systematic attempt to disconnect spirituality from religion. In this book, he claims that spirituality mainly consists of realizing that the self is an illusion, and the most reliable way to achieve this is through mindfulness and meditation. Yet, this whole project of trying to demolish the self seems to many to be quite unscientific, for critics wonder: can science actually prove that the self is an illusion? That doesn't impede Harris from trying to wrest spirituality from religion and developing an understanding of spirituality that allows for a deep investigation of consciousness.

Sam Harris also has a strong presence on social media. His podcast, *Making Sense*, deals with controversial issues such as psychedelics, politics, and current events. Due to its popularity, it has been named one of iTunes' best podcasts. His app, *Waking Up with Sam Harris*, is also popular and has thousands of subscribers. The app not only helps people to start or maintain a meditation practice but unlike many of its competitors, it also covers the theory and concepts behind mindfulness and features guest lectures from experts in the field.

The topics Harris explores are wide-ranging, and his positions are provocative. Not surprisingly, he has inspired both fans and foes. The contributors to this volume, mostly neither fervent admirers nor vitriolic critics, tend to fall within the middle of this spectrum. While they use Harris's ideas as their basis, they make conceptual connections to other notable thinkers such as B.F. Skinner, Aristotle, Robert Nozick, Karl Popper, and David Hume, and offer unique contributions to discussions on timeless issues such as morality, religion, and free will. More importantly, the contributors claim to identify gaps in Harris's thinking that perhaps warrant more attention.

SANDRA WOIEN

I

What Human Life Is For

[1]
Another Red Pill

SANDRA WOIEN

I am not a mediocre thinker. My consciousness is vast enough to contain all contradictions, but within me, they become complementary to each other.

—OSHO

In the 1999 sci-fi blockbuster *The Matrix*, Neo, Morpheus, and Cypher are unplugged from a simulated reality known as the Matrix. After their liberation, they wake up from their illusions and see the world as it actually is.

While their perceptions are now truthful, Cypher, one of the antagonists, doesn't enjoy life in the real world. He finds it so unbearable that he makes a deal with Agent Smith that if Cypher provides critical information he will be plugged back in. He does this deal because life outside the Matrix—real life—is unpleasant. He doesn't value the truth. He's tired of dressing in rags, eating gruel, and trusting Morpheus's far-fetched prophecies. Instead, he wants to have pleasant experiences and believe that he is eating steak and cavorting with beautiful women. He wants this so badly that he betrays his only real friends.

Cypher's betrayal is morally deplorable due to the tragedy it causes, yet understandable from the point of view of trying to maximize subjective well-being. Living in austere conditions on the *Nebuchadnezzar* and fighting sentinels and agents was stressful, to say the least.

According to Sam Harris, most of us are like those hapless people plugged into the Matrix. We live in a dream world and sleepwalk through life. We, however, are not literally imprisoned by machines. Rather we are self-imprisoned, so our keys to liberation—to the good life—lie elsewhere.

How to Measure the Quality of a Life

Like Cypher, we want our lives to go well. Yet, how can we tell? Is there a method to measure the quality of a life? For any initial skeptics, Harris employs an analogy between health and well-being. If I asked your doctor if you were healthy, I would be provided with evidence and data about your blood pressure, cholesterol, body-mass index, diet, physical activity, and so forth. Armed with such accurate data, a judgment can be made about how healthy you are. Similarly, what evidence could you give to judge how well your life is going? In other words, assume you were on your deathbed and asked if you lived a good life; what data could you provide to convince your interlocutor that your life had indeed been a wonderful one?

Theories of well-being (or welfare) are paramount in answering such a question. Philosophically speaking, well-being captures the notion of what it means for a life to go well for the person living it, so theories of well-being determine what kinds of states of affairs are non-instrumentally or intrinsically good *for* a person. As such, according to Fred Feldman, they attempt to provide an account of what makes life good *for* the person who lives that life. These theories also capture the negative aspects of a person's life, so in dire cases, like with a terminal illness, we may claim that someone's well-being is negative. States of affairs, however, that have a causal impact on well-being, such as wealth or bad luck, are only considered to be instrumentally good or bad. Focusing only on what is intrinsically good (or bad) for a person, a theory of well-being describes what makes a life good for the person living that life, thereby judging a person's life from one particular perspective.

Lives can be measured via different metrics. Feldman notes that there are at least four ways to judge the quality of a life: the morally good life, the useful life, the beautiful life, and a life good in itself for the person who lives it. Consider how a morally good life and a life good in itself can diverge. Feldman uses Mother Teresa as an example. In her case, she tried to help others, do her duty, and abstain from sin. Yet, in her letters, she admitted to suffering from chronic depression, painful physical ailments, and feelings of meaninglessness. Feldman concludes that she lived a morally good life, but not a good life in terms of well-being. Similarly, we can assert that Cypher did not live a morally good life; he killed, maimed, and sabotaged his only true friends. Yet, was he right about it being good *for* him to re-enter the Matrix, sustained by a myriad of pleasant, but false experiences?

Philosophers have traditionally divided theories of well-being into three broad categories: mental state theories, desire satisfaction theories, and objective list theories. Mental state accounts maintain that experiential states are the only states of affairs that improve or diminish well-being. Such theories uphold what James Griffin calls the experience requirement; this keeps well-being within reasonable bounds and excludes states of affairs external to our experiences. As the saying goes, "What you don't know won't hurt you."

The most prevalent example of a mental state theory is hedonism; it maintains that no experience can be good for a person unless she finds pleasure in it. Since pleasure is intrinsically good for a person while pain is intrinsically bad, well-being consists of the maximization of pleasure and the minimization of pain. A life, therefore, is judged to be good or bad (and various degrees in between) by the quantity and intensity of pleasures, so a life with a vast preponderance of pleasure and just a little pain would indeed be a very good one.

Desire satisfaction theories comprise the second category. What unifies these types of theories is that they maintain that well-being consists of the satisfaction of desires. So, what is intrinsically good for a person is to have her desires, or some subset of them such as informed desires, satisfied, and it is intrinsically bad for a person to have her desires frustrated.

Then, there are objective list theories. These theories maintain that the presence of certain objective goods is intrinsically good for us, and their absence is bad. While different versions may have different lists, they all agree that the presence of more than one objective good, whether virtue, knowledge, or friendship, determines well-being.

In keeping with Harris's health analogy, when the hedonist says that pleasure is good for you or the objective list theorist says being deceived is bad for you, it's similar to your physician claiming that kale is good for you while cigarettes are bad.

Harris's Murky Notions Regarding Well-Being

At the outset of *The Moral Landscape*, Harris's exposition of well-being begins. The moral landscape is a hypothetical "space of real and potential outcomes whose peaks correspond to the heights of potential well-being and whose valleys represent the deepest possible suffering" (p. 7). In other words, it's a type of topological map for judging lives. The peaks represent the myriad ways lives can go well; the valleys represent the countless ways lives can go awry.

Now, we may wonder, what does Harris mean by well-being? Well, he doesn't tell us. Instead, he claims that "the concept of well-being . . . resists precise definition" (pp. 11–12). Yet, he unequivocally states that "human well-being entirely depends on events in the world and on states of the human brain" (p. 2). So, we do know that our location on the moral landscape depends, to some extent, on our mental states.

Later, in *Waking Up*, he explores "consciousness and its contents" and reminds us that "your mind will determine the quality of your life" (p. 204). He writes:

> Some people are content in the midst of deprivation and danger, while others are miserable despite having all the luck in the world. This is not to say that external circumstances do not matter. But it is your mind, rather than circumstances themselves, that determines the quality of your life. (*Waking Up*, p. 47)

So, what states of affairs improve or diminish well-being? Like the concept itself, this too is unclear. Since Harris is a scientist and claims that science is the way to understand morality, it certainly can't be like the late Justice Stewart's obscenity test: "I know it when I see it." Harris claims that "the concept of 'well-being' captures all we can intelligibly value" (*The Moral Landscape*, p. 32). Such an axiomatic concept deserves precision.

From a philosophical perspective, Harris conflates two issues. The first one is conceptual. It's about how to define well-being, and we can answer it by conducting a conceptual investigation that leads us to a definition. The second one is substantive. It is about what determines well-being, and we can answer it by identifying the features needed to fulfill the given definition. For example, a young child doesn't know what a square is, but I tell her it is a shape with four equal sides. I could also draw one for her and point out examples. Doing so gives her the concept of a square. Now with the concept, she can identify what shapes are squares and what ones are not, and she knows what people are talking about when they talk about squares.

In other words, a difference exists between a definition of the concept of well-being and a theory that purports to tell us what contributes to well-being. Failing to distinguish between the conceptual and the substantive issues—the latter of which ties into his account of normative ethics—causes problems for Harris. First, because he ignores a rich philosophical history of well-being, in which well-being has an accepted definition as what is intrinsically good *for* a person, he ends up awkwardly claiming that the concept resists a precise definition. Second, instead of Harris telling us the determinants of well-being, we're left sifting through innumerable examples that, as we will ultimately see, lack coherence.

One example Harris gives is a sketch of two lives. The first he calls "The Bad Life." In this scenario, a young widow is living in a war-torn country. Her daughter was raped and killed by her son, who was forced to do so at machete point by a brutal gang. She is now running through the jungle, attempting to escape being murdered. Since its inception, her life has been devoid of joys like travel, reading, and hot showers. Instead, it has been a series of unpleasant experiences like hunger, fear, loss, confusion, and sadness. Contrast this with Harris's vision of "The Good Life." In this scenario, a person has a wonderful spouse, an engaging career, strong social connections, plenty of money, and superb physical health. She also helps others and finds her life immensely rewarding. Her life, absent of privation or misfortune, has been a source of deep satisfaction and contentment (pp. 15–16).

From this sketch and other passages, we gather that determinants of well-being seem to include mental states like pleasure, compassion, love, and contentment. Mental states that diminish well-being include pain, fear, doubt, illusion, terror, and cruelty. So, how should we categorize Harris's theory of well-being?

Navigating Muddy Waters

First, Harris's theory could be a form of hedonism. This interpretation makes sense if all the positive mental states he mentions are reducible to pleasure. Yet, in the same manner that he smugly dismisses the contributions of moral philosophy—in a footnote—he also professes to reject "a strictly hedonic measure of the 'good'" (p. 196). Thus, it would seem odd for him to write an entire book just to discover that he is a hedonic utilitarian—a person, like Jeremy Bentham, who thinks that pleasure is the only intrinsic good and who judges actions as right or wrong in terms of their ability to maximize pleasure and minimize pain. So, let's take him at his word and reject this possibility.

Second, his theory could be a type of pluralistic mental statism, a type of mental list theory that can be plugged in to his consequentialist framework. This is a more plausible interpretation, yet it also faces problems. It leaves us wondering: what unifies all these mental states? Since these disparate mental states have no unifying property, it risks begging the question. What mental states are good for us? Those that contribute to well-being. Well, that implies that we already know what its determinants are!

Also, can a mental state interpretation be reconciled with other passages? He claims, for example, that psychopaths seek forms of well-being that we understand, such as excitement and freedom from pain. Then, he writes, "a psychopath like Ted Bundy takes satisfaction *in the wrong things* [italics mine], because living a life purposed toward raping and killing women does not allow for deeper and more generalizable forms of human flourishing" (p. 205). He also writes, "Some pleasures are intrinsically ethical—feelings like love, gratitude, devotion, and compassion. To inhabit these states of mind is, by definition, to be brought into alignment with others" (*Waking Up*, p. 49). Now, what does it mean for any mental state theorist to say that a person takes pleasure in the wrong things? Is 'ethical' a property of a mental state— or can some property called 'ethical' affect our mental states?

Third, well-being could depend "on events in the world and on states of the human brain" (*The Moral Landscape*, p. 2), making it a hybridized account in which both states of mind and states of the world matter. So, we may query, what objective goods matter? Again, we have no idea. At certain points, he makes it explicitly clear that things, commonly thought to be objective goods like knowledge, have only instrumental value. About those people who claim to value knowledge for its own sake, Harris writes that "they are merely describing the mental pleasure that comes with understanding the world" (p. 203). As for another alleged objective good, fairness, he vacillates a bit before concluding that fairness is not intrinsically good for a person (p. 209).

Harris's position drifts too much to be classified. Yet, one thing we know for sure: Harris fails to provide an operationalized account of well-being. This poses a problem for his moral philosophy. According to Harris, what's good is that which contributes to well-being (p. 12), and morality is "the principles of behavior that allow people to flourish" (p. 19). Thus, the ultimate goal of morality is to maximize the well-being of conscious creatures. But how can we do that if we don't know how to define or determine well-being?

The Waters Get Muddier

Harris unequivocally maintains that well-being comprises all that is good. Yet, I get a distinct impression that another philosophical distinction eludes Harris: that well-being may be different from moral goodness. In other words, a theory of well-being need not be coextensive with a theory of the good. Thus, agent-relativity about the good (to be good is to be intrinsically good *for* someone) may be distinct from intrinsic goodness (good in itself). A theory of well-being, which determines the states of affairs that are good for a person, focuses on the former, while a theory of the good focuses on the latter.

Well-being may indeed capture everything that has intrinsic value, as a hedonic utilitarian such as Jeremy Bentham believed; in this case, hedonism functions both as a theory of well-being and a theory of the good. But well-being may just be one component of the good. For example, I believe that pleasure is the only thing intrinsically good for conscious creatures, but I also believe in other intrinsic goods such as truth, liberty, and beauty. This makes me a welfare hedonist, but not a hedonic utilitarian.

Harris endorses consequentialism, a category of ethical theory that maintains that only consequences determine the rightness or wrongness of an action. Thus, for a consequentialist, an action is right if and only if it produces the best result. Yet, how do we determine what result is the best? To do this, we now need a theory of the good. Harris claims that "well-being is the gold standard by which to measure what is good" ("A Response to Critics"). Yet, his theory of well-being isn't clear. His moral theory, therefore, is incomplete; moral terrain exists, but we don't have a clear map to reach those lofty peaks.

Dismissing Such Gravitas

Harris is vaguely aware of problems in his account of well-being. In a reply to critics, he sums this up as a counterargument. "Even if we did agree to grant 'well-being' primacy in any discussion of morality, it is difficult or impossible to define it with rigor. It is, therefore, impossible to measure well-being scientifically. Thus, there can be no science of morality" ("A Response to Critics").

Now, we may ask, what exactly does Harris mean by "science of morality"? One possibility is that it would help us answer conceptual questions—maybe it will help us define the very concept of well-being. Perhaps using this scientific approach, we would arrive at a different definition than philosophers use. Another possibility is that it is about what determines well-being, so it tells us what makes a life go well for the person living that life. A third possibility is that we could use such a science to figure out what is the morally right thing to do. If this is the case, it's intended to tell us what makes actions right or wrong.

These three philosophical distinctions appear to be conflated in Harris's mind, so even his understanding of the counterargument is off base. He seems to think that he can fail to define well-being, while at the same time, he can 'see' answers to what makes a life go well versus poorly. Like a type of divining rod, he can then determine right from wrong.

Yet, well-being is possible to define: a philosophical consensus exists on how to define it. And while disagreement exists over what determines well-being, it's still possible to provide a consistent account of its determinants and to distinguish between a theory of well-being and a theory of the good. In terms of unpacking these issues, being conversant with the philosophical literature would have helped Harris immensely. By avoiding it, clarity is sacrificed, and confusion wrought. He has ignored Aristotle at his peril.

Indeterminacy or Illusion

Harris is committed to the idea that moral questions, like scientific ones, theoretically have answers. Yet, in practice, indeterminacy is common; our inability to answer a question ultimately tells us nothing about whether the question has an answer. For example, in practice, it may be virtually impossible to determine how many hairs I have on my head or how many pandas live in the wild. Answers to such questions, however, exist. Likewise, for moral questions like: How well is my life going? What would make my life better? What should I do? In such cases, definite answers may elude us, but we can distinguish answers close to the mark from those that miss it entirely.

Harris, however, uses indeterminacy as a shield, or perhaps, it simply blinds him from giving a clear account of the constituents of well-being. No matter what the case, it is inexcusable. Harris should care more about clarifying the determinants of well-being, which is foundational for his moral architecture. Even non-philosophers should expect more from an ethical theory, especially if they, like Harris, are committed to moral realism.

Despite being unable to define or precisely determine well-being, Harris still believes that judgments regarding well-being can be made to some degree. However, what he says about the possible constituents of well-being shifts around too much: one minute, he appears to be a hedonist, the next minute a desire-satisfaction theorist, and the next, some type of objective list theorist. Hence, Harris gives us no clear metric to judge the quality of a life, so his confidence in his ability to do so is ungrounded.

A Spillover

In his later books, *Lying* and *Waking Up,* truth plays a central role in Harris's vision of the good life. Yet, since he hasn't provided a clear account of well-being, we are confronted with a dilemma: if positive mental states are all that contribute to well-being, how does it fundamentally matter if a person doesn't want to wake up or realize the truth? If positive mental states are not all that contribute to well-being, for well-being consists in the maximization of a variety of states of mind and states of the world, then how can it be true that "the quality of your mind determines the quality of your life"? In other words, how does truth matter under his account of well-being? Is it an instrumental good or an intrinsic one?

The experience machine is a thought experiment by Robert Nozick. Unlike in the Matrix, we can choose our experiences in this machine. In fact, by plugging in, we can have any experience we want, for it produces the identical mental states as if we were actually doing these things. If, like Cypher, we want to think we're eating steaks and enjoying pleasurable encounters with beautiful women while also being ridiculously wealthy, we will have the same mental states as we would in a real world where all this were true. Our experiences would be identical; it would be impossible to distinguish between reality and fantasy. It could even simulate the same experiences as in Harris's sketch of the good life: we could be programmed to believe that we have rich and rewarding relationships with people we love, a fulfilling career, and a long, healthy life. According to mental state theories, by plugging in, we could max out our well-being by having an abundance of positive mental states. Moreover, like those in the Matrix, once in, we're deprived of any knowledge of our connection. Our lack of awareness would be so profound that worries about abandoning our friends or loved ones could never even enter our minds.

While this may be alluring, Nozick rejected mental statism and claimed that we should ultimately resist plugging in. He thinks it is better for us to *do* actual things and *be* a certain way. Sure, most of us would prefer to *really* be successful, cocooned from the travesties of life by good genes and relationships. But what if our lives were going very poorly? What if we had to choose between plugging in or dying a slow, painful death, or between plugging in and being the woman in Harris's bad life scenario? When faced with such dire prospects, plugging in certainly seems the best choice.

If truth is only instrumentally valuable, Harris's positions about the illusory nature of the self, free will, or even God are weakened. Sure, free will and God may not exist, but what if it makes me happy to believe they do? Harris, in this case, is forced to accept that false information may increase a person's well-being. For example, it might cripple a person to discover that God, free will, and the self are illusions. In such a case, it seems as if it would be good *for* this person to continue to believe otherwise. Harris, failing to account for individual differences, assumes that certain beliefs like the belief in a self or a God are undeniable sources of suffering. Yet, while Harris finds such beliefs unpalatable, it could be the case that you or I take pleasure in them. Hence, they are good for us, but bad for him.

However, if the truth is intrinsically good for a person, what he says about the illusory nature of the self, free will, and God makes more sense. Yet, it entails that his account of well-being is not a mental state account, so claiming "the quality of your mind determines the quality of your life" is implausible. Moreover, his overall position in *The Moral Landscape* is undermined because, without providing a compelling account of how truth can directly impact mental states, facts about well-being are no longer reducible to facts about the brain.

Harris is at an impasse; he either has to admit that a person who chooses to plug into the experience machine may be living a very good life, or he has to accept that the presence of objective goods like truth contribute to well-being. But he cannot simply claim that a life of illusion can't have more positive mental states than a life of veridical experiences.

Can Harris swallow such a bitter pill, or is clinging to indeterminacy regarding the constituents of well-being the one comforting illusion he is unwilling to surrender? Tried and true philosophical paths out of this briar patch are available. Harris, however, hasn't found any of them, so he remains mired.

Coda

Harris stands resolute in his endeavor for a scientific morality that allows us all to flourish, for this project may lead to a terrestrial nirvana. (As Harris repeatedly reminds his readers, it is naive to hope for paradise elsewhere.) "Consider how we would view a situation," he writes, "in which all of us miraculously began to behave so as to maximize our collective well-being. Imagine that on the basis of remarkable breakthroughs in technology, and politic[al] skill, we create a genuine utopia on earth" ("A Response to Critics").

Toward the end of *The Matrix,* Agent Smith, during his interrogation of Morpheus, divulges that the first version of the Matrix was designed to be a utopia, where everyone was happy, and suffering was absent. This would be akin to transforming Harris's moral landscape with many peaks and sloping valleys into a plateau. Yet, while this iteration attempted to maximize the good, Smith laments, it was a disaster.

Like the architect in *The Matrix*, Harris seems confident that if moral experts were in charge, a utopia, a Heaven on Earth, would be within our reach. He writes, "We must also include the possibility (in principle, if not in practice) of changing people's desires, preferences, and intuitions as a means of moving across the moral landscape." Let the experts take the reins, he urges. Forget autonomy. Most people need a strong dose of paternalism to propel themselves up those lofty peaks. Better yet, they should be shepherded by the wise.

Utopian visions, whether real or fictionalized, from those of Osho and Karl Marx to the architect of *The Matrix*, inevitably fail, but many of the faithful naively cling to hope—*it will be different next time*. Thankfully, those outside the grip of such despots and their delusions still have choices. Like Neo, we may decide to take the Red Pill and wake up, no matter the suffering it entails, or like Cypher, we may prefer to go back to sleep so we can be absorbed in blissful fantasies.

No matter life's dilemmas, we should choose for ourselves rather than hand the reins of power to others. Harris may be the high priest of meditation in the West, yet in terms of grasping the philosophical issues surrounding morality, Jesus's exhortation seems best: "Beware of false prophets."

References

Bentham, Jeremy. 1988. *The Principles of Morals and Legislation*. Prometheus.

Feldman, Fred. 2004. *Pleasure and The Good Life: Concerning the Nature, Varieties and Plausibility of Hedonism*. Oxford University Press.

Griffin, James. 1986. *Well-Being: Its Meaning, Measurement, and Moral Importance*. Clarendon.

Harris, Sam. 2010. *The Moral Landscape: How Science Can Determine Human Values*. Free Press.

———. 2011. A Response to Critics <www.huffpost.com/entry/a-response-to-critics_b_815742>.

———. 2013. *Lying*. Four Elephants Press.

———. 2015. *Waking Up: A Guide to Spirituality without Religion*. Simon and Schuster.

Nozick, Robert. 1974. *Anarchy, State, and Utopia*. Basic Books.

Osho. 2010. I Am Vast, Okay? <www.youtube.com/watch?v=awB4EWcOJXg>.

Wachowski, Lana and Lilly, directors. 1999. *The Matrix*. Warner Brothers.

[2]
My Life Gives the Moral Landscape Its Relief

MARC CHAMPAGNE

> The basic clue is that life says "yes" to itself. By clinging to itself it declares that it values itself. But one clings only to what can be taken away. From the organism, which has being strictly on loan, it can be taken and will be unless from moment to moment reclaimed. Continued metabolism is such a reclaiming, which ever reasserts the value of Being against its lapsing into nothingness. . . . Are we then, perhaps, allowed to say that mortality is the narrow gate through which alone *value*—the addressee of a "yes"— could enter the otherwise indifferent universe?
>
> —HANS JONAS, *Mortality and Morality*, p. 91

Sam Harris was spurred to intellectual activism by the events of September 11th 2001. As Harris observes, people confronting religiously-motivated murder-suicide often "imagine that science cannot pose, much less answer, questions" about whether the values prompting such acts are "inferior to our own" (*The Moral Landscape*, p. 1). He disagrees.

In drastic cases like 9/11, a person might think that their indignation is based in some sort of timeless truth (about nonviolence, the right to live, or whatever). But Richard Rorty, Harris's one-time professor, expressed a common sentiment when he wrote that "sentences like . . . 'Truth is independent of the human mind' are simply platitudes used to inculcate . . . the common sense of the West" (*Contingency, Irony, and Solidarity*, pp. 76–77). Harris wants a principled way of escaping this conclusion.

17

To distance himself from such cultural relativism, Harris converts "questions about values . . . meaning, morality, and life's larger purpose" into "questions about the well-being of conscious creatures" (*The Moral Landscape*, p. 1). This conversion is pivotal, since it is only once we unpack the notions of good and bad as promotions or curtailments of conscious well-being that values can be translated "into facts that can be scientifically understood." Such a scientific understanding is rendered possible because conscious states are caused by the brain, which can in turn be studied. Harris thus claims that "The more we understand ourselves at the level of the brain, the more we will see that there are right and wrong answers to questions of human values" (p. 2).

A Vantage from Which to Judge

Naturally, on the neuroscience front, a lot of work remains to be done. Still, the mere fact that we can understand the brain—and thereby conscious states—and thereby well-being—is enough to restore objectivity in discussions of morality. As Harris rightly warns, "mistaking *no answers in practice* for *no answers in principle* is a great source of moral confusion" (p. 3). We may not have all the answers right now, but those answers are out there—or more precisely in here, inside our skulls.

Like all organs, brains serve a function. As Harris says in a 2016 TED talk: "Intelligence is a matter of information processing in physical systems." My kidney may be a bit smaller or larger than yours, but as a kidney it performs the same function, namely to filter blood. Likewise, my brain may have been shaped by environmental stimuli that differ from yours, but both perform the same function, namely to process information. The senses provide inputs (a brick flying at me, say) which the brain converts into behavioral outputs (dodging the brick, say). Evolution and experience beat such input-output relations into shape. Since morality is simply in the business of maximizing a particular brain state—well-being—morality should be understandable.

Cross-cultural complexity and an overdone sense of respect can often make it seem as if "cultures are too different to compare" (Shah, "Cross-Cultural View of Rape," p. 92).

Membership in a shared species, however, ensures that law-like generalizations can nevertheless be made. Clearly, deriving happiness from a Hollywood movie is no different than deriving happiness from a Bollywood movie. The fact that there can be different ways to flourish makes ample room for cultural variation. Yet, just as a biological phenomenon like "Cancer in the highlands of New Guinea is still cancer" (*The Moral Landscape*, p. 2), a social phenomenon like rape is wrong, irrespective of whether it happens in India or the United States. It is *not* imperialistic to say so.

To make this vision of ethical objectivity tangible and memorable, Harris ties it together with a metaphor: moral assessments yield a landscape, where the "peaks correspond to the heights of potential well-being and whose valleys represent the deepest possible suffering" (p. 7). In a real landscape, there needn't be only one mountaintop. Likewise, we needn't assume "that we will necessarily discover one right answer to every moral question or a single best way for human beings to live." We must therefore be prepared to accept that "Some questions may admit of many answers, each more or less equivalent." This pluralism, however, does not leave us unable to judge abhorrent practices. As Harris explains, "the existence of multiple peaks on the moral landscape does not make them any less real," since there is a "difference between being on a peak and being stuck deep in a valley" (p. 7). This difference is felt by experiencing subjects, so persons undergoing "female genital excision, blood feuds, infanticide, the torture of animals, scarification, foot binding, cannibalism, ceremonial rape, human sacrifice, dangerous male initiations, restricting the diet of pregnant and lactating mothers, slavery, potlatch, the killing of the elderly, sati, irrational dietary and agricultural taboos attended by chronic hunger and malnourishment, the use of heavy metals to treat illness" (p. 20) are *not* experiencing the best that life has to offer.

This is the vision developed in Harris's book, *The Moral Landscape: How Science can Determine Human Values*. I am ambivalent about that work. On the one hand, I regard Harris as an ally. In fact, on September 11th 2010—exactly nine years after the events that triggered Harris's career (and mine)—I presented kindred ideas before the British Psychological Society ("Axiomatizing Umwelt Normativity"). My pivot, however, is life itself, not the conscious experience of well-being, so there are interesting differences worth fleshing out. Harris takes our ability to compare degrees of well-being as his starting point, but I think that the analysis can be pushed further. There is a (non-religious) reason *why* well-being is desirable, namely the finite life of an individual organism. It is because death is a constant possibility that things can be assessed as "for" or "against" someone. Such an account lets us objectively adjudicate moral questions, as Harris desires. However, by anchoring itself in the mortal body as a whole and pivoting on an affirmation of life, such an account dampens the claim that neuroscience would have all the answers. The trade-off is nevertheless worthwhile.

Knowledge of the Means, Desire for the End

Harris's first book, *The End of Faith* (2004), told us where values do *not* come from, namely faith. The sequel, *Letter to a Christian Nation* (2006), essentially did the same, albeit in a more focused way. Obeying the pottery barn rule that says when you break something you have to replace it, *The Moral Landscape* (2010) complements these critiques of faith and religion with a positive account of the origins of values.

Harris's starting premise, which he regards as "very simple" and beyond controversy, is that "human well-being entirely depends on events in the world and on states of the human brain" (*The Moral Landscape*, p. 2). Events and brain states are both needed, I take it, because an event that is not cognized cannot be evaluated and a brain state with no basis in fact cannot have any practical utility. What happens in the world naturally affects what happens in the mind. We can thus use the promotion or curtailment of conscious well-being to handle questions of right and wrong. The disagreement about science that I am about to develop should not eclipse the large areas of agreement, namely that moral objectivity *is* possible and that religion is *not* the way to get it. However, the inference "Not religion, therefore science" does not follow.

Like many, Harris takes science to be the paradigm of what solid knowledge looks like. Harris may dismiss the work done by professional ethicists (p. 197), but one thing gained by engaging in philosophy is a realization that something can be "objective" without being "scientific." Mathematical knowledge is one such example. Morality is another. Harris writes that "no one wants utter, interminable misery," so "if someone *claims* to want to be truly miserable, we are free to treat them like someone who claims to believe that 2 + 2 = 5" (p. 205). Yet, Harris does not seem to realize that, if claims like "2 + 2 = 4" and "I want to be happy" cannot be shown wrong, then they are ejected from the realm of science. Rational deliberations about well-being are definitely tethered to something, but not to natural science (as it is typically understood).

Harris wants to say that discussions of ethics can be objective. But, by accident or design, he conveys this message by saying that discussions of ethics can be scientific. This slide burdens Harris with adopting a stronger stance than he should. The non-scientific status of life-striving does not mean, however, that anything goes or that moral truths rest only on mystical insight. Anchoring morality to well-being may sound revolutionary to those acquainted only with religious accounts, but secular thinkers like Jeremy Bentham and John Stuart Mill said essentially this, with Aristotle and Epicurus saying it better several centuries before them. Harris, however, gives the insight about well-being a newfangled twist: neuroscience should ultimately be our guide. This turn to neuroscience is admittedly trendy (Legrenzi and Umiltà, *Neuromania*). Yet, how much science is needed to seek happiness and steer clear of whatever impedes it? Empirical discoveries might enlarge the list of what counts as poison, but such discoveries will never revolutionize the idea that poison is to be avoided. The 'poison' part is chemistry, the 'avoidance' part is ethics.

Increases in knowledge fine-tune the means, not the end. To see this, consider the case of radon. We have advances in science (and technology) to thank for letting us know when and where to avoid this colorless and odorless radioactive gas. Hence, in contrast with a prehistoric caveman, my knowledge about naturally-occurring radon (and access to contemporary detection instruments) can tell me to regard a particular cave as a bad choice of dwelling. But, why should

I or the caveman *care* about the adverse effects of radon? As labeling on cigarette packages reveals, no number of facts will force one to live well. There is a tunnel in Germany where people willingly expose themselves to radon, so science should certainly be consulted to settle whether low doses of this radioactive gas indeed have any health benefits, as some claim. If, however, someone were to openly grant radon's danger yet walk through the radioactive caves with a clear suicidal intent, it is hard to see what science could say.

Why should a description of the universe worry that a particular patch of matter is on the verge of becoming inanimate, when it is bound to become inanimate anyway? The scientific method cultivates a "view from nowhere" (Nagel, *The View from Nowhere*). However, if Harris is right that "anything of value must be valuable *to* someone (whether actually or potentially)" (*The Moral Landscape*, p. 180), then the living subject is vital to valuing. Values may not be subjective but they are subject-involving (Smith, "The Importance of the Subject"), just as "parenthood involves a subject" in no way leads to "parenthood is subjective." In other words, values involve you but are not up to you. We can thus say, objectively, that radon is worth avoiding, but such a predicate is incomplete. Worth avoiding? *For whom?*

The precarity of my embodied life entails that I cannot do whatever I want. This moral objectivity, however, does not mean that values exist out there like regular things. A precipice on the early surface of this planet wasn't 'dangerous' prior to the advent of creatures liable to fall off the edge. It is not just that a brain must be brought into relation with a precipice to deem it worth avoiding. Rather, the relation must involve a living thing, perhaps with a brain, that wants to keep on living. Only by appealing to this standard can we explain the otherwise bizarre fact that the predicate "is dangerous" attaches to a fifty-feet deep trench but not a one-foot deep one. Our worldly landscape gets overlaid with a moral landscape only when it is appraised by a living entity concerned to remain so.

The universe is replete with differences (how many things currently differ from your cup of coffee?). So, to show up on our moral radar, a difference between fifty-feet and one-foot depths must make a difference to some organism

(Bateson, *Steps to an Ecology of Mind*, p. 453). Indeed, were I much taller or suicidal, the fifty-feet deep trench might not bother me or trigger my avoidance. Since whatever badness attaches to a fifty-feet deep trench is subject-involving, it cannot be confirmed solely with a measuring tape. While I agree with Harris that moral assessments are factual, the usual interpretation of what counts as a 'fact' tends to be quite crude, so care must be taken to properly characterize the relational complexity of moral assessments ("Axiomatizing Umwelt Normativity," pp. 28–30). My crucial contribution to the transaction needs to be factored in.

Life and Death

Inquiry into the foundation of ethics is difficult because it seeks to account for distinctions that normally seem obvious. It is a bit like asking what distinguishes the ground from the sky. We are all tempted to dismiss such a question as spurious and answer: Can't you just *see*? Harris, for instance, juxtaposes the following cases (*The Moral Landscape*, pp. 15–16; descriptions and labels from Meacham's review, p. 42):

Life A: Imagine that you are an illiterate and homeless . . . woman whose husband has disappeared. You have just seen your seven-year-old daughter raped and murdered at the hands of drug-crazed soldiers, and now you're fearing for your life. Unfortunately, this is not an unusual predicament for you. From the moment you were born, your life has been marred by cruelty and violence.

Life B: Imagine that you are a respected professional in a wealthy country, married to a loving, intelligent and charismatic mate. Your employment is intellectually stimulating and pays you very well. For decades your wealth and social connections have allowed you immense personal satisfaction from meaningful work which makes a real difference in the world. You and your closest family will live long, prosperous lives, virtually untouched by crime, sudden bereavements, and other major misfortunes.

Harris holds that most of us would place life B "atop" life A. I sure would. The moral landscape thus seems to have its relief already there, waiting for us to notice. Yet, even if such ranking seems obvious (especially in stark contrasts involving few or dramatic options), it is a methodological mistake to equate 'psychologically intuitive' with 'philosophically primitive'. The fact that we evaluate and rank options so quickly may precisely hide, not reveal, the mechanisms or standards that we rely on.

So, what's going on? Here is one analogy. There is a light in my home controlled by a dimmer switch. I can turn that knob clockwise to increase the brightness level or counter-clockwise to diminish it. If I turn clockwise all the way, I max out to the brightest level possible (which can vary, based on the type of light bulb used). If, however, I keep turning the knob counter-clockwise, I eventually hear a sharp 'click' and the light goes out. Everything on the dimmer is on a continuous (analog) spectrum—except for the 'off' setting, which is marked by a sharp (digital) distinction. The existence of a living organism can be compared to such a dimmer switch, with degrees of well-being capped by the 'click' of death at one end.

As a precarious state that battles the decay and heat-loss characteristic of all material things (Schrödinger, *What Is Life?*, pp. 70–75), life places demands that we ignore at our own peril. There are many such demands, ranging from the obvious to the barely detectable. The effects of water deprivation will be felt fairly soon, whereas the effects of an unrewarding career will be felt through a host of seemingly-unrelated mood changes. Maximal well-being thus requires that many things fall into place, especially when the organism in question is social and capable of monitoring its own thoughts and actions. Because cruelty and violence are inimical to life, they turn life A in a deathward direction. Conversely, safety and a stimulating career take life B farther from the state of nonbeing that makes comparisons of brightness levels consequential.

Even in the best case, living organisms who keep entropy at bay are fated to lose the battle. In every painting, we ought to put the Grim Reaper somewhere in the background. Yet, until death comes, the constant alternative between life and non-life gives rise to values and forces one to make choices. Poison? Not good. Smoothie? Good. Only a living entity could make such value judgments—on the assumption, of course, that the living entity wants to continue being one.

Life-affirmation as Outside the Scope of Science

The account of values that I am developing draws more heavily on biology than neuroscience. Yet, even if we switch the emphasis from neuroscience to biology, there are features of well-being that make the labels 'science' and 'scientific' inapplicable.

To see this, consider the following. I want to continue to be happy and to flourish, right now, even though by everyone's admission no one yet has given a full account of how the brain works. My well-being—being healthy, well fed, in good company, busy with useful and challenging tasks, and so on—is its own reward. What could we learn about such a state of well-being? Lots of things: we could learn how blood sugar levels regulate moods, we could track correlations between personality types, careers, and recreational activities, we could catalog hereditary traits that predispose a person to stay calm under stressors, and so on. We could also learn which social, economic, and political arrangements best promote well-being. In fact, we are learning many of those things right now. Yet, no matter what discoveries await, it seems unlikely that science could ever show that happiness is something to be avoided. This is simply off the table. So, if a panel of experts showed up at my door with charts and data to convince me, on a scientific basis, to give up joy and embrace misery, I would doubt their findings, not my desire to live.

I can know this outcome before any demonstration or argument. This may not seem like a big deal, but it is disastrous for Harris's account. Indeed, my non-negotiable desire to live—to be happy, flourish, and envelop a select group of people (like my family) in that sustained project—commits the cardinal sin of science, which is to put the conclusion before the premises. In other words, my desire to be happy is not falsifiable. Science, however, is distinguished from other intellectual pursuits by its readiness to be shown wrong (Popper, *Conjectures and Refutations*, pp. 43–78). A good scientist should actively try to disprove her theories, not prove them. Like a boxing champion routinely putting a title on the line against the best contenders, it is only when we try to genuinely defeat a claim and it wins that we can be confident in it. Absent such exposure to the real possibility of defeat, a claim's alleged "truth" means nothing. Problematically though, the claim 'My life is worth living' can't be shown wrong. The bedrock of morality, then, cannot possibly be science.

Countering cultural relativists by appealing to science is thus overkill and actually backfires. I agree with Susan Haack that "we need to avoid *both* under-estimating the value of science, *and* over-estimating it" ("Six Signs of Scientism," p. 76). Harris is on the right track when he objects to moral relativism and points to well-being as the compass by which to adjudicate moral questions. However, he is led astray when he presents the resulting account as "scientific." Specific proposals on *how* to maximize the best state possible can definitely be falsified in light of new evidence. However, the desirability of that state itself is not falsifiable.

What are we to make of this? As a vocal critic of religious dogma, Harris knows that an account which enshrines a claim come-what-may cannot count as scientific. This results in a dilemma: either his proposal must leave open the possibility that scientists could one day discover that happiness is *not* to be sought (which is absurd), or his proposal cannot be "scientific" in the normal sense. I think we should champion the second horn of this dilemma.

Not 'Why Mountaineering?' but Rather 'Why Mountains?'

Two closely-related issues must be distinguished. One is the issue of what motivates persons to strive for well-being as opposed to self-destruction. Wherever you find yourself on the moral landscape, you must act and those actions must head somewhere. Why do some people embrace mountaineering while others cannot muster the drive to seek a higher plane? As Harris correctly observes, "Many of us spend our lives marching with open eyes toward remorse, regret, guilt, and disappointment" (*Lying*, p. 1). Yet, Harris's observation that we often fail to seek the best life possible presupposes that the highs and lows of the moral landscape have already been differentiated. We must therefore distinguish the psychological question about motivation from another, logically prior, philosophical question: what gives the moral landscape its relief? *Why* is 'up' up and 'down' down? This is the question that my appeal to mortal life seeks to answer.

The physical world that we perceive is indifferent to our plight. We take an interest in the world (for instance, tsunamis), but it does not take an interest in us (for instance, tsunamis). So, despite the rapid speed of our intuitive assessments, we cannot assume that the peaks and valleys of the moral landscape exist apart from our involvement. Indeed, puzzlement about human motivation to seek what is best (or better) only makes sense once some piece of behavior has been foregrounded as worth emulating. Why is the firefighter a good guy and the arsonist a bad guy? After all, from a purely physical standpoint, they are indistinguishable: both are chunks of matter acting in accordance with natural laws. Such material bodies (and the events they generate) must therefore be given a valence to be placed in a hierarchy, with the firefighter 'above' the arsonist. The same goes for lives A and B above.

Alas, Harris never does any 'moral geology': the highs and lows of the moral landscape are just there, somehow. This is insufficient, because well-being is the expression of something more fundamental, namely the finitude of life. Moreover, to the extent that values are rooted in the phenomenon of life, there's no pressing reason to think that the brain is the organ that matters most. Indeed, "Much ordinary thinking about plants . . . reflects implicit recognition of life as the source of value judgments. When we assess certain events as beneficial or harmful for plants . . . What allows these evaluations is not the fact that one experiences varying feelings in reaction to such events. Rather, it is the fact that the organisms stand to gain from them; their lives can be strengthened or set back" (Smith, *Viable Values*, p. 87). Well-being must therefore be indexed to the species in question.

Surely, for a typical plant, some spot near a well-lit window is more desirable than some dark corner behind a door. To point out that plants are sessile and thus can do very little to reach more preferable locations would be to change the topic from the end (life) to the means (anatomy). Naturally, plants have no nervous system. It doesn't matter: they want to live. Hence, on my account, even a greenhouse with no humans houses a moral landscape. It may be too much to claim that "If plants or amoebas are not conscious, yet can still be subject to things of value to them, then Harris's . . . argument fails" (Meacham's review, p. 43). But, it seems fair to say that even a completed neuroscience thousands of years from now would not have all the answers.

The word "flourishing" comes from the Latin *"florere"* which means "to bloom" or "to flower." This state is the ultimate accomplishment of a living thing, something that happens when all of its needs are met and surpassed. When organs like kidneys and brains co-operate, they add up to an organism, whose 'function' or aim is to live. This aim can be achieved with varying degrees of success, with emotions (in humans) acting as a report card on how well we are living. Now, our grammar and lexicon can often trick us into making needless philosophical commitments, so it may be helpful to recall that the concatenated word 'well-being' simply means 'being well'. Nothing more, nothing less. Once we keep that simplicity in mind, the idea that all living beings face a moral landscape becomes less contentious. We won't find a 'neural correlate' of flourishing, any more than a well-functioning car has a precise spot where its 'well-function' happens.

If the foundation of morality is mortality and the momentous life-or-death alternative it constantly poses, then the answers to moral questions stem from our perishable body, not just what is inside our skull. A full belly, for instance, is valuable—quite apart from a brain registering that fullness. If anyone doubts this, we could doctor cortical stimulations that fool their brain into feeling satiated while depriving their stomach wall of actual hydration and nutrients. The consequences for such a person would objectively suck, in the same way that exposure to radiation sucks even when you are unaware of it. We feed on food, not knowledge of food.

Beings with Skin in the Game

The revised picture that emerges from the foregoing is as follows. Harris correctly notes that "the difference between a healthy person and a dead one is about as clear and consequential a distinction as we ever make in science" and that "The differences between the heights of human fulfillment and the depths of human misery are no less clear" (*The Moral Landscape*, p. 12). I wholeheartedly agree. These stark contrasts lead Harris to oppose relativists who "imagine that science cannot pose, much less answer, questions" about which "way of life is better, or more moral, than another" (p. 1). I have argued, however, that science can do so only by appealing to a criterion—well-being—whose desirability can be sought but not justified. Requests for explanation of well-being's desirability thus bottom out in the premise "Because my life is worth living," which is no explanation at all. This, however, is fine. Life is not an argument (Nietzsche, *The Gay Science*, p. 117).

We can try to reduce the desire to live to facts about the brain, but by then we have moved the discussion to a place where the very notions of 'life', 'feeling', and 'good' vanish. You won't see those under a microscope, no matter how sophisticated those instruments get. Consider the absurdity of looking at a brain scan, pointing to a patch of color, and saying to your spouse: '*That, there*, is my love for you' (see Uttal, *The New Phrenology*). I am unsure what people hope to find in a skull. I thus agree with John McDowell that "Where mental life takes place need not be pinpointed any more precisely than saying that it takes place where our lives take place" ("Putnam on Mind and Meaning," p. 40).

Despite this deflated role for neuroscience, we can marshal the "clear and consequential" distinction between life and death to make "very precise claims about which of our behaviors and uses of attention are morally good, which are neutral, and which are worth abandoning" (*The Moral Landscape*, p. 8). Happenings involving fleshy tissues mean nothing without an individual organism (me) who cares to live, so it is only in virtue of such caring that clipping your nails gets differentiated from amputating your arm.

Harris helps himself to a ready-made notion of well-being and assumes, without defense, that it is to be sought. I certainly seek it. But, if we ask *why* well-being is desirable, we are met with a bizarre answer: it is desirable for its own sake, not for the sake of anything else. Moreover, an individual must willingly assent to this, in some strange sense of 'assent' where the alternative would be self-annihilation. This may not be drastic, especially if we accept that "Science and rationality generally are based on intuitions and concepts that cannot be reduced or justified" (*The Moral Landscape*, p. 204). So, who knows: maybe in time we will make individual acts of self-affirmation a part of a scientifically-respectable picture of the human condition. If we are open-minded enough, we might even rethink some traditional moral tenets.

I realize that there is a whole cottage industry of people delineating no-go zones for science. Harris deems it "inevitable . . . that science will gradually encompass life's deepest questions" and anticipates that this ever-increasing encroachment "is guaranteed to provoke a backlash" (p. 7). Although elements of my stance could presumably be used to grease a slippery slope to religion, I believe that "The concepts of value hierarchy and topmost value [that some ascribe to God] can be brought down to Earth and made compatible with our ability to err. All one needs to do is match the religious devotee's enthusiasm while acknowledging that one's yearning for a full life, no matter how ardent, cannot guide one about what to do next. That, like most things, requires fallible inquiry" ("Stone, Stone-Soup, and Soup," p. 111). You may not need—and indeed-could never rely on—science to tell you *to* live; but you definitely want science to counsel you on *how* to best achieve that end.

Using a helpful terminology (proposed in "Stone, Stone-Soup, and Soup," p. 110), we might say that desiring the end is *non-rational* (unrelated to reason), determining the means-end fit is *rational* (justified by reasons), but nothing in the sum is *irrational* (against reason). Given that religion and mysticism have no foothold in such an account, I think a tenable account of right and wrong rooted in well-being should explicitly countenance an individual life-affirming assent, instead of hoping, as Harris does, that everyone will take predicates like 'is worth seeking' and 'is scientific'—and their troublesome conjunction—for granted.

Moral Truths, Arranged in a Hierarchy, and Invested with Value from Without

Harris and I agree that moral judgments can be objective. The people who went to work in the Twin Towers and the maniacs who flew planes into those buildings were not just having a cultural difference, akin to preferring falafels over hotdogs. Most people can see this. However, unlike Harris, I want my account of moral objectivity to rest on deeper foundations than intuitive responses. To that end, I have grounded morality in the phenomenon of life, more specifically in the individual decision to live and avoid death.

The fine-tuning that results from this approach may be illustrated as follows. Imagine that all possible ethical statements are written on small cards. Such statements would include "It is good to eat a balanced breakfast," "It is wrong to pursue a career you dislike," "It is wrong to beat your partner senseless with a crowbar,"—you name it. We could then separate the cards into two stacks of dos and don'ts. We can even order them within those groups, since some are more serious than others. This hierarchical sorting relies on pairs like 'right' and 'wrong' that don't just describe the way the world *is* but rather prescribe the way the world *should* be. Although "science can . . . help us understand what we *should* do and *should* want" (*The Moral Landscape*, p. 28), this understanding is conditional on a prior desire to live the best life possible, which is an essential spark that science cannot supply. So, on my telling, all the cards need to be rewritten into conditional statements '*If you want to live/flourish, then* it is good to eat a balanced breakfast', '*If you want to live/flourish, then* it is wrong to pursue a career you dislike', '*If you want to live/flourish, then* it is wrong to beat your partner senseless with a crowbar',—and so on.

Now, as any first-year student of logic knows, conditional statements can be true or false (for example, it can be true that 'If someone smashes the vase, then it will break', even when no one smashes it). Hence, keeping in mind the peculiarities of our anatomies and environments, I see no reason why science could not determine the truth or falsity of the conditional statements listed on the cards. Still, having fully determined such truths, nothing would compel one to act as the cards recommend. For such statements to be morally binding, one needs to affirm the first part of their if-then statements, thereby turning the conditional structure into what is called a *modus ponens*:

> If you want to live/flourish, then it is good to do x, y, and z.
>
> I want to live/flourish.
>
> Therefore,
>
> It is good to do x, y, and z.

There are different ways for propositions to be true. So, if the proposition 'I want to live/flourish' has any truth-conditions, then its truth-maker is my *want*. I make it true. This explains why, when it comes to seeking happiness, the caveman and I are on equal footing. It is my mortality, not my two PhDs, which compels me to regard radon—and the Taliban—as worth avoiding.

In most contexts, we can omit life-affirmation of the second premise for the sake of brevity. Harris (*The Moral Landscape*, pp. 15–16) certainly omits it when he juxtaposes his desirable and undesirable lives. Here is essentially what he says:

> *x*, *y*, and *z* are good.
>
> Therefore,
>
> It is good to do *x*, *y*, and *z*.

The most tangible sign that Harris takes the most basic ethical polarities for granted is that, in his original text, he labels the lives A and B "the bad life" and "the good life" respectively (p. 15)—thus employing the very terms that stand in need of justification. Similarly, Harris banks on our recoil from a scenario involving "The Worst Possible Misery for Everyone" (p. 38). Yet, a choice to favor life over death must be operative for such scenarios to have any moral significance and inform our conduct (see the telling anecdote in *The Moral Landscape*, p. 182). This desire should be made explicit, as in the *modus ponens* just proposed. I thus see my account as making room for the more relationally complex fact that "anything of value must be valuable *to* someone" (p. 180).

According to this augmented picture, we can line up all the cards like dominoes, with life-promoting behaviors at one end, death-promoting behaviors at the other end, and a slew in between. Science can and should be tasked with assisting this ordering. Why, for example, is lying not conducive to a good life? It is not obvious, so we need an explanation (of the sort offered by Harris in *Lying*). Yet, as home-buyers know, no amount of argument or data-gathering will amount to a decision. Hence, even if the cards are organized like dominoes, something outside the cards needs to topple the first in the series.

When, like a marriage vow, I express my love of life by affirming (not necessarily verbally) that *I do* want to live/flourish, the second parts of the if-then statements sequentially get unlocked and all the cards fall like dominoes (the organization is actually a lattice, see my "Axiomatizing Umwelt Normativity," p. 30). The set of now-binding prescriptions, taken as a corporate body, constitute a morality—a principled blueprint on how I should act. I may then evaluate any object, person, or event that I cross paths with. The arsonist and 9/11 attacker objectively become bad guys, whereas the firefighter and office worker objectively become good guys.

You have to live and wish to extend that precious gift for morality to get into gear. Nature (your parents) gave you life, but you must do as professional actors say and *own it*. Since an affirmation of the second premise's "I want to live/flourish" can only come from the individual, it would seem that "we have a prerogative which some would attribute only to God: each of us, when we act, is a prime mover unmoved" (Chisholm, *Human Freedom and the Self*, p. 12). Indeed, despite my antipathy toward religious dogma, I find it interesting that, in the Biblical creation myth, God says after each stepwise ingredient that "it was good." Such valuation only seems 'god-like' because we haven't (yet) invented a better vocabulary for the purpose.

Harris could perhaps invoke his critique of free will (*Free Will*) to insist that, under normal circumstances, an organism is compelled to turn the conditional of the first premise into a *modus ponens*. Clinging to life is indeed the default (which explains the relative rarity and difficulty of suicide). But, one of the things we need, in my estimate, is an account of how living organisms, as real wholes, possess genuine agency. Yet, even if we assume that it was ordained from the moment of the Big Bang that determinists like Harris would serve as the mouthpieces of the universe itself, we should still favor an account that factors in an organism's regard for its life.

Cherishing My Life in the Aftermath of God's Death

A lifeward (or death-avoiding) orientation distinguishes the people in the Twin Towers from their attackers. As befits a murder-suicide, both died. But, one wanted to live while the other didn't. This wanting makes all the difference. Indeed, unlike Harris, my account is not susceptible of being upturned by the presence of "rapists, liars, and thieves" who "would experience the same depth of happiness as the saints" (*The Moral Landscape*, p. 189), since those folks would hinder *my* life (see my "What About Suicide Bombers?" for a fuller discussion of this crucial nuance).

It is thus important to underscore that the moral standard here is not some disembodied concept of "Life" with a capital L, but one's *individual* life, flesh and all. I have argued elsewhere that Harris's "wilful disregard of professional work in ethics leads him to reinvent utilitarianism (the greatest happiness for the greatest number)—in a version completely unresponsive to the criticisms that this view underwent in actual debates" (*Myth, Meaning, and Antifragile Individualism*, p. 181). Indeed, "It is not at all clear why, starting from a 'moral' desire to enhance our own well-being, we should move to a concern for the well-being of conscious creatures generally. A crucial premise is missing" (Meacham's review, p. 44). Life, in general, may endure, but only particular beings die and only particular beings (strive to) experience well-being. The account I am proposing is thus self-centered, in the strict non-pejorative sense of the term:

Suppose that eventually a living system arose from the primordial soup—or wherever it was. Then we will have to ask: Who was the subject to whom the differences worked on by such a system should make a difference? If one admits at all, that living systems are information processing entities, then the only possible answer to this question is: *the system itself is the subject. Therefore a living system must 'exist' for itself,* and in this sense it is more than an imaginary invention of ours: . . . Self-reference is the fundament on which life evolves, the most basal requirement. (Hoffmeyer, "Code Duality Revisited," pp. 101–02; emphasis added)

This is why *my* life gives the moral landscape its relief.

To gloss this as "autism rebranded" ("How to Lose Readers [Without Even Trying]") would not only be to confess cynicism about the human ability to weigh larger contexts (in a manner reminiscent of game theory), but also to confess that one is still in the grip of religious admonitions. Harris may be an atheist, but Nietzsche warned that even though "God is dead; . . . there may still for millennia be caves in which [people] show his shadow" (*The Gay Science*, p. 109). In his debate with Harris, the Christian apologist William Lane Craig expressed confidence that both men would agree on practically all ethical issues. Yet, to say, for example, that lies overburden one's mental accounting (*Lying*, p. 33) and needlessly complicate one's life (p. 41) is to say something very different from what most religions say. Providing reasons instead of commandments is already a game-changer, but the truly revolutionary suggestion is that lying is not in one's long-term best interest (compare Harris's case for honesty with Smith, *Ayn Rand's Normative Ethics*, pp. 75–105, who doesn't airbrush her appeal to self-interest).

In his work on lying and elsewhere, Harris contends that "I should do the right thing," but he denies that "I" even exist (since there is supposedly no self) or that I could "do" anything anyway (since there is supposedly no free will). Maybe I need to meditate more or take "pharmacological shortcuts" (*Waking Up*, p. 93), but it seems to me that Harris undermines his own moral project. Even those promulgating a dialogue between cognitive science and meditation think that Harris's stance is "nonsensical" (Thompson, *Why I Am Not a Buddhist*, p. 45). In any event, until I plumb the depths of such mysteries, I prefer to bite down hard on all the concepts that "I should do the right thing" presupposes (see my "Can 'I' Prevent You from Entering My Mind?" for a defense of the

"I," "Axiomatizing Umwelt Normativity" for a defense of the "should," and "Just Do It" for a defense of the "do").

What *is* the right thing to do? If we stop waving our hands and start looking at applied cases, it quickly becomes a complicated question, with plenty of room for reasonable disagreement. One thing is for sure, there is no way to switch the anchor from God's will to my life and emerge with an identical list of dos and don'ts. Jesus, for example, viewed pride as a vice. Aristotle, the founder of biology, viewed pride as the crown of all the virtues. There is substantial disagreement here. It should be clear where I side. "Self" is not a four-letter word (see Salmieri, "Aristotle on Selfishness?"). Some will undoubtedly try to make appeals to well-being square with traditional religious tenets, but reshaping someone else's intuitions is a fool's errand, so I will not endeavor to "defeat God's shadow as well" (*The Gay Science*, p. 109). Time will do that for me.

Harris notes that "one of the greatest challenges facing civilization in the twenty-first century is for human beings to learn to speak about their deepest personal concerns . . . about ethics . . . in ways that are not flagrantly irrational" (*Letter to a Christian Nation*, p. 87). I agree. One of the most valuable things we humans have at our disposal is rationality, since that mutation allows us to critically scrutinize what our elders taught us, to determine which values are truly worth pursuing. Rationality also allows us to go beyond here-and-now gratification to ascertain what is really in our best interest. Since the written statements in my thought-experiment exhaustively covered every conceivable moral truth, there must be a card in the mix that reads: "If you want to live/flourish, then it is good to learn more about the nature of your wanting." The individual desire to live at the heart of such a rational ethic may not be "scientific" in the strict sense of being falsifiable. But, hopefully, this chapter has shed light on the fundamental life-or-death alternative that gives the moral landscape its relief.

References

Bateson, Gregory. 1977. *Steps to an Ecology of Mind*. Ballantine.

Champagne, Marc. 2011a. Axiomatizing Umwelt Normativity. *Sign Systems Studies* 39:1.

———. 2011b. What About Suicide Bombers? A Terse Response to a Terse Objection. *The Journal of Ayn Rand Studies* 11:2.

———. 2013. Can 'I' Prevent You from Entering My Mind? *Phenomenology and the Cognitive Sciences* 12:1.

———. 2014. Just Do It: Schopenhauer and Peirce on the Immediacy of Agency. *Symposium: Canadian Journal of Continental Philosophy* 18:2.

———. 2020. *Myth, Meaning, and Antifragile Individualism: On the Ideas of Jordan Peterson*. Imprint Academic.

———. 2022. Stone, Stone-Soup, and Soup. In *Jordan Peterson: Critical Responses*, edited by Sandra L. Woien. Open Universe.

Chisholm, Roderick M. 1964. *Human Freedom and the Self*. University of Kansas Press.

Haack, Susan. 2012. Six Signs of Scientism. *Logos and Episteme* 3:1.

Harris, Sam. 2004. *The End of Faith: Religion, Terror, and the Future of Reason*. Norton.

———. 2006. *Letter to a Christian Nation*. Random House.

———. 2010. *The Moral Landscape: How Science Can Determine Human Values*. Free Press.

———. 2011. How to Lose Readers (Without Even Trying). samharris.org blog post (August 24th) <www.samharris.org/blog/how-to-lose-readers-without-even-trying>.

———. 2012. *Free Will*. Free Press.

———. 2013. *Lying*. Four Elephants Press.

———. 2014. *Waking Up: A Guide to Spirituality Without Religion*. Simon and Schuster.

———. 2016. Can We Build AI Without Losing Control Over It? TED Summit (June 29th) <https://www.youtube.com/watch?v=8nt3edWLgIg>.

Hoffmeyer, Jesper. 2002. Code Duality Revisited. *S.E.E.D. (Semiotics, Evolution, Energy, and Development)* 2:1.

Jonas, Hans. 1996. *Mortality and Morality: A Search for the Good after Auschwitz*. Northwestern University Press.

Legrenzi, Paolo, and Carlo Umiltà. 2011. *Neuromania: On the Limits of Brain Science*. Oxford University Press.

McDowell, John. 1992. Putnam on Mind and Meaning. *Philosophical Topics* 20:1.

Meacham, Bill. 2012. Review of *The Moral Landscape: How Science Can Determine Human Values*. *Philosophy Now* 90.

Nagel, Thomas. 1986. *The View from Nowhere*. Oxford University Press.

Nietzsche, Friedrich. 2001. *The Gay Science*. Cambridge University Press.

Popper, Karl R. 2002. *Conjectures and Refutations: The Growth of Scientific Knowledge*. Routledge.

Rorty, Richard. 1989. *Contingency, Irony, and Solidarity*. Cambridge University Press.

Salmieri, Gregory. 2014. Aristotle on Selfishness? Understanding the Iconoclasm of *Nicomachean Ethics* ix 8. *Ancient Philosophy* 34:1.

Schrödinger, Erwin. 1992. *What Is Life?* Cambridge University Press.

Shah, Shuchee. 2016. Cross-Cultural View of Rape. *Southern California Review of Law and Social Justice* 26:1.

Smith, Tara. 2000. *Viable Values: A Study of Life as the Root and Reward of Morality*. Rowman and Littlefield.

———. 2006. *Ayn Rand's Normative Ethics: The Virtuous Egoist*. Cambridge University Press.

———. 2008. The Importance of the Subject in Objective Morality: Distinguishing Objective from Intrinsic Value. *Social Philosophy and Policy* 25:1.

Thompson, Evan. 2020. *Why I Am Not a Buddhist*. Yale University Press.

Uttal, William R. 2001. *The New Phrenology: The Limits of Localizing Cognitive Processes in the Brain*. MIT Press.

II

Liberal Values

[3]
Spotting Dangerous Ideas

DAVID RAMSAY STEELE

The thing that most struck me when I first read *The End of Faith* was Sam Harris's unashamed advocacy of intolerance, arising out of his preoccupation with dangerous ideas.

Harris made a point of putting on record—no one was twisting his arm—his opinion that it's entirely permissible, indeed right and proper, to kill people who have done nothing wrong, simply because they believe things which he judges to be dangerous. You think I must be distorting what Harris says?

> Some propositions are so dangerous that it may even be ethical to kill people for believing them. This may seem an extraordinary claim, but it merely enunciates an ordinary fact about the world in which we live. Certain beliefs place their adherents beyond the reach of every peaceful means of persuasion, while inspiring them to commit extraordinary acts of violence against others. There is, in fact, no talking to some people. If they cannot be captured, and they often cannot, otherwise tolerant people may be justified in killing them in self-defense. (pp. 52–53)

Several misunderstandings here. A moral judgment or a policy recommendation cannot merely enunciate a fact. Some former terrorists have given up their commitment to terrorism after coming to terms with their experience and being confronted with arguments, so terrorists are not always beyond the reach of peaceful persuasion. Killing someone because you believe they hold to ideas that might lead them to commit acts of violence in the future is not self-defense.

Harris insists that there can be no "private" ideas (p. 44). It follows that your innermost thoughts are the business of the police. And he says:

> I hope to show that the very ideal of religious tolerance—born of the notion that every human being should be free to believe whatever he wants about God—is one of the principal forces driving us toward the abyss. (p. 15)

Harris never does show this. He never even produces an argument that we're being driven toward any abyss by anything. But he does make plain that he's against religious tolerance—I like the old-fashioned term, 'liberty of conscience'. If you find yourself inclined to believe something of a religious nature, you not only have to decide whether it might be true; you also have to run it by Harris in case it's one of those conclusions that would persuade him that you need to be deleted.

Harris's view that it's okay, or perhaps even morally obligatory, to kill folks who embrace dangerous ideas should be clearly distinguished from his general willingness to criticize Islam as an erroneous system of thought, like Christianity or Judaism—or, I would add, like Marxism, Psychoanalysis, or Postmodernism. The Wokish wee folk have condemned Harris and have spitefully disseminated untruths about him, because he has drawn attention to the fact that Islam is, like Christianity, largely composed of falsehoods. He has also irritated the Wokish by dwelling on the fact that the 9/11 attacks and many other recent terrorist outrages have been perpetrated by Muslims. And he's not reluctant to call attention to the oppressive treatment of women and other groups within some traditional Muslim cultures, something which our progressive feminists consider iniquitous to mention, because . . . ? Well, ask them.

In being willing to criticize Islam as well as Christianity, and in pointing out certain facts about terrorist acts by some Muslims, Sam Harris is entirely in the right. However, I beg to differ with Harris with respect to three of his contentions: 1. that the liberal principle of liberty of conscience should be abandoned, as it applies to Muslims, or some subset of Muslims; 2. that it's morally okay to kill people who have broken no law because we judge (or someone judges) that their ideas are dangerous; and 3. that suicide bombings can be simply explained by the theory that Muslims do what the *Quran* tells them to do.

Harris's Two Theses

There are two theses running through *The End of Faith*. Harris sees these two theses as being entirely at home with each other. But I think they require separate treatment.

First, there is the thesis that there exists something called "religion," distinguished by accepting beliefs "on faith," which Harris unpacks as accepting beliefs on insufficient evidence or as accepting *unjustified* beliefs. Second, there is a peculiar problem with Islam, because Muslims revere the *Quran*, the *Quran* tells them to kill unbelievers, and this explains why there is suicide bombing.

At first glance these two theses may seem to be compatible, because identifying the *Quran* (or the *New Testament*) as the infallible word of God doesn't appear to be well supported by evidence. But as we look more closely, we notice that the two theses are mutually independent and don't sit very well together.

While Muslims might be supposed to believe things on inadequate evidence, Harris makes no attempt to show that they're more susceptible to "faith" than many other people, religious or irreligious. Although Harris doesn't quite commit himself on this point, he seems open to the idea that non-Muslims can be just as prone to accepting unjustified beliefs as Muslims. By Harris's own standards, everyone, or very nearly everyone, believes a whole lot of things without adequate evidence.

There's a difference between saying that Muslim ideas are dangerous because they are accepted on faith, and saying that Muslim ideas are dangerous because of their specific content. The latter is Harris's position, so faith drops out as an explanatory variable.

We observe that the vast majority of Muslims, even the most devout and fundamentalist ones, are not suicide bombers. It's true that quite a large number of Muslims have some sympathy with today's Muslim suicide bombers. I explain this in much the way that I explain why many Irish Catholics (encompassing Irish Catholic Americans), including some who would never directly support Sinn Fein, have some sympathy with IRA-Sinn Fein: they see these people as fighting (perhaps not always in the best way) for the defense of their own national ethnic population.

Muslims, like Christians, do take propositions on faith, meaning, as Harris tells us, that the truth of these proposition has not been justified. I thought I was going to have to take up a bit of space to explain to Sam Harris that *no proposition can ever be justified*, except within a theoretical framework requiring assumptions which cannot themselves be justified. But I'm now relieved to see that there's no need for this, because Harris has more recently stated that "Science and rationality generally are based on intuitions and concepts that cannot be reduced or justified" (*The Moral Landscape*, p. 204n21).

Motives for Suicide Bombing

In Harris's view, Muslim suicide bombers do it because the *Quran* tells them to—it's just that simple. In some cases we may want to say 'the *Quran* and the *hadith*', but, as far as I understand it, the *hadith* gain their authority from helping us to clarify the meaning of the *Quran*.

Robert Pape and his associates have presented a mass of detailed evidence on the motives of suicide bombers, and this evidence excludes the conjectured explanation for suicide bombing that Muslims read the *Quran* and then do what it says.

Pape analyzed all the recorded suicide bombings between 1980 and 2003; later the database was continued to 2009. About a quarter of suicide bombings between 1983 and 2003 had been committed by atheists, mostly members of the Tamil Tigers (the Liberation Tigers of Tamil Eelam), a Sri Lankan group aiming at independence for the Tamil minority in Sri Lanka. Though of Hindu background, the Tamil Tigers were Marxist-Leninists, fiercely opposed to theistic religion. Another atheist group which perpetrated suicide bombings was the PKK (Kurdistan Workers Party), a Kurdish separatist group in Turkey, adherents of Marxism-Leninism, whose victims were Muslims.

So, when *The End of Faith* was being written, a quarter of recent suicide bombings were by atheists, not Muslims, and some of these targeted Muslims. Harris seems to have been unaware of this when he wrote *The End of Faith*. After 2003, the Tamil Tigers and the PKK ceased to be operative, so that nearly all subsequent suicide bombings are by people of Muslim background, though many of these (around fifty percent) are atheist or more broadly secular-minded adherents of leftist ideologies. (These generalizations are drawn from Pape's two books, which summarize his detailed files on every recorded case of a suicide bombing.)

Two conclusions emerge very clearly from the data. First, groups which organize terrorist attacks mostly represent militarily weak ethnic populations who perceive their homeland to be under foreign occupation. They see themselves as resistance fighters conducting defensive warfare against an aggressive and brutal enemy. It would not be very promising to look into Catholic theology for the 'terrorist outrages' of the French Resistance against German occupation in 1940–45.

Second, suicide bombing has come into favor among terrorist organizations because it works; it's an entirely rational technique which achieves results. The announced goal of 9/11 was to get the approximately 25,000 US troops to leave Saudi Arabia. The US troops were removed from Saudi Arabia. The operation achieved its goal.

There were no suicide attacks by people of Muslim background in the period prior to 1981—and that in itself should raise a doubt about Harris's theory. The pivotal event in modern suicide bombing occurred in Lebanon in October 1983. A single member of Hezbollah (an organization newly formed in response to the Israeli occupation of Lebanon) detonated a truckload of explosives, taking out 241 US marines, as well as himself. President Reagan withdrew the US troops from Lebanon, so this operation was a complete success. Around the same time the French, who had suffered a similar though less spectacular suicide bombing, also withdrew their troops.

It has been estimated that on average someone prepared to die in an attack can take out twelve times as many of the enemy as someone who plans to escape with his life. Would Reagan have reacted the same if the death toll had been only twenty? Suicide bombings as well as non-suicide terrorist attacks are organized by intelligent, educated people who follow the news. The atheist Tamil Tigers were quick to draw the logical conclusion from the successful suicide bombing in Lebanon. (Some people would say that Lebanon 1983, while it was a suicide attack, was not a case of 'terrorism' since US troops stationed in a country whose population seriously doesn't want them to be there are neither innocent nor civilians. But Pape extends the use of 'terrorism' to such cases, and I won't quibble.)

It shouldn't be necessary to remind anyone that all pro-war narratives, for example American or British movies about World War II, represent it as the summit of patriotic virtue and glory when someone strikes a blow against the enemy knowing that it will result in his own death. Celebrating the voluntary self-destruction of soldiers in wartime, patriotic Christians would often apply the famous saying of Jesus: "Greater love hath no man than this, that a man lay down his life for his friends" (*John* 15:13).

Nor should it need to be recalled that a major part of Allied military operations in that war was devoted to the mass slaughter of non-combatants (the 'area bombing' of working-class housing in German cities and similar bombings of civilian dwellings in Japan, culminating in Hiroshima and Nagasaki). The stated aim of this systematic extermination of civilian non-combatants was to "break the morale" of the enemy population.

History is studded with suicide attacks, though these were limited in effectiveness before the invention of dynamite in 1867. We're told that Samson, with God's help, killed himself and three thousand Philistine men and women by collapsing the building they were in (*Judges* 16:30), no doubt a prophecy of 9/11. A high percentage of Roman emperors were assassinated or violently injured in assassination attempts, usually by people who knew this would automatically mean their own deaths. The assassination of Tsar Alexander II in 1881 and of Russian minister Plehve in 1904 were suicide bombings. Suicide squads and individual suicide bombings were frequently employed in the Chinese wars from 1911 to 1949, both between different Chinese war lords and against the occupying Japanese. The Japanese military employed the famous *kamikaze* suicide bombings against the US, beginning in October 1944, and the Luftwaffe flew 'self-sacrifice missions' (*Selbstopfereinsatz*) against the Soviets in the Battle for Berlin, April 1945.

Suicide attack is the continuation of a policy of non-suicide attack by suicidal means. If the suicide attackers could do as much damage to the enemy without suicide, they would always opt to do so.

In nineteenth-century Europe there were anarchist suicide assassins who were generally atheists. These killings are not usually labeled suicide attacks but it's clear that the attackers often didn't expect to survive the attacks. This phenomenon became a theme in Victorian popular culture, reflected in "The Stolen Bacillus," by H.G. Wells and *The Secret Agent* by Joseph Conrad.

A Dangerous System of Ideas

Suicide bombing is horrible, but it's a vanishingly tiny part of "man's inhumanity to man." Suicide bombing (with the exceptions of the *Selbstopfereinsatz* and *kamikaze* pilots, and even those were cases of last-ditch desperation) is done by weak groups out of power, whereas more than 99 percent of major atrocities are carried out by strong groups in full command of a state.

So, by way of a change, let's turn our attention to the hundred-ton titanosaur in the room—Bolshevism, alias Marxism-Leninism, alias Communism, alias the Fraternal Socialist Camp. Communism killed 90 million innocent people. (I talk about killings for brevity, though we have to understand that for every killing there are dozens of less bothersome inconveniences, such as imprisonment and torture, visited on the Communists' hapless "human material.") Communism, in the twentieth century, killed hundreds of times more innocent victims than Christianity and Islam combined, in their entire historical existence.

There are various ways of putting this in numerical perspective; I'll mention just one example. The Spanish Inquisition (Ha! You didn't expect *that*) lasted 356 years, from 1478 to 1834. Estimates of the total number executed by the Inquisition range from 1,250 to 5,000. Compare this with 15,000 killed *in two months*, under the Lenin-Trotsky government in the fall of 1918. Everyone executed by order of the Holy Office of the Inquisition had their day in court, and most people accused were acquitted. The Bolshevik victims were just names on a list, picked up and disposed of, with a bracing proletarian disdain for bourgeois hang-ups like human rights or due process. Not that the Bolsheviks were proletarians, but they affected to be proletarians (we can call them trans proletarians). The Bolsheviks had managed to divine the true interests of the proletariat, or so they devoutly believed, and had therefore—scientifically— anointed themselves the vanguard of the proletariat.

Harris's Unsatisfactory Response

Harris naturally attempts to answer the most obvious criticisms of his position. In support of his claim that there's something uniquely Muslim about suicide bombing, he points out that various non-Muslim populations have faced poverty and oppression without turning to suicide bombing (p. 109). This side-steps the key causal factor, occupation by foreign troops, and ignores the many non-Muslim suicide bombers.

In a direct comment on Pape's work, Harris calls it "obscurantist" to attribute nationalist political motives to Osama bin Laden (p. 261). Of course, a fundamentalist Muslim resistance fighter will justify his actions in fundamentalist Muslim terms, just as a Marxist-Leninist resistance fighter will justify his actions in Marxist-Leninist terms. Yet bin Laden scoffed at the suggestion that al-Qaeda was motivated by general hatred of the unbelieving West, emphasizing repeatedly that al-Qaeda was a response to Western military occupation.

No, we fight because we are free men who don't sleep under oppression. . . . contrary to Bush's claim that we hate freedom. If so, let him explain why we don't strike, for example, Sweden. (bin Laden video, quoted in *Cutting the Fuse*, p. 51)

Harris asks, "Where are the Palestinian Christian suicide bombers? . . . Where, for that matter, are the Tibetan Buddhist suicide bombers? . . . The difference lies in the specific tenets of Islam" (p. 233).

Does it really? There have been some Palestinian Christian fighters against Israel and its Western backers. The best known is George Habash, founder and leader of the Popular Front for the Liberation of Palestine (PFLP). There were no Middle Eastern suicide bombers before 1981 but there were both Muslim and Christian Palestinian resistance fighters or 'terrorists'.

What about Christian suicide bombers specifically? I have not found a total count so I can't compare the number with other Palestinian suicide attacks. Christians comprise 1.5 percent of Palestinians living in the Middle East. It does seem from Pape's published materials that in all likelihood Palestinian Christians account for a decidedly bigger percentage than 1.5 percent of suicide attacks against Israel and Israel's Western backers. For example, in the resistance to the Israeli occupation of Lebanon, from 1982 to 1999, there were 32 successful suicide attacks, where the ideology of the attackers can be identified. Five were Christians (15.6 percent), while 22 were leftists with no commitment to religious extremism, leaving five whose outlooks were primarily Muslim fundamentalist (*Cutting the Fuse*, p. 196). So, in that admittedly non-probative case, Christians are more than ten times as well-represented among suicide bombers as their proportion of the Palestinian population. This is what we might expect, as Palestinian Christians are distinguished by a high average level of education, and education is a predictor of involvement in resistance/terrorism.

As for Harris's rhetorical query about the Tibetan Buddhists, it's well documented that the people who organize suicide bombings believe that these actions work more effectively against democracies than against totalitarian states. Totalitarian states can prevent their general population (and sometimes the outside world) from getting news about such events, and do not have to face domestic anti-war movements. There were very few suicide bombings against the Soviet occupation of Afghanistan, but very many against the later US occupation. If China were to become a democracy, we should expect to see some elements in various ethnic groups within China become more violent, and some of them become suicide bombers.

Naturally, Harris tries to respond to the fact that atheists have been responsible for more and bigger atrocities than theists. He says that "communism was little more than a political region." Communist beliefs "were both cultic and irrational" (p. 79; and see p. 231). But this amounts to equivocation. Harris made his name and his fortune by boldly proclaiming that Muslims are particularly prone to become mass murderers, because of what it says in the *Quran*; confronted with the fact that atheists are historically vastly more likely to commit mass murder than Muslims, his response is that Communism is a religion.

As far as Muslim suicide bombings go, the solution does not lie in killing devotees of the *Quran* before they get around to suicide bombing. That will reliably increase the incidence of anti-US suicide bombing. The solution lies in ending military interventions against Muslim populations. (Surely it's a point in favor of such a policy that these interventions are, from the point of view of US self-interest, costly and most often disastrous, even not counting the terrorist attacks they automatically provoke. What did the US gain from the 2003–2011 Iraq war, which killed 100,000 innocent civilians?) No doubt there will still be occasional rare attacks in response to blasphemous cartoons or the like, but more than 99 percent of anti-US suicide bombings will immediately and permanently cease, if the US stops intervening militarily against Muslim populations. (In arguing for total non-intervention, I go further than Pape's group, who favor a more indirect and sensitive mode of intervention.)

Pape's theory propounded in 2005 elicited some serious criticisms, such as those of Assaf Moghadam and Scott Attran. Subsequent events have powerfully corroborated Pape's position (*Cutting the Fuse*, pp. 44–83); yet, in any case, Pape's competent critics did not endorse Harris's simple theory that suicide attacks are caused by doing what the *Quran* tells you to do.

Dangerous Ideas, Old and New

Within industrialized capitalist societies, theistic religion withers on the vine. We observe that this holds in all cases—

the notion that the United States was ever an exception is a simple misunderstanding, arising from the fact that for two centuries the United States contained within its borders a third-world country: the South. Now that the South has industrialized, America is rapidly becoming exactly like Europe, as far as theistic religion goes.

Sam Harris ignores the big fact that the theistic or supernaturalistic belief systems of pre-industrial cultures are succeeded by the non-theistic, non-supernaturalistic belief systems of industrialized cultures. These latter 'scientific' belief systems are just as much filled with absurdities and preposterous nonsense as the earlier belief systems. The Oedipus Complex, the class struggle, or intersectionality are just as much intellectual dross and drivel as the doctrines of the Trinity or blood sacrifice for sin. And they are just as likely to lead to atrocities, perhaps more so.

As a simple matter of fact, the historical atrocities deriving from purportedly scientific belief systems vastly outweigh the historical atrocities deriving from theistic or supernaturalistic belief systems. Does this mean that atheism is inherently more prone to commit mass murder than theism? Not necessarily. The greater death toll attributable to secular ideologies could be wholly or partly due to the fact that the rise of non-supernaturalistic ideologies coincides with the emergence of bigger populations and more efficient techniques to mobilize the state's mass-murder machine.

Voltaire's motto was *Écrasez l'infâme!*, crush the appalling monstrosity of ecclesiastical Christendom. It never crossed his mind that theistic belief systems would be replaced by new ideologies avowedly based on reason and science, and that these ideologies would turn out to be far more murderous, far more devastating for human well-being, than theism or supernatural belief had ever been.

The eclipse of theistic religion in the industrialized world has been much less of a gain for humankind than rationalists and freethinkers expected. There has been hardly any diminution of gross error in people's thinking, rather a limitation of one narrow type of error and the proliferation of many new errors, nearly always presenting themselves as scientific.

The driving narrative of Sam Harris and all the New Atheists is that we face a peculiar menace from theistic religion, which threatens to push us into the abyss, because it accepts propositions without sufficient evidence. Through my old atheist eyes, I see theistic religion as an enfeebled and increasingly irrelevant force in the world (as long as net global economic growth continues), being replaced by atheistic and purportedly scientific belief systems, which swallow just as many impossible things before breakfast, and threaten us with atrocities more horrendous than anything the theists could have dreamed up.

The Paradox of Tolerance

Harris's principle that we're entitled to kill people for holding dangerous ideas naturally brings to mind the Paradox of Tolerance, briefly formulated by Karl Popper in *The Open Society and Its Enemies* (Volume 1, p. 265n4). Popper holds that we ought to be selectively intolerant of intolerant ideas (though not routinely, but only under very rare and specific conditions), in other words, we ought sometimes to deny the usual liberal freedom of expression to those who advocate policies which would deny the usual liberal freedoms to everyone.

Popper's argument is superficially persuasive, but it falls apart upon closer examination. Its incoherence becomes visible when we pose the question 'Who is the we?' Is the 'we' an extra-dimensional wraith, who can observe the growth of the intolerant group and intervene from outside the political process to restrict people's freedom of speech? Presumably not. But then we have the situation where the 'we' is itself part of the political system, socially interacting with the intolerance-advocating group as well as other groups. And we have to assume that the 'we' is able to deny freedom to the intolerance-advocating group while not being able to counteract the intolerance-advocating group by peaceful persuasion. Right off the bat, that looks unlikely.

Surely if the 'we' is able to deny freedom to the group advocating intolerance, the 'we' must be in a strong position, while the apparent inability of the 'we' to combat the influence of the intolerance-advocating group by peaceful persuasion must imply that the 'we' is weak. Furthermore, suppression of the group's activities might very well stimulate sympathy for the group, and play into the hands of those who say that tolerance is a sham, that the so-called tolerant are only tolerant as long as their key interests are not threatened, and so on. The government of the Weimar Republic prohibited Adolf Hitler from speaking publicly; whether this ultimately hurt or helped his chances of getting into power is debatable.

All in all, then, selectively practicing intolerance against those who would install an intolerant regime if they could, is not a superior strategy to defending the principle of liberty of conscience all the time. Ultimately, ideas expressed in words are the only weapon available to combat intolerance, just as ideas expressed in words are the only weapon available to spread intolerant ideas in the first place.

From Out of Left Field

Where are future atrocities going to come from? It's not obvious which ideas and which ideological groups are going to turn out to be the most dangerous.

Prior to 1917, the basic principles of Marxism were widely known. They included the following propositions: Minority coups or insurrections are wrong, and to be actively discouraged. (When I use words like 'wrong' here, I'm translating from Marxese into English.) The socialist movement must be fully democratic and must take part in the democratic process to "win the battle of democracy." Even in non-democratic polities like Germany, Marx and Engels thought it wrong to use violence, as long as progress towards democracy could be made by non-violent means (Hunt, pp. 325–336). Among other key tenets of classical Marxism, no socialist revolution is to be expected in a predominantly peasant society and the worst fate will befall anyone who tries to carry through a social revolution before the economic conditions are ripe for it.

These principles were fully accepted by all Marxists, including even the Bolsheviks. And when the Bolsheviks acted contrary to these Marxist principles by seizing power, shutting down the democratically elected assembly, and killing their intellectual critics, all leading Marxists in the world, without exception, denounced the Bolsheviks. Top of the targets on the Bolshevik hit list were those Marxists who remained true to elementary Marxist principles, notably the Mensheviks.

Before 1917 it would have seemed fantastic beyond all possibility of ridicule to hypothesize that by far the bloodiest empires in all of human history were about to be founded by a sect of Marxism, albeit a bizarrely heretical sect. If I were to predict now that five years in the future, the most murderous regime of all time will be set up by fanatical followers of Sam Harris, that would be about as plausible as a similar prediction about Marxism in 1912 (in fact a little more plausible, since Marx, unlike Harris, did not preach that people holding dangerous ideas should be wasted).

There's no litmus test to determine where the biggest danger is going to come from next—and no simple formula to decide in advance, when things get really bleak, who's going to be the ally who may possibly save your family's life.

Bibliography

Attran, Scott. 2006. The Moral Logic and Growth of Suicide Terrorism. *Washington Quarterly* 29:2.

Collard-Wexler, Simon, Constantino Pischedda, and Michael G. Smith. 2014. Do Foreign Occupations Cause Suicide Attacks? *Journal of Conflict Resolution* 58:4.

Conrad, Joseph. 2007 [1907]. *The Secret Agent: A Simple Tale.* Penguin.

Courtois, Stéphane, et al. 1999. *The Black Book of Communism: Crimes, Terror, Repression.* Harvard University Press.

Exposing Theism. 2012. Sam Harris vs Robert Pape on Suicide Terrorism. <www.youtube.com/watch?v=emiwacyap0Q&t=4s>.

Harris, Sam. 2005 [2004]. *The End of Faith: Religion, Terror, and the Future of Reason.* Norton.

———. 2010. *The Moral Landscape: How Science Can Determine Human Values.* Free Press.

Moghadam, Assaf. 2006. Suicide Terrorism, Occupation, and the Globalization of Martyrdom: A Critique of *Dying to Win.* *Studies in Conflict and Terrorism* 9:8.

<www.tandfonline.com/doi/full/10.1080/10576100600561907>.

Pape, Robert A. 2005. *Dying to Win: The Strategic Logic of Suicide Terrorism*. Random House.

Pape, Robert A., and James K. Feldman. 2010. *Cutting the Fuse: The Explosion of Global Suicide Terrorism and How to Stop It*. University of Chicago Press.

Popper, Karl Raimund. 1966 [1945]. *The Open Society and Its Enemies. Volume I: The Spell of Plato*. Two volumes. Princeton University Press.

Smith, George H. 2013. *The System of Liberty: Themes in the History of Classical Liberalism*. Cambridge University Press.

Steele, David Ramsay. 2008. *Atheism Explained: From Folly to Philosophy*. Open Court.

———. 2010. Is God Coming or Going? *Philosophy Now* 78. Reprinted in Steele 2019.

———. 2014. The Bigotry of the New Atheism (by an Old Atheist). The London Libertarian blog. Reprinted in Steele 2019.

———. 2019. *The Mystery of Fascism: David Ramsay Steele's Greatest Hits*. St. Augustine's Press.

Wells, H.G. 2017 [1894]. The Stolen Bacillus. In H.G. Wells, *H.G. Wells Short Stories*. Flame Tree.

Williams, Jeffrey William. 2013. The Human Use of Human Beings: A Brief History of Suicide Bombing. *Origins: Current Events in Historical Perspective* <https://origins.osu.edu/article/human-use-human-beings-brief-history-suicide-bombing?language_content_entity=en>.

[4]
Intellectual Integrity or Social Justice?

Lucas Rijana

As a key component of New Atheism's early rise to popularity, Sam Harris's critique of religion is incredibly influential. That's why it might come as a surprise to know that Harris would not call himself an atheist. In *The End of Faith* (2004), the word does not appear even once. In fact, during a speech given at the 2007 Atheist Alliance conference, Harris decried the use of the term, arguing that it is unhelpful and unnecessary. By adopting the term, he argued, we unwittingly uphold religion's hegemony over public discourse, when we should aim for its complete ostracization.

To illustrate this, Harris uses the analogy of racism: "How have people of good will and common sense gone about combating racism? There was a civil rights movement, of course . . . There have been important and, I think, irrevocable changes in the way we talk about race . . . But, ask yourself, how many people have had to identify themselves as "non-racists" to participate in this process? Is there a 'non-racist alliance' somewhere for me to join?" (Harris, "The Problem with Atheism").

Fast forward to the present day, and non-racist alliances abound. *Antiracism* is not only more intelligible and more present in public discourse today than ever before, but it's also quickly becoming a theoretical cornerstone of many academic, media, and political elites. If the analogy of racism did not age well, is it because such a strategy is, after all, necessary? Or is it because, as Harris would suggest, we've lost our way?

Sam Harris's views on modern forms of social justice activism resemble his early critique of atheism's struggle against religious dogma. Both pursuits share the same kind of end goal, the same strategic and philosophical problems to get there, and the same vital precondition: intellectual integrity.

What Antiracism?

A minimal definition of antiracism refers to: "Those forms of thought and/or practice that seek to confront, eradicate and/or ameliorate racism" (Bonnett, *Anti-Racism*, p. 3). Of course, different forms of antiracism often operate with different definitions of racism. For Sam Harris, both racism and religion are beliefs or ideas held by individuals. Understanding racism as a belief held by an identifiable person can be contrasted with understanding racism as structural or systemic. In the latter case, an institution may be deemed racist if unequal outcomes exist. This is true even if no individual within that institution holds racist beliefs, because the unit of analysis is a collective (*Anti-Racism*, p. 4). These are ultimately complementary perspectives and not mutually exclusive. Nevertheless, the kind of antiracism that Harris objects to is based upon an overly lax definition that doesn't require individuals to consciously hold beliefs. As a result, it risks hurting its cause by diluting conscious racism into a sea of bad jokes, microaggresions, and suspected unintentional biases. On the other hand, atheists can likewise adopt loose conceptions of religious dogma that mistakenly include, for instance, practical forms of spiritual pursuit that have traditionally been associated with religion. Mindfulness meditation and similar activities do not need to believe anything on faith and rely on experiential evidence accessible to anyone. Their utility is often cast aside by atheists, when they should instead focus on more harmful religious practices ("The Problem with Atheism").

While the popular and sometimes pejorative term "Critical Race Theory" is not specific enough, the writings of Ibram Kendi (*How to Be an Antiracist*) and Robin DiAngelo (*White Fragility*) are straightforward examples of this form of antiracism. Many institutions such as universities have adopted it in their speech codes and admissions policies. *The*

New York Times and other influential newspapers have embraced antiracism through initiatives such as *The 1619 Project*, while science-oriented magazines like *Nature* and *Scientific American* continue to dedicate resources to find and purge racism in science (articles in *Nature* and *Scientific American*). Some of the most powerful corporations in the world, like Google, have explicitly endorsed antiracism (Pichai, "Our Commitment to Racial Equality"). Antiracism in education has become a staple of US political discourse, with Republican politicians routinely concerned about the teaching of Critical Race Theory in schools and democrats denouncing these concerns as "accepting of racism" (Lemon, "AOC Suggests").

Some suggest that antiracism today has become a kind of religious cult that is here to stay (McWhorter, *Woke Racism*; Murray, *The War on the West*). Of course, many would argue that this is all an exaggeration and most people in high positions are not 'passionate antiracists'. However, the question of this ideological strain's actual reach and intensity is a separate issue altogether, while its existence cannot be denied. As Sam Harris describes it: "People by the millions are now surrendering themselves to a kind of religious awakening. But like most religious awakenings, this movement is not showing itself eager to make honest contact with reality" ("Can We Pull Back from the Brink?"). As we will see, this refusal to accurately depict the facts is the most significant hazard affecting these movements today.

The End Goal

For Harris, the battle against religious beliefs and the struggle against racism share a common end goal. A world where religious beliefs no longer play a relevant role in public deliberation is one where "atheism is scarcely intelligible as a concept," because theism is no longer as prevalent as it currently is. In this world, people simply "cease to praise one another for pretending to know things they do not know" ("The Problem with Atheism"). Likewise, victory against racism: "certainly won't be a world in which a majority of people profess that they are 'nonracist'. Most likely, it will be a world in which the very concept of separate races has lost its meaning" ("Can We Pull Back from the Brink?"). These pursuits will end when the categories of thought they seek to extirpate are no longer in use, if not just for referencing a tumultuous past. Racist and religious people might still exist, but there will be a consensus that their claims do not command any discursive respect, especially in scientific or political matters. Harris believes that, were racism finally defeated, "skin color would become like hair color in its political and moral significance—which is to say that it would have none."

Nevertheless, the goal of color-blindness is often denounced as an excuse to pay less attention to the problem of present-day racism and maintain the status quo (Bonilla-Silva, *Racism without Racists*). For some, this ideal only reasserts the dominant ideology of the most powerful and privileged racial group. Many would gladly call color-blindness a form of racism (Williams, "Colorblind Ideology Is a Form of Racism"). The whole project of liberalism, with its assertion of neutrality, has also been deemed to enable and perpetuate racism (Sheth, *Toward a Political Philosophy of Race*).

Indeed, color-blindness is regularly used to oppose race-based social programs like affirmative action and other ways to improve minorities' standing. It has also been used in tandem with the belief that we already live in a 'post-racial society', a recurrent phrase in the years after Barack Obama's presidency. However, as argued by Phillip Mazzocco (*The Psychology of Racial Colorblindness*, p. 35), there are different varieties of color-blindness, and these "antagonist" or "protectionist" interpretations do not correspond to Harris's "visionary" understanding of it. Harris remains open-minded about reparations and other possible short-term correctives ("Can We Pull Back from the Brink?"), and acknowledges that we are nowhere near a post-racial society. Additionally, critics such as Mazzocco and Williams propose 'multiculturalism' as an alternative to color-blindness. Some believe that being proud of our race or gender and recognizing and even celebrating these categories is the only way to live harmoniously in a diverse society. But this is a false dichotomy. Nothing would impede color-blindness from working alongside a multicultural model (in fact, they complement each other). Nevertheless, Harris advises against imbuing our circumstantial traits with deep meaning and asking others to judge us accordingly. We did not choose where to be born or what body to inhabit. There is nothing about ourselves that we should be 'proud' of, for we are ultimately not the authors of ourselves. Harris's experience in meditation informs his opinions on identity politics and race, and his realization that free will and the self are illusions also plays a role (*Free Will*, *Waking Up*).

The Activist Paradox

Both pursuits, Harris suggests, share a sort of dilemma regarding their end goal: if we want a world where religion or prejudice cease to be influential, then it seems counterintuitive to give increasing presence and attention to these concepts. To *get past* race, we should eventually focus *less* on race, not more. Antiracism, just as atheism or antitheism, requires continuous vigilance against what it opposes and is meaningless without it, thus perpetuating a kind of vicious dialectical cycle.

If we continue to insist on categorizing people according to the variable of race, even when no one believes in the inferiority of any given group, stereotypes, stigma and consciously differentiated attitudes will remain. As Harris puts it, "the more progress we make on issues of race, the less racism there will be to find, and the more likely we'll find ourselves chasing after its ghost . . . The future we want is not one in which we have all become passionate anti-racists. It's not a future in which we are forever on our guard against the slightest insult—the bad joke, the awkward compliment, the tweet that didn't age well." ("Can We Pull Back from the Brink?"). Giving more power and relevance to organizations whose sole purpose is to find and denounce racism is a recipe for more 'moral panics' to come in the long run.

Clearly, this depends on the context, and Harris makes the point specifically for the present conditions. To be sure, racism is still alive in the United States, but these are not the times of Martin Luther King either and the state of race relations has no doubt improved since then. Of course, the determinate degree of progress is still in question. Critics might suggest that Harris assumes that we have already achieved a satisfactory level of non-discrimination,which is why he recommends not to 'fix what isn't broken'. However,

Sam Harris is not arguing we should do nothing about whatever consequences prejudice has today, but argues that we should do it from a more denoting viewpoint like 'liberalism' or 'humanism', or better still, from no unique viewpoint at all.

The Perils of Labels

Having a single defining label is generally seen as an essential part of social movements, while nameless movements have little chance of success. What's more, terms like 'secularism', 'liberalism' or 'civic republicanism' are too abstract or open to interpretation in the public's eye. They don't have the same galvanizing effect against a particular complaint that 'antiracism' does. So what's the problem with naming ourselves this way?

Public discourse in the United States has formed an unattractive stereotype around these labels. Atheists appear as arrogant, provoking, intolerant, and obstinate in their beliefs. Antiracists are not far behind, given the viral character of college debates and confrontations involving 'social justice warriors'. Adversaries regularly presuppose what both self-identified atheists and antiracists think, making the possibility of agreement ever more far-fetched. What's more, these groups' worthwhile ideas and achievements are obfuscated by what gets amplified in the media and exploited by political leaders.

But the issue Harris sees goes deeper than that. It's worth quoting his thoughts on atheism at length here:

> Atheism is too blunt an instrument to use at moments like this. It's as though we have a landscape of human ignorance and bewilderment—with peaks and valleys and local attractors—and the concept of atheism causes us to fixate on one part of this landscape, the part related to theistic religion, and then just flattens it. Because to be consistent as atheists we must oppose, or seem to oppose, all faith claims equally. This is a waste of precious time and energy, and it squanders the trust of people who would otherwise agree with us on specific issues. ("The Problem with Atheism")

Atheists tend to be either tempted or cornered into focusing on the 'theistic' part of religion, at the expense of pointing out its detrimental real-life consequences, like holy war, oppression of minorities, and scientific stagnation. By doing so, they equate all faiths on the common denominator of metaphysical confusion. This is a costly mistake since some strains of religious belief are more problematic than others and deserve more attention (nobody is losing sleep over Amish or Jain fundamentalism, as opposed to other kinds).

Similarly, social justice advocates who primarily identify as antiracists are led to focus on racism as the leading cause of racial injustice at the expense of alternative variables that might be just as consequential. It is undeniably true, for instance, that the legacy of slavery and segregation is the original reason for education and wealth inequality among black and white people in the United States, but whether it is discrimination and racist sentiment that keeps it that way today remains a matter of debate. The welfare state, cultural trends, and the breakdown of the family structure have all been suggested as important variables by Thomas Sowell (*Discrimination and Disparities*), among others. Whether this is right or not, antiracists tend to gloss over explanations such as these and alienate those who share their commitment but worry about getting the facts straight.

Atheists' focus on theism and their opposition to religion 'as a whole' allow them to selectively criticize the more politically correct targets, such as Christianity, and be moral relativists towards other religions, like Islam. In the same way, antiracists' permissive definitions of racism allow the same kind of cherry-picking. For example, Ibram Kendi argues that the Arab-run slave trade, though much larger and longer than the transatlantic slave-trade (Murray, *The War on the West*, p. 103), is somehow not as reprimandable because "they were not pursuing racist policies—they were enslaving what we now consider to be Africans, Arabs, and Europeans alike" (Kendi, *How to Be an Antiracist*, p. 39). Overall, while these might seem helpful tactics to employ for our cause, they destroy credibility, misdiagnose root problems, overlook potential solutions, deepen polarization, and strengthen the enemy.

The Way Forward: Intellectual Integrity

So, what *can* we do instead? If we aim to carry out this fight effectively and efficiently (that is, in a way that accomplishes its objective without creating additional problems), then there is something we *must* do. According to Harris, whatever we do, we must "advocate reason and intellectual honesty" ("The Problem with Atheism"). When people fail to live up to this ideal of intellectual integrity for reputational safety, emotional compromise, or ideological commitment, they increase the risk of ending up on the losing side of the war of ideas.

'Intellectual integrity' refers to the capacity that people exhibit in varying degrees to make unbiased observations of the facts. It is an ideal that might never be fully realized but can be aimed at. It is a commitment to objectivity and trying to represent the world as accurately as possible (of course, we should first define such things as 'facts', 'reality' and 'truth', but who shouldn't). 'Intellectual honesty', used interchangeably, refers to the conscious efforts of correcting our judgment based on new evidence and resisting the urge to 'strawman' opposing arguments. It may be easier to describe it by stating what it is *not*:

> It's the other who will not listen to reason, who has no interest in facts, who can't join a conversation that converges on the truth, because he knows in advance what the truth must be. We should fear the other who thinks that dogmatism and cognitive bias aren't something to be corrected for, because they're the very foundations of his epistemology. We should fear the other who can't distinguish activism from journalism or politics from science. Or worse, can make these distinctions, but refuses to. And we're all capable of becoming this person. If only for minutes or hours at a time. And this is a bug in our operating system, not a feature. We have to continually correct for it. ("Can We Pull Back from the Brink?")

Harris is referring to one of the central values of positivism and the Enlightenment. Richard Feynman's first principle of science "You must not fool yourself—and you are the easiest person to fool" sums it up. Humans have enduring cognitive biases and irrational tendencies (Ariely, *Predictably Irrational*; Kahneman, *Thinking Fast and Slow*). Yet, Harris

argues that getting to know the facts by continually correcting for these biases is the best (and maybe the only) basis
for determining our values (*The Moral Landscape*). Thus,
intellectual integrity is a key component of wise political
decisions. Wherever we stand on the issue of whether it is
worthwhile to defend this ideal for its own sake, the point
here is that it is indispensable to effectively and efficiently
pursue ulterior goals, especially social transformation.

Naturally, disagreements are not only the result of intellectual dishonesty, which is why intellectual honesty cannot
by itself resolve our differences. We regularly find brilliant
and informed people who value logical consistency on both
sides of any political issue. Atheists and antiracists are not
necessarily 'misinformed' or lacking integrity when their
interpretation of the facts is contrary to ours. Alas, intellectual honesty is not a solution, though it *is* a necessary condition. It is a guiding principle, an intention, or a desire,
more than a guarantee of converging opinions. If this precondition is absent, no level of consensus can guarantee that
we are not just right by accident.

The Way Backward: Tribalism

Intellectual honesty is hard to cultivate but very easy to
erode, especially when put to the task of pursuing a collective
goal. Harris notes: "The desire to know what is actually going
on in the world is very difficult to argue with. Insofar as we
represent that desire, we become difficult to argue with. And
this desire is not reducible to an interest group. It's not a
club or an affiliation, and I think trying to make it one diminishes its power" ("The Problem with Atheism").

Tragically, the intellectual honesty ideal is disserved by
the very dynamics of social change. It amounts to yet another
kind of dilemma: by joining together into pressure groups to
advance a cause, as we inevitably must, we become susceptible to cognitive biases that ultimately hurt the cause
(hence the tragedy). Both atheists and antiracists are, like
everyone else, vulnerable to the pitfall of tribalism, given the
right circumstances.

Agents who develop an ideological attachment to the
established group identity are particularly capable of disre-

garding intellectual honesty to favor a noble cause. This is nothing new. Collectives with a specific aim create a sense of meaning in life, especially when the objective is to oppose another collective (Elnakouri et al., "Hate and Meaning in Life"). This gives rise to several cognitive biases, particularly when the adversary is deemed more powerful, creating an 'underdog effect' (Vandello et al., "The Appeal of the Underdog"). Crucially, people disagree on factual questions such as climate change not because of divergent information, but because their positions convey oaths of allegiance to different cultural and political groups (Kahan et al., "The Tragedy of the Risk-Perception Commons"). In any case, the point here is not to rehearse the typical arguments against tribalism, but to warn social movements about adopting the *modus operandi* of identity politics, loosely understood as a particular way to pursue social change from the standpoint of identity.

Identity can no doubt be a powerful motor of positive collective action, and we should channel its potential as much as possible. But there is no need to stifle our judgment for it to be a force for good. We would then almost guarantee to have the opposite effect. Identity politics makes the systematic disregard for intellectual integrity a permanent feature of politics and a legitimate way to play the game, not only for us but for everyone, including the opposite side. As Harris has commented, the renewed primacy of this style of social justice activism ended up breeding the 'white identity politics' that helped elect President Donald Trump in 2016 (This Week in Startups).

Consequently, we should neither identify ourselves as atheists nor antiracists. These terms are double-edged swords that we can and must outgrow in favor of a more widely shared standard of deliberation. We should instead "go under the radar—for the rest of our lives. And while there, we should be decent, responsible people who destroy bad ideas wherever we find them" ("The Problem with Atheism").

Ultimately, Sam Harris's recommendation to those who also pursue secularism and social justice can be summed up as a more extensive caution against the lure of tribalism and a constant reminder that the ideal of intellectual integrity should always be upheld, no matter the circumstances. This benefits everyone and harms no one. We ought to realize that accurately interpreting the world is vital to changing it for the better. Only then will we be able to take a confident step towards moral progress.

References

Ariely, Dan. 2009. *Predictably Irrational: The Hidden Forces that Shape Our Decisions*. Harper Perennial.

Bonilla-Silva, Eduardo. 2010. *Racism without Racists: Color-Blind Racism and the Persistence of Racial Inequality in the United States*. Rowman and Littlefield

Bonnett, Alastair. 2000. *Anti-Racism*. Routledge.

DiAngelo, Robin J. 2020. *White Fragility: Why It's So Hard for White People to Talk about Racism*. Beacon Press.

Elnakouri, Abdo, Candice Hubley, and Ian McGregor. 2022. Hate and Meaning in Life: How Collective, but Not Personal, Hate Quells Threat and Spurs Meaning in Life. *Journal of Experimental Social Psychology* 98 (January): 104227. <https://doi.org/10.1016/j.jesp.2021.104227>.

Hannah-Jones, Nikole, Caitlin Roper, Ilena Silverman, and Jake Silverstein. 2021 [2019]. *The 1619 Project: A New Origin Story*. One World.

Harris, Sam. 2005 [2004]. *The End of Faith: Religion, Terror, and the Future of Reason*. Norton.

———. 2007. The Problem with Atheism. *Sam Harris* (blog). <www.samharris.org/blog/the-problem-with-atheism>.

———. 2010. *The Moral Landscape: How Science Can Determine Human Values*. Free Press.

———. 2012. *Free Will*. Free Press.

———. 2015. *Waking Up*. Black Swan.

———. 2020. Can We Pull Back from the Brink? Sam Harris (blog). <www.samharris.org/blog/can-pull-back-brink>.

Kahan, Dan M., Maggie Wittlin, Ellen Peters, Paul Slovic, Lisa Larrimore Ouellette, Donald Braman, and Gregory N. Mandel. 2011. The Tragedy of the Risk-Perception Commons: Culture Conflict, Rationality Conflict, and Climate Change. *SSRN Electronic Journal*. <https://doi.org/10.2139/ssrn.1871503>.

Kahneman, Daniel. 2011. *Thinking, Fast and Slow*. Farrar, Straus, and Giroux.

Kendi, Ibram X. 2019. *How to Be an Antiracist*. Vintage.

Lemon, Jason. 2021. AOC Suggests CRT Opponents 'Accepting of Racism' as GOP Bills Against It Pile Up. *Newsweek*, December 18, 2021.
<www.newsweek.com/aoc-suggests-crt-opponents-accepting-racism-gop-bills-against-it-pile-1660874>.

Mazzocco, Philip J. 2017. *The Psychology of Racial Colorblindness*. Palgrave Macmillan.

McLemore, Monica R. 2021. The Complicated Legacy of E.O. Wilson. *Scientific American* (December 29th)
<www.scientificamerican.com/article/the-complicated-legacy-of-e-o-wilson>.

McWhorter, John H. 2021. *Woke Racism: How a New Religion Has Betrayed Black America*. Penguin.

Murray, Douglas. 2022. *The War on the West: How to Prevail in the Age of Unreason*. HarperCollins.

Nature. 2020. Systemic Racism: Science Must Listen, Learn and Change. *Nature* 582:7811.
<https://doi.org/10.1038/d41586-020-01678-x>.

———. 2021. Tackling Systemic Racism Requires the System of Science to Change. *Nature* 593:7859.
<https://doi.org/10.1038/d41586-021-01312-4>.

Pichai, Sundar. 2020. Our Commitments to Racial Equity. The Keyword (blog).
<https://blog.google/inside-google/company-announcements/commitments-racial-equity>.

Sheth, Falguni A. 2009. *Toward a Political Philosophy of Race*. SUNY Press.

Sowell, Thomas. 2019. *Discrimination and Disparities*. Basic Books.

This Week in Startups. 2017. #706 Sam Harris "Waking Up": Trump Asymmetric Warfare, Jihadism Prob and How to Avoid AI Apocalypse (podcast).
<www.youtube.com/watch?v=UoeDN_BvGFw>.

Vandello, Joseph A., Nadav P. Goldschmied, and David A.R. Richards. 2007. The Appeal of the Underdog. *Personality and Social Psychology Bulletin* 33:12.
<https://doi.org/10.1177/0146167207307488>.

Williams, Monnica. 2011. Colorblind Ideology Is a Form of Racism. Culturally Speaking (blog).
<www.psychologytoday.com/intl/blog/culturally-speaking/201112/colorblind-ideology-is-form-racism>.

[5]
Is Redistribution the Endgame?

ANTONY SAMMEROFF

"Redistribution is the endgame," says Sam Harris on *The Joe Rogan Experience*, "because you can't have a society where trillionaires are living in gated compounds while everyone else is out on the street."

Sam Harris probably speaks for most when he states that inequality is a major problem, and that it has to be solved by the redistribution of wealth. In fact, his position is pretty moderate against the backdrop of a political climate where hostility to capitalism and the accumulation of wealth is the norm. Most people consider government policy to be the *only* tool for addressing social problems. The market is rarely perceived as a means of solving problems, but it does this every day by testing the success of different solutions for meeting people's needs against their actual willingness to pay for those solutions.

Harris favors a mixed economy, with a strongly regulated market. He agrees that we want to retain the incentive for talented people to do "creative work that makes the world better and better," and rise to riches as entrepreneurs, and acknowledges that capitalists provide value to customers and their employees. This makes him a little bit more pro-market than many intellectuals today who reflexively advocate for heavy socialization of the economy. Harris deprecates "the quasi-socialist demonization of wealth of the sort that one hears from AOC or Elizabeth Warren" (Making Sense, January 5th 2021).

Harris presents his position as a balanced one, somewhere between laissez faire and outright socialism. He states that people who are "just railing at the mere existence of billionaires" are "just confused about economics," but that on the other hand, "anyone for whom terms like inequality and redistribution have become radioactive is just confused about ethics."

Redistribution Creates Poverty

Sam Harris—ever moderate—states that, "There are good faith debates to be had about how much inequality is too much, but there really is no question that this is a problem that decent, compassionate people—or even merely self-interested people are now wise to worry about. I mean, however rich and insulated you are, if you don't think you've lost something when the level of homelessness and crime soars in your city, well then, you've lost your mind."

This runs into an empirical problem. Homelessness and crime soar where there is more redistribution (Los Angeles, San Francisco, New York), and do not soar where there is less redistribution (Miami, Houston). This correlation is pretty reliable, at all times and places, at least between nations and within advanced industrial cultures. The more redistribution, the more poverty. Redistribution creates poverty. If you implement more redistribution you make a lot of people poorer. This is predicted by economic theory, which holds that you get more of what you incentivize.

Since the War on Poverty was inaugurated in 1964 by President Lyndon B. Johnson, the US government has spent well over $15 trillion on welfare payments. Given that the US is home to only a tiny fraction of the world's poor, poverty should have been abolished here long ago if redistribution were an effective solution, but it hasn't been. In fact, redistribution of wealth has never resulted in the end of poverty anywhere. $40–50 billion is spent by the US on foreign aid annually with little to show for it—in fact some argue, as in the documentary *Poverty, Inc.*, that foreign aid has done more harm than good to the recipients.

You may say that redistribution usually goes along with other kinds of intrusive government activity, and so the turning of once-beautiful and prosperous San Francisco into a hell-hole of violence and squalor might not be due to redistribution but more due to these other 'progressive' measures. In principle that's correct, but these policies usually all go together, and Harris treats them as though they automatically go together, his discussion moving easily from one to the other and back.

Most philosophers who have looked at Harris's *The Moral Landscape* have expressed some surprise at the author's neglect of hundreds of contributions in three thousand years of philosophical ethics which look as though they might be relevant to his discussion. Harris claims that science can tell us what moral values to hold and that all ethics reduces to a concern with human well-being, something which, he admits, is impossible to precisely define.

Few have pointed out that there are two other scholarly disciplines which Harris also almost completely ignores, though they have things to tell him which are vitally relevant to his argument about ethics and well-being.

One is welfare economics, the branch of economic theory concerned with what institutional arrangements and policies maximize utility. Utility is one way of looking at the knotty question of well-being. Utility is not happiness; it is satisfaction of people's demonstrated wants. Of course, we can debate whether it's always good for people to get what they want. I will say no more here about welfare economics, though some of the arguments I make may reflect a simplified recollection of some welfare economics I have read.

The other relevant discipline is the empirical study of happiness, defined as subjective well-being (SWB). Researchers in this branch of social psychology have arrived at a number of pretty firm conclusions. First, the great majority of people are happy. Second, higher income yields more happiness (though at a steeply diminishing rate once a fairly modest minimum of comfort has been attained). Consistent with that, people in advanced industrial societies are, on average, considerably happier than people in less developed countries. Inequality does not reduce happiness; in fact happiness is positively correlated with inequality: the more inequality there is, the happier people are. And poor people in rich countries are happier than poor people in poor countries. Whether you live in a rich or a poor country, it turns out, is a better predictor of how happy you will be than how rich or poor you personally are. Freedom is important for happiness, and far and away the most weighty form of freedom is economic freedom. Economic freedom not only makes people happier by increasing their incomes, but additional to that, gives them a happiness bonus just because they live in an economically free society.

All these empirical results are surely relevant to Sam Harris's project of deriving ethics from science and well-being, and specifically, to the question of how much, if any, redistribution of income governments ought to attempt to bring about.

Poverty Is Not the Same Thing as Inequality

Like so many people, Harris tends to conflate the issues of poverty and inequality. We want everybody, especially the poorest, to be better off. But the process of economic development—which makes them better off—automatically generates inequalities.

Poverty and inequality do not always go hand in hand. Afghanistan is a very 'equal' country in terms of living standards, but people there are generally extremely poor, and most people would much rather be poor in the more 'unequal' America. There is also the question of whether America really is more unequal. I mean, while the difference between the people who are at the top and bottom may look bigger so far as dollar amounts go, the way they live is far closer. Both ends of the income spectrum have cars, clothes, beds, flush toilets, running water, soap, electricity and appliances, Internet access to all the education, art, music, culture and social media that brings as well as access to more food than they can ever eat.

In the 'poor but more equal' countries in the developing world, people at the top live in mansions while people at the bottom literally starve to death. The nature of the inequality is completely different. So, it would be fair to say, inequality alone says nothing about how well or badly people are doing, only that some people are doing better than others. If you looked solely at the rate of inequality among blacks in South Africa compared to a few decades ago, you'd have to conclude that this situation has gotten worse. But we know that's not true. The inequality figures only look worse because over six million black people have left poverty and entered the middle class.

I once attended a Humanist meeting where I pointed out that poverty had dropped in India (prior to the 1980s, many observers had said that India would *never* develop), since they adopted free market policies in place of socialism, and another attendee *literally* opposed me, stating that: "Poverty may have gone down but inequality has gotten much worse!"; giving support to the claim that *some* people *really would* rather that everyone was poorer so long as we are more equal—as Margaret Thatcher famously alleged.

But would you? Would you rather have a society with a wide range of incomes and a high general level of income, or a society with a much narrower range of incomes and a much lower general level of income?

We Have a Lot of Redistribution

When we talk casually about 'redistribution', we may imagine sums of money taken from those with highest incomes and sent through the mail to those with lowest incomes. The first thing to notice is that this is already happening on a huge scale. Large sums of money are taken from higher-income people in taxes, and spent by the government on whatever the government chooses to spend it on. Some of that spending undoubtedly reaches the lowest-income segment of the population. So, the question isn't whether to redistribute income, but whether to do more redistribution or less.

Harris freely admits that there is a downside to equalizing by redistribution: he acknowledges that redistribution may reduce incomes generally. So, we who read Harris or listen to him might say, maybe there's far too much redistribution already, and it ought to be considerably reduced. We can't know until we look at the facts, and give them some thought. Harris does not inform us how we would be able to tell whether there was far too much redistribution. He seems to assume that the case for ever more redistribution is made by the fact that there are poor people. But redistribution always generates poverty. This is an endless escalating cycle: redistribution creates poverty, people like Sam Harris deduce that we need more redistribution to fix the poverty, then more redistribution creates even more poverty, and so on.

The top 1 percent of income earners pay 38.8 percent of all federal income tax, the top 10 percent pay 70.8 percent, the top 25 percent pay 86.6 percent, and the top 50 percent pay 96.9 percent. We can conclude that the 'bottom' 40 percent of income earners pay no federal income tax. (It's roughly similar with state income taxes, and higher-income people pay the most in property taxes.) So, the first part of 'redistribution' is already being done, in a very big way.

What about the second part, actually giving this money to the worst off? Here things are a bit more complicated. Of the total US national budget, 40 percent goes to 'welfare', so we can say that some of the second part of 'redistribution' is also being done, though less than 40 percent because much of 'welfare' spending pays for the costs of administering the welfare system, which is a lot more expensive than if the money taken from higher-income people really were just sent to the lowest-income people through the mail. On the other hand, some products of government spending, such as public libraries and paving the streets do benefit those who pay no taxes, so the total redistributed may, after all, be more like 40 percent, or perhaps a good bit more.

For the sake of not being misleading, we should note that there are also governmental transfers from lower- and middle-income groups to higher-income groups, and from some middle-income groups to others. The political market has its own laws, operating independently of what we might like, just as the economic market does: one observable theme is that income is transferred from poorly-organized segments of the population to well-organized segments. Recent proposals to 'forgive' student debt, that is, to get all of us non-students to pay for it, would have the effect over several years of transferring money from lower- and middle-income groups to higher-income groups.

The More Redistribution, the More Poverty

Sam Harris is not suggesting flattening everything out and making everyone equally poor. He's only arguing that a somewhat bigger redistribution of the gains of the world's billionaires should be added to the already large amount of redistribution. Yet, contrary to what Harris seems to assume, there's nothing self-evidently morally right about proposing more redistribution. The equation looks simple enough: on one hand we have people with too little money, and on the other we have people with too much of it. Surely, all we need to do is take some from the big pile on the right and add it to the little pile on the left. But when you do this, you change behavior, both the behavior of those from whom you take and the behavior of those to whom you give.

Harris does appear to acknowledge there is an incentive problem. If you tax higher incomes heavily, you reduce the incentive to benefit the public by satisfying consumer needs. This isn't just a problem of motivation, but also of information. If there is a way to make a fortune by starting a business and running it in a particular way, this shows that there is a gain to consumers from the products of that business. If all the price signals are dimmed, because the possibility of making such fortunes is concealed by high marginal taxation, entrepreneurs will be less likely to shell out the money on risky possibilities. Redistributing income or wealth can also harm the poor by making the whole of society less wealthy, and it does this in a way that compounds over time.

What we call poverty is the natural state of humankind. It requires no special explanation. We are all born naked, with nothing. What requires special explanation is sustained and cumulative emergence from poverty—economic growth. Throughout recorded history up until the agricultural revolution, human beings lived on under $3 a day. After 200 years of accelerating incomes, the world average is now around $33 a day. And in the richer, more successful countries, most people live on around $100 a day. The poverty rate halved worldwide between 1990 and 2010, falling from 43 percent to 21 percent. Some African nations still struggle in extreme poverty, while other nations like Ethiopia—which used to have periodic famines under socialism, and Rwanda—which suffered a devastating genocide—are doing extremely well in comparison to their neighbors and their former selves. So, we must be getting poverty reduction right in some places at least some of the time. One thing we know with absolute certainty is that it never involved redistribution. Understanding how that has been accomplished will provide alternative policy prescriptions to redistribution that will be more successful in abolishing poverty.

Taking money from people of roughly average income and above, and directing some of that money to the poorest attacks wealth creation that ultimately benefits everyone. It leads to the present reality, where cutting tax rates for higher incomes would lead to higher-income people paying more in taxes, because productive activity currently vetoed by high taxes on higher incomes would become possible.

But what about the poorest who get some of this bounty? Aren't they made better off? Unfortunately, they tend to get caught in the well-known 'welfare trap'. It takes tremendous fortitude to keep on working for the future when it pays you in the short run to quit work and become a professional dependent. Some people do possess such fortitude, but many don't. Welfare dependency destroys the monogamous family unit, by rewarding couples for separating and penalizing fathers for providing for their children, and it destroys the cultivation of desirable work habits by rewarding perpetual unemployment, since if you refuse to work, your need is greater, and you get more benefits. Neither mothers nor fathers have any incentive to care much about their kids' well-being, because that is the state's job, not theirs. This whole mess is compounded by the minimum wage, which makes it a crime to hire the least productive workers—and this mostly means inexperienced teenagers, so a big proportion of them don't get hired and don't acquire the elementary skills of holding down a job that they don't like. Added to all this, the majority of people on welfare seize the opportunity to supplement their income by illegal activities, most commonly drug dealing. Thus the system which was designed to eliminate poverty, squalor, wretchedness, and crime creates a permanent underclass of endless poverty, endless squalor, endless wretchedness, and endless criminality.

Do Billionaires Do Any Good?

Talk about billionaires and even trillionaires can be misleading, because there aren't enough billionaires to pay for very much. The fabled 'top one percent' of income earners are people making over $500,000 a year (households) or $360,000 a year (individuals). Far more tax revenue comes from the 'bottom' 99 percent than from the top one percent, because there are so many more of them.

To economists, 'capital' means physical stocks of goods used for producing more goods—machines, factory buildings, trucks, power stations. 'Investment' means adding to those stocks of physical goods—making machines, constructing buildings, manufacturing trucks, or building power stations. In ordinary speech, 'capital' means a sum of money or savings in a form that can quickly be turned into money, while 'investment' means allocating part of your income to some interest-bearing asset, such as a deposit in a savings account, a 401k, or a mutual fund. Obviously these two senses of 'capital' and 'investment' are closely related, but they are distinct.

If you have savings, it's going to do you no good to keep your stash under a mattress. If you want to receive an income from your savings (which you need just to keep up with inflation), you have to invest them in producing something that other people actually want to consume. This aligns the self-interest of the individual with the interests of society in a way that seems to be very little understood today—the less by left-wing intellectuals who, as humanists, should be deeply concerned with understanding it.

People who save make possible the increases in productive output that benefit us all, because that money goes into buying all the machines, factories, and natural resources, as well as funding all the research, development and personnel required to make society more materially affluent. Most of these people are not rich. The total assets of workers' retirement funds in the US amount to $30 trillion—six times the combined wealth of the billionaires. And that's not counting the even greater total of savings held by the less-rich-than-billionaires outside retirement funds.

Everyone can save if they want to, but the richer people are the more they tend to save. Imagine someone who invests $500 million into a chemical plant that reduces the average cost of plastics by one percent; they have just made everyone in the world who will ever buy a plastic product better off. The effect would be immeasurably more beneficial to human welfare than simply redistributing the $500 million.

Cumulatively, over time, these modest steps forward add up to tremendous increases in living standards. These would never happen without the initial investment, and it is exactly this form of investment that accounts for why most regular people in Europe, North America, and some countries in Asia (South Korea, Japan and Singapore) are so much richer than most people in South America or Africa and other parts of Asia (like Cambodia and Myanmar).

If you reduce the wealth of the highest earners by taxation for redistribution you reduce total capital investment, and people of all income levels will be impoverished relative to what they would have been if you had allowed the money to be invested into the machines and factories. If, when John D. Rockefeller, the first billionaire, began to accumulate his wealth, all we had done was taken his wealth and redistributed it evenly among the poor, perhaps everyone would have eaten like a king for a week or two, but we would not have got tar for paving roads, lubricating oil, Vaseline, and the countless other by-products that were developed from crude by Standard Oil. This includes paraffin for making candles, at a time when only the rich could afford whale oil and candles. We enjoy luxuries today that even a king, before the days of John D. Rockefeller and Standard Oil, could not even have dreamed of.

Leftists suppose that some people are poor *because* some people are rich. If that were true, there would certainly be a strong case to expropriate the rich. But the exact opposite is true. At least to the degree we have market economies—where amassing wealth is largely dependent on providing a service to customers—people get rich generating wealth—not just for themselves, but for others.

It's people *saving* that makes the poor rich, or at least, less poor. All that saved money is not just lying under a mattress, but buying all the machines and factories, and funding all the research and development that has driven us into the space-age world of luxury, comfort, and leisure. It's taking the invention that someone's crazy uncle came up with in their basement out of their head, and channeling it through development teams, focus groups, safety testers, online marketers, and a hundred other experts, before transporting it—via a massive, worldwide network of distributors—into the houses of millions and millions of people who have decided, that out of the almost-infinite number of things they could spend their limited resources on, this is the thing they want to buy. Since they seem to value whatever this thingamajig is more than the money they pay for it, we can conclude that they consider themselves better off for having bought it.

Capital Investment Makes Things Better and Cheaper

As the amount of capital increases, more stuff is produced, and that stuff becomes cheaper. More saved wealth means more efficient production techniques allow us to produce more with less land and fewer resources. Another reason is that machines allow one person to do the work of several people. For example, a forklift. This reduces production costs, and the reduction must be passed on to the consumer in order for firms to remain competitive.

Consequently, we're living in the era of the most affordable food, appliances, clothing, and transportation in history. As well as a downward pressure on price, markets place an upward pressure on the quality of products as competitors muscle in to seduce customers with a better deal. When you compare a flat screen TV you would get today for a couple of hundred bucks it so far transcends the machine you would buy in the 1970s for $500—at a time when $500 meant a lot more money than it does now. This explains why so many items that were once considered luxuries (such as personal computers, smart phones, household appliances, cars, and holidays abroad) are the norm—even in relatively poor households in the 'rich but unequal' West. Usually when it comes to the luxury end of goods like mobile phones and laptops, wealthy people buy them first at high prices, and some few years later, what *was* a luxury becomes affordable to more and more consumers.

As average incomes rise, an ever-smaller percentage of people's incomes are spent on basics like food, shelter, clothing, and cars. People have more time for leisure because they have to work less to afford the lifestyle they desire. Between 1870 and 2015 the average work week fell from 57 hours to 37. There are some sectors in which real-term costs have gone up in the last few decades, but those are largely where there is the most government provision, or intervention from government into the economy to regulate the terms of provision, for example, in education, healthcare, housing, transportation, and the provision of childcare. If there were little government interference to stand in the way, cheaper schools, hospitals and accommodation would soon be cropping up everywhere— and the standard of provision would be far better.

Who Really Controls the Wealth of the Wealthy?

In order to profit from their wealth, people with savings— investors or capitalists, and that includes low-income people with a savings account or a 401k—need to invest in things that people actually want.

The capitalist can't just invest in any old thing he fancies. People have so many choices when it comes to how they spend their money, that in order to win out in this grand auction where millions of sellers hock their wares to billions of buyers, you really have to serve lots of people and do it more efficiently than the next guy. Because capitalism is mass production *for* the masses, in order to become extremely rich, it's usually necessary to sell a huge number of products to a tremendous number of people. The most decisive influencer of the economy is not the capitalist but the consumer—you, me, and Sam Harris. It's the man on the street who makes or breaks the capitalist.

What this effectively means is that the buying public determines what all the machines, and factories owned by all the corporations of the world are to produce. We dictate what the engines crank out and which laboratories get funding for new gadgets (subject to some distortion by government intervention). If coffee is going out of fashion this season, then the plantations had better be quick to switch over to growing tea. Effectively, the market's mechanism of profit and loss puts private wealth in the hands of the public. It might look as if the wealthy just get to boss everyone around and make decisions, but if someone does it better than any one of them, they are out of luck. They will be replaced by a competitor. All of this is coordinated by the mechanism of profit and loss.

Profit and Loss Distributes Resources in a way that Serves the Public

When someone invests money, what they're effectively doing is choosing *not* to spend it themselves, on a world tour by private jet, for example.

In pursuit of profit, the investor attempts an educated guess as to what the buying public are going to want in the future. If he succeeds, his lines of investment become profitable and grow in value. Some considerable expertise must be required to perform this feat, or else we'd all be millionaires. On the other hand, if he invests in businesses making products that no one's interested in, he will never see his money again. His resources will be unceremoniously ripped from his hands without mercy or compensation. All the factories and machines that his assets represent pass into the ownership of people who think they can do a better job of employing them to the greater satisfaction of the buying public.

The intelligence of this process is that the capital is constantly getting allocated and reallocated to those who show a good record of managing those resources. You could say that the returns on investments are society's way of saying: 'Thanks, you did a great job of employing those factories in ways that people want, here are some more to manage. Please decide what to do with those, as well.' Similarly, if someone fails and their lines of investment go bankrupt, that is the equivalent of society saying: 'You clearly don't know what you are doing with these! We're going to take them from you and sell them off to someone who can perform better.' We assume the new buyer has the best chance of doing a good job with those assets since if they're willing to take the biggest financial risk then they must be the most confident in their idea. It's not a perfect system, but it's the only system where all the incentives are pointed in the right direction.

This constant process of wealth flowing out of the hands of bad investors and into those of better ones is effectively the constant reallocation of capital to those who can manage it best. Whether the public knows (or approves of) the big names of the richest people in the world, their assets are working to provide them with cheaper goods and services of greater quality. Their wealth is serving us! The moment it stops serving us they start losing it.

There is no comparable mechanism of testing public servants, politicians or policy-makers for their aptitude at allocating funds. This explains why more market-oriented countries are so much wealthier than countries which severely restrict markets. The capital gets directed to those who know how to use it in capitalist countries. Those who consistently guess what consumers want get to allocate more resources in the future—because they are proven entities. This makes sense as you wouldn't want people who didn't know what they were doing in charge of deciding who runs the factories and what the factories will produce.

In dictatorships of all forms, left or right, the decision makers are those who seize power. They have to guess what to produce. The more totalitarian the dictatorship, the worse of a job they will end up doing because they have to make decisions over everything without having their plans tested against the wants of the buying public. This is why, for all the good intentions of the Communists in countries like Cuba and Venezuela they have never been able to provide their people with the gains in well-being the Communist revolution promised, or even to maintain the living standards of the pre-revolutionary society. We take for granted wealth in less controlled—and less 'redistributed'—societies and some of us curse the excesses of capitalism. But it's exactly the excesses of capitalism that afford us the luxury of leisure time to complain of anything other than being poor.

The Government as Investor and Arbitrator

When you redistribute the savings of the billionaires—and the many more above-average income people who are less than billionaires—via government programs, you're not putting those resources in the hands of anyone tested to be competent at making decisions with them. At best they have shown their aptitude at getting into power. If they were good administrators of wealth they'd probably be in the private sector making a fortune. What's more they don't have the mechanism of profit and loss to guide them as to what to produce because they gain their income through the tax system, whether the people want to pay for public services or not, so command over funds does not depend upon performance.

They also have lots of perverse incentives to pay off major supporters with corporate welfare or preferential legislation while bribing constituents to vote for them with public money. This presents a major incentive problem in mixed economies because instead of spending all their money on making, distributing, and advertising better products corporations start wasting resources on lobbying the government for favors. Innovation and living standards are reduced and huge sums of money are wasted paying lobbyists, accountants, actuaries, lawyers, regulators, public sector workers and politicians who do busy work—and would otherwise have to get jobs creating wealth and making society richer.

Putting Wealth to Work

Sam Harris says that "Our infrastructure and education and everything else in our society needs to be funded and there is no one in a better position to fund these things than the wealthy!"

Let's think about that for a moment. The wealth of the wealthy (along with the greater total wealth of the not-so-wealthy) is already fully employed in funding grocery stores, auto manufacture, computer production, trucking, farming, housing construction, and everything else. None of it is just lying idle. As we've seen, it's all spoken for, and it's already making possible our historically high and growing standards of living. So what Harris means about funding infrastructure and education is taking money from the highly efficient funding of grocery stores, auto manufacture, and the rest, and allocating it to the highly inefficient funding of infrastructure and education.

You can't get something from nothing. Redistributing wealth is eating the seeds of next year's harvest. And we've already been doing this on a mass scale. In most Western nations government spending represents 30–50 percent of total spending in the economy. (Think how much richer we'd all be if it weren't!) We're already funding schools and infrastructure by money taken from the wealthy and the not-so-wealthy. Most of this money is taken out of earnings rather than savings, but generally speaking people with higher incomes tend to accumulate more savings. By reducing them we're trading future prosperity for more government.

The qualifying difference between private investment and government spending is that the first is voluntary and guided by what the consumer wants. Because "the customer is king" and he wants the best product at the best price, auto manufacture and grocery stores tend to be extremely efficient. If you don't like a product and return it, you usually get a refund. Try that with a government service! You have to lobby, involve your neighbors, write letters to the paper, complain to your congressman, start a pressure group, change your vote, drive your family to distraction in the attempt to reform their dysfunctional leftist views on politics—and still you usually get nothing! Schools and infrastructure are operated by the government and extremely inefficient and there is little the public can do to help it. James Tooley wrote *The Beautiful Tree*, a book on how poor people across the world manage to educate themselves cheaply, then began a project to open a chain of low-cost private schools charging only £2,700 a year—something like half what the government spends on average per student in state schools.

Extensive meta-analyses combining the results from multiple studies have consistently shown that government services are on average twice as expensive as the same services provided by the private sector (John Hilke, *Cost Savings from Privatization*). And this does not even account for the differences in the quality of services, which are typically far better on the market because 'you get what you pay for'. The government has been consistent in ignoring seventy years of pedagogical research on how to create learning environments where children thrive, for example, and everyone constantly complains about the state of the roads.

If schools and infrastructure operated privately for profit, they would soon be able to discover the best ways to educate people and fix potholes at a price that was affordable. If one company did a poor job, they'd lose out to someone who was willing and able to do a better one. So much wealth would be saved that every man woman and child in the country would be richer.

This could be accomplished most directly by just getting the government out of the way and letting anyone who wants to open a school open a school. If that's too radical for moderates like Harris, the government could, during a transition period, continue to provide public schools for the poor and offer tax rebates to families taking their children out of public school to help them pay for better private schools, since they are saving the state money.

According to Harris, "Government mismanagement isn't an argument for not paying taxes, and it isn't an argument for lower taxes, it's an argument for better government." Sounds snappy enough, but it presumes that Harris knows the secret which has eluded all governments for thousands of years: finding a way to get government enterprises to operate efficiently. The inefficiency of government does not arise because no one has hit upon the trick to make government operations efficient, but because inefficiency is inherent in governments, due to the distinctive incentive structure of governmental organization.

Government departments are not in competition with other service providers, so they don't have anyone to compare their performance to and improve what they are doing relative to. There is no trial and error. They are paid for out of the public purse, whether the service they are providing is considered satisfactory by the user or not. This removes the primary incentive placed upon private companies to find ways of lowering delivery costs: pressure from customers who always want the best quality service at the best price. Since consumers can't take their business elsewhere, they just have to take what they get.

Imagine if instead of having a market in the provision of coffee, there was only one legal provider of coffee, and people were forced to pay for it whether they liked it or not. Would the coffee available likely be any good? Private organizations cannot get lax in their methods of provision or set in their ways. If they do, they will soon face competition from innovators and people will stop paying for their services. This even goes for charities and nonprofit organizations, to the extent that the donors are willing to be discerning and do research as to who will use their money best before donating.

Naturally, we can look at government enterprises and improve their organization structure in various minor ways, but they can never come close to private enterprises, because they are not answerable to paying consumers and don't face competition, which in the world of the free market, can come from any direction at any time.

Get the Billionaires to Fund Our Schools!

I've pointed out that it's the consumer who decides what the billionaires do with their billions because these are allocated to producing whatever is in demand. And this applies also to the millions of people with above average incomes but less than billionaire incomes. So, Sam Harris is partly right when he says that billionaires are in the best position to fund infrastructure, schools, and everything else in our society. Only partly right because people of higher than average income but below billionaire status pay far more taxes than billionaires because there are far more of them. The fact is that higher-than-average income people, including billionaires, already do fund infrastructure and schools, but inefficiently and wastefully through taxation.

If people democratically decide that the government ought to be responsible for *funding* services like healthcare and education, then this could be done through a voucher system. If people are given vouchers, backed by taxation, to spend on school and hospitals, this will partially emulate a free market; providers will compete for cashable vouchers by improving services. This would radically improve the standard of provision of education and untold fortunes would be saved in the enhanced efficiency. We would be making the poor rich and reducing inequality in the sense that their lifestyle would climb closer to what the rich enjoy now.

The End of Poverty

"Redistribution is the endgame, because you can't have a society where trillionaires are living in gated compounds while everyone else is out on the street."

Lots of people live in gated communities and they are not trillionaires, or even billionaires. My friend in Las Vegas lives in one. It even has grass. Imagine having grass in Vegas! Higher-income people pioneer the living standards of the poor. Much of what we take for granted, such as hot running water or air conditioning, was once considered a luxury item only for the very wealthy. If economic growth is allowed to continue, then perhaps even people on the lowest incomes will one day live in gated communities that have plenty of grass despite the desert heat.

As for everyone else being out on the street, this sounds as though we'll all be living in homeless encampments, and this isn't seriously likely. I have written extensively (including in my book *Universal Basic Income*) to demonstrate that house prices are through the roof due to government intervention on the economy, and pointed out that a Los Angeles musician crowdfunded $100,000 to build tiny solar-paneled homes for the homeless at a cost of $1,200 each—only to have the city tear them down. Who exactly will the trillionaires sell their products to if everyone else is poor? Storing all those products and machines in factories and warehouses will become an expensive burden and the trillionaires will just have to give them away— or even pay someone to take them off their hands because that is cheaper than keeping them! (So much for Sam Harris's worry that 3D printing, AI, and automation are going to make everyone poor.)

Once you understand that it's capital investment made possible by *savings*—the combined wealth of the wealthy and the not-so-wealthy—that has vastly improved conditions for the great mass of people, redistribution is revealed as the process of taking water from the shallow end of the swimming pool and throwing it in the deep end, after spilling half of it along the way. Redistribution reduces total output by reducing capital investment. Resources are diverted from future prosperity to current consumption, analogous to eating seeds that could be sown.

What makes societies better off is functioning markets. The freer the better. Hong Kong and Singapore were once as poor as many of the poorest countries in Africa but in a generation became two of the richest countries in the world due to policies of comparatively unregulated free trade. Of the former eastern bloc countries, Estonia is likely the most free-market orientated and conspicuously more prosperous than its neighbors. In South America, socialism has proven near impossible to recover from wherever it has been tried, which is why most of South America is poor. Chile is the most free-market country in Latin America and the richest. New Zealand, once in the vanguard of welfare state redistributionism, did extremely well after implementing free market reforms in the 1990s, and Sweden—still thought by many to be socialist—was most prosperous *before* it adopted socialistic policies beginning in the 1960s, many of which have now been scaled back because they were such a disaster.

Redistribution is not the endgame. In fact, redistribution has destroyed so much wealth that it threatens to ensure that the game will never end.

Bibliography

Andrzejewski, Adam. 2021. New Report: Nearly $300 Billion in Foreign Aid Spent by US Government. Forbes <www.forbes.com/sites/adamandrzejewski/2021/08/04/new-report-nearly-300-in-foreign-aid-spent-by-us-government/?sh=1649e4d44374>.

Bennett, James T., and M.H. Johnson. 1981. *Better Government at Half the Price: Private Production of Public Services*. Green Hill.

Borcherding, T.E. 1977. The Sources of Growth in Public Expenditures in the U.S.: 1902–1970. In T.E. Borcherding, ed., *Budgets and Bureaucrats: The Sources of Government Growth*. Duke University Press.

Diener, Ed, and C. Diener. 1996. Most People Are Happy. *Psychological Science* 7.

Diener, Ed, and Shigehiro Oishi. 2000. Money and Happiness: Incomes and Subjective Well-Being Across Cultures. In Diener and Suh 2000.

Diener, Ed, and Eunkook M. Suh, eds. 2000. *Culture and Subjective Well-Being*. MIT Press.

Friedman, Milton, and Rose D. Friedman. 1990 [1979]. *Free to Choose: A Personal Statement*. Harcourt.

Harris, Sam. 2010. *The Moral Landscape: How Science Can Determine Human Values*. Simon and Schuster.

————. 2019. The Joe Rogan Experience #1241. <www.jrepodcast.com/episode/joe-rogan-experience-1241-sam-harris>.

————. 2021. Making Sense #229: A Few Thoughts for a New Year <www.samharris.org/podcasts/making-sense-episodes/229-a-few-thoughts-for-a-new-year>.

Hilke, John. 1993. *Cost Savings from Privatization: A Compilation of Study Findings,* Reason How-To Guide #6 (March).

Kertscher, Tom. 2021. Confiscating US Billionaires' Wealth Would Run the US Government About 8 Months. Politifact. The Poynter Institute. <www.politifact.com/factchecks/2021/nov/02/viral-image/con-fiscating-us-billionaires-wealth-would-run-us-g>.

McCloskey, Deirdre N. 2016. *Bourgeois Equality: How Ideas, Not Capital or Institutions, Enriched the World.* University of Chicago Press.

Miller, Michael Matheson, director. 2014. *Poverty, Inc.* <povertyinc.org>.

Murray, Charles. 2015 [1984]. *Losing Ground: American Social Policy, 1950–1980.* Basic Books.

Sammeroff, Antony. 2019. *Universal Basic Income: For and Against.* Rational Rise Press.

Shellenberger, Michael. 2020. *Apocalypse Never: Why Environmental Alarmism Hurts Us All.* HarperCollins.

————. 2022. *San Fransicko: Why Progressives Ruin Cities.* HarperCollins.

Sowell, Thomas. 2016 [2015]. *Wealth, Poverty, and Politics.* Basic Books.

————. 2012. *'Trickle down Theory' and 'Tax Cuts for the Rich'.* Hoover Institution Press.

Steele, David Ramsay. 2005. Life, Liberty, and the Treadmill. *Liberty* 19:2 (February). Reprinted in Steele 2019.

————. 2019. *The Mystery of Fascism: David Ramsay Steele's Greatest Hits.* St. Augustine's Press.

Tax Foundation. 2022. Summary of the Latest Federal Income Tax Data, 2022 Update. <https://taxfoundation.org/publications/latest-federal-income-tax-data>.

Tooley, James. 2013 [2009]. *The Beautiful Tree: A Personal Journey into How the World's Poorest People Are Educating Themselves.* Cato Institute.

Veenhoven, Ruut. 2000. Freedom and Happiness: A Comparative Study in Forty-Four Nations in the Early 1990s. In Diener and Suh 2000.

Part III

Science and
Ethics

[6]
The Mantle
of Neuroscience

RAY SCOTT PERCIVAL

Fancy being unable to distinguish between the reason for a thing,
and the condition without which the reason couldn't be operative!

—SOCRATES, *The Phaedo*

Neuroscience is a serious and fascinating area of human
knowledge. Harris has studied and contributed to this discipline. Armed with this mastery of the domain of brain science, he appears on the stage as a public intellectual with
some bold claims about ethics likely to raise a rumpus in any
philosophy conference.

Harris asserts that David Hume's esteemed distinction
between Is and Ought doesn't hold water and that morals
are just a subset of the total set of facts. You can logically
derive how we ought to live from facts alone, specifically from
brain states. Not only that, but he is going to help build a
systematic science of ethics. The subtitle of his book *The
Moral Landscape* is *How Science Can Determine Human
Values*. That's "determine," not simply help us achieve or
understand our moral values. It's all-embracing in its bold
claim: morality is completely captured by the idea of subjec-
tively experienced human well-being and "human well-being
entirely depends on events in the world and on states of the
brain."

You would think that Harris might have backed up his
neuroscience with a decent study of the history of the problems of ethics. However, in Harris's *The Moral Landscape* and

other presentations, you'll be astonished by his lack of engagement with the millennia-old tradition of philosophical inquiry into ethics, stretching right back to Plato and beyond.

How Should We Live?

When Socrates asked 'How should we live?' Plato and Aristotle answered that we should live a life of virtue. Plato claimed there were four great virtues: Temperance, Justice, Prudence, and Courage. Plato posited these as abstract universal forms that particular actions may participate in. Both Plato and Aristotle asked the question, 'Could a man be virtuous in some respects and not in others?' Could a bad person, someone dishonest or intemperate, for example, be courageous? Plato and Aristotle inclined to the view that this was not possible, because all the virtues were different aspects of a coherent, indivisible wisdom.

Aristotle posited many more virtues, seeing them, like Plato, as abstract but, in contrast to Plato, conceiving them as embodied in achievements of character and excellence of skilled activity. He developed his famous theory of the mean, that being courageous, for example, is a mean state between the deficiency of cowardice and excess of rashness, or that being witty is the mean state between the excess of buffoonery and the deficiency of boorishness.

It's arguable whether he succeeded with the idea of the mean, as it fails to apply to the virtue of truthfulness understood broadly. He could have deployed a theory of aptness, that virtue is the excellence of showing a certain propensity or skill at the right time and place in the right way. This was Aristotle's normal heuristic when thinking about skills, as is clear in his books *The Art of Rhetoric* and *Poetics*, in which different kinds and devices of rhetoric and poetry are described as apt to different purposes and audiences. Aptness is more general than the mean because many inaptnesses, such as untruthfulness, are cases of neither deficiency nor excess. Aristotle's crowning definition of happiness, the ultimate aim of the good life, is that it consists in virtuous activity, and perfect happiness lies in the best activity, which is philosophical contemplation.

Much later the Christian Church added three more virtues: Faith, Hope, and Love—not any kind of 'love', but specifically the love called *agapé*, translated in the King James Bible as 'charity'. These would have struck Plato and Aristotle as alien, and Nietzsche portrayed them as subverting the strength of the human spirit by a slave mentality. Alasdair Macintyre declared, more diplomatically, that we in the West have inherited a mixture of incompatible standards from Ancient Greece and Christianity.

But where does the motivation for virtue come from? Do we need rules to tell us how to behave or can we rely on our feelings of benevolence, compassion, and empathy towards other human beings? Influenced by the clockwork universe idea of Galileo and by William Harvey's insight into the heart as a pumping machine, Thomas Hobbes thought humans were rational robots and were constantly calculating the costs and benefits of their actions for self-preservation, including the helping of others. Joseph Butler refuted that notion by pointing to the instantaneous altruism that people evince in risking their own lives for others, leaving insufficient time for such calculations and, in Hobbesian terms, risking everything.

I have to say something about the Is-Ought issue, what Dawkins in the book's blurb calls "the hectoring myth that science can say nothing about morals." David Hume is the source of the misplaced indignation that Harris (and Dawkins) display against ethical philosophy. In his *Treatise of Human Nature*, Hume argues that reason, our capacity to apprehend logical relations, mathematical and empirical facts, cannot *alone* motivate any emotion and therefore any moral passion. "'Tis not contrary to reason to prefer the destruction of the world to the scratching of my finger." Hume's point is that that preference would strike anyone as ludicrous, yet there's nothing contrary to logic about it. Only to a superficial reading might it seem that Hume is denying any connection between morals and facts. He's careful to say, just before this, that reason can undermine a moral passion by showing the passion to be founded on a falsehood (you mistake the postman for a burglar) or chooses ineffective means for the end (you exhort a person who's shouting and swearing to be polite, but then discover they have Tourette

Syndrome). Hume's discussion is intricate and substantial and mixes psychology with purely logical considerations.

In modern, more formal language, one of Hume's points is that a factual description, taken alone, cannot yield by deduction any 'ought' statement. For example, consider the following argument, which has only a factual statement as a premise:

1. **Everyone shakes hands when they meet.**

2. **Therefore, everyone ought to shake hands when they meet.**

That would be considered invalid. However, consider this one, which has a mixture of factual and moral sentences:

1. **Everyone shakes hands when they meet.**

2. **Whatever everyone does is the custom.**

3. **Everyone ought to do whatever is the custom.**

4. **It is the custom to shake hands when you meet.**

5. **Therefore, everyone ought to shake hands when they meet.**

This, Hume might have accepted, is perfectly valid. If the premises are correct, the conclusion must also be correct. Harris is often confused in the world of logic. Harris tweeted this:

@SamHarrisOrg
Question for fans of the is-ought impasse in ethics: why don't we have a similar problem with reasoning itself? Why aren't we tempted to worry, for instance: "The fact that A *is* bigger than B doesn't allow us to say that we *ought* to believe that A is bigger than B ... ?
6:23 PM · Dec 31, 2021.

I replied:

Replying to
@SamHarrisOrg
This is not a case of deriving an ought from solely factual premises. It's an enthymeme, an argument in which some premises are suppressed (typically because everyone accepts them). With a

combination of factual *and* moral premises it is possible to derive interesting morals.
2:06 PM · Jan 2, 2022

The full and perfectly valid argument would be:

1. **One ought to believe what is true.**

2. **It is true that A is bigger than B.**

Therefore, one ought to believe that A is bigger than B.

So much for the hectoring myth.

In his masterful work, David Hume also explored the question, neglected by Harris, how do subjective feelings of moral approbation and disapprobation give us the important objective abstract institutions of private property and law? Hume created a beautifully subtle theory about how repeated reciprocal expressions of feeling and promises could evolve into social institutions, the very pillars of civilization.

Harris sweeps all these specific deep questions and historic advances aside and with nothing but token allusions in his notes section to the participants in this colossal debate, Harris presses ahead with his claim that science can tell us how we ought to behave. More recent thinkers are completely ignored—for example, Alasdair MacIntyre, Michael Slote, Roger Crisp, and Philippa Foot. These four thinkers have spearheaded a return to the original questions about character virtues, as opposed to the more amorphous concept of 'human well-being'. Virtue ethics is a vibrant research program, already sprouting healthy variants.

The physical sciences currently enjoy authority with the public. Therefore, a neuroscientist who wants to be a public intellectual will typically present his opinion, supposedly authorized by a physical science, clothed in a mixture of psychology and philosophy, hoping that we won't notice that it's the latter—the clothing—that constitutes the substantial element of what he's saying.

A Built-in Immunization Stratagem

What exactly is Harris claiming? Is he really saying that neuroscience can determine how we should live? That would be a bold and arguable thesis open to criticism. However, it's unclear whether Harris wants to say anything like that. The central thesis deployed in *The Moral Landscape* is carefully formulated, hedged, and qualified in such a way as to evade making a definite claim and therefore a thorough evaluation is guaranteed to give a conscientious reviewer a splitting headache.

For distinctive impact, Harris wants his thesis to be about neuroscience and morals:

> The more we understand ourselves at the level of the brain, the more we will see that there are right and wrong answers to questions of human values. (p. 12)

But, just in case neuroscience fails to supply the explanatory goods, he hedges his bets, making it about the enterprise of science as a whole, talking about any events of the world that may be relevant:

> the argument I make . . . rests on a very simple premise: human well-being entirely depends on events in the world and on states of the human brain. (p. 13.)

But, wait for it, Harris gives science a correspondingly inordinately broad conception:

> Science simply represents our best effort to understand what is going on in this universe, and the boundary between it and the rest of rational thought cannot always be drawn.

Thus, by definition nothing is out of court, from how to build a Tesla, a theory of crystal formation, a description of your brain, a theory of harmony, epigenetics, a theory of unintended consequences of policies such as tariffs or minimum wages, how to grow chrysanthemums, and so on . . .

Harris thus seems to be saying that if any factual enquiry whatsoever bears upon human well-being, that supports his approach. The promised and much heralded moral insights specifically of Neuroscience—a Neuroethics—evaporate. You could remove every bit of neuroscience from the book without affecting his actual moral arguments. Instead Harris floods his rhetoric with blatant and outrageous cases of immorality that we in the West can easily agree on, such as honor killings, the psychopathic behavior of serial killers like Ted Bundy, fanatical Muslims throwing homosexuals off roofs, and the mutilation of young girls. Harris is, typically, mostly concerned to bang his anti-religious drum. Some of his arguments are fine. For example:

> It is wrong to force women and girls to wear burqas because it is unpleasant and impractical to live fully veiled, because this practice perpetuates a view of women as being the property of men, and because it keeps the men who enforce it brutally obtuse to the possibility of real equality and communication between the sexes. Hobbling half of the population also directly subtracts from the economic, social, and intellectual wealth of a society. (*The Moral Landscape*, p. 266)

That's a good argument against the veil, but it has nothing whatsoever specifically to do with neuroscience, or any science explicitly except admittedly a slight nod to the sciences of economics and sociology. In sum, it's an argument mostly from common wisdom and everyday economics.

Like all the unexceptionable moral arguments in the book, it's an argument at the level of persons in a world of beliefs, goals, ideals, ethical standards, achievements, and failures. It employs the conceptual scheme of the world of ordinary conversation, not neuroscience.

Amorphous Well-Being

There's a problem with the amorphous idea of well-being. The general idea that morality is about human well-being is common to nearly all systems of ethical theory, most conspicuously the various kinds of utilitarianism. What philosophical analysis in these areas shows is that 'human well-being' is too vague to have detailed implications, and that when we come to apply it to practical examples, we encounter numerous unexpected pitfalls and paradoxes. So, arguing from human well-being to practical issues is not simple. Harris brushes all this aside and won't look at what has turned up in this vast field of human inquiry.

Harris argues in defense of the generality and vagueness of the concept of well-being by comparing it with the standard of health and sickness, which are themselves vague but no less fundamental and useful because of that. Karl Popper put it better than Harris did, when he pointed out that although there is no general criterion for health and sickness, we nevertheless successfully make standards of health and sickness as we progress through a tentative process of conjecture and refutation in which medicine addresses specific ailments and puzzles. Before we had batteries of tests for tuberculosis, doctors knew what they meant by tuberculosis and were often successful in identifying cases of it. Sometimes a researcher suspects intuitively that someone is afflicted by some ailment, but struggles to pin down what it is and this may take a great deal of imaginative theoretical and experimental probing, only to find it is a previously unknown condition.

In other words, even though we don't have a general criterion of health, just as we don't have one for truth or knowledge, we successfully surmise specific theoretical standards and tests of health and sickness as medicine advances. Our conception and standard of disease may change surprisingly. For example, the process of aging has long been considered a normal phase of a healthy life. However, recently some— Aubrey de Grey and David Sinclair—have argued, each for different reasons, that aging itself is a disease and may be cured. In other words, there's no general criterion or standard of health and sickness that completely captures all that is to be said about health and sickness. What happens if we turn this point around on Harris's thesis?

What if we follow Harris's suggestion and argue by analogy that health = virtue and sickness = vice? Remember, Harris is claiming that ethics is "completely captured by the notion of well-being." Just as illness and health have to be unpacked in terms of specific kinds of health and illness, this notion of human well-being has similarly to be unpacked in terms of specific virtues and vices of character and feeling.

So we can agree with Harris that the call for a precise definition or criterion of well-being is misplaced, but we cannot agree that the notion is comprehensive and exhaustive and that it is all we need to care about in ethics.

Coinciding with a perceived inadequacy in the notion of well-being, there is a serious resurgence in ethics of an inter-

est in virtue as a character disposition and personal knowledge and wisdom. Key thinkers here are Michael Slote,
Roger Crisp, and Philippa Foot.

My own humble argument is that the virtues are objec-
tives in their own right, and that human well-being is derivative of our pursuit of virtue. In all our ethical struggles we're
aiming at inventing particular virtuous solutions to particular problems according to the standards of one or more
virtues, rather than aiming directly at well-being as such.

Two Thought Experiments

Honesty is an achievement.
—DAVID MCDONOUGH

Aristotle holds that virtue consists in having a disposition to
have the right feeling and take the right action, in the right
way, at the right time and place, in response to the right person. It's a form of practical knowledge or wisdom, and its performance is a skill with standards of achievement. Hence
McDonough's motto. But we can substitute any of the virtues
for honesty. They are all achievements.

Now, even if there were a state of well-being that satisfied
the stipulates of Harris's thesis, I'm arguing that it would
necessarily have to be instantiated in specific virtues. And
these virtues can only be understood at a certain level of
description, the description we are all familiar with in our
ordinary conversation about good and bad characters and
behaviors, and not at the level of brain processes and states.

Experiment 1: Trying to be Good by Collecting Utils

Utilitarianism is the thesis that there is a common currency
for calculating moral goodness and this is happiness. The
imperative of this precept is that we ought to act in such a
way as to maximize the greatest happiness for the greatest
number of people.

However, if the ultimate standard of morality is the maximizing of the greatest happiness for the greater number, the
maximization of utility, and this is the universal currency of
virtues, then why would I not simply go around maximizing
opportunities to be virtuous? Why would I not, for example,

set off one day to see how many opportunities I can find or arrange to be honest, witty. and temperate? Maybe the next day, after a morning tea, I should set off to be courageous at least twice before lunch, evince warm compassion thrice before dinner, and then magnanimity throughout a whole evening's Socratic dialogue with enthusiastic critics of my latest thesis? What if my guests can't turn up? What can I do to compensate for the unexpected shortfall in virtue-utility that day? How many witty comments, for example, should I have to make that evening at the local bar to at least equal in value the foregone magnanimity at my evening symposium?

Any such man continuously and feverishly auditing his "virtue balance" would strike us as ludicrous. It might appear to others as buffoonery or otherwise sham, undermining the very effort to be virtuous. A paradox of trying too hard to be good? Aristotle might have said that it's a case of intemperance or incontinence, and thus an argument for his idea that the virtues are an indivisible whole, a pearl of unified wisdom. A contemporary version of this ludicrous 'trying to be good' behavior would be Wokist virtue-signaling on social media. This latter might more justly deserve the contemporary metaphorical meaning of the word 'incontinence'—verbal diarrhea.

Perhaps there's no common moral currency and virtue is won as an accomplishment by meeting challenges thrown at us by life's vicissitudes. Even virtues themselves in the abstract aren't what we directly focus on in the flow of life. They are more like tacit, subsidiary constraints on our actions. For example, there are many desires and actions over which we can be temperate; in attempting to exercise appropriate control in each case, we find that either we are or are not temperate in general. Unsullied virtue is an incidental beauty to our actions in pursuit of specific goals, and not accomplished by a pro-active systematic virtue-hunting similar to stamp collecting. Virtues are non-collectible, non-exchangeable, adventitious flowers of human existence.

Experiment 2. Neural Control Buttons

Suppose you found that by boosting the activity of a certain region of the brain you could enhance someone's honesty: the more activity, the stronger the urge to be honest. If you were given a remote control on that, would you press it to make yourself more honest? Whether you would or not is one question; it's significant, I think, that you could sensibly ask yourself, should I? It's not obviously a good idea to do so. Perhaps in real situations the best solution involves a trade-off between honesty and other virtues, say pity or compassion. Therefore, even if you had a controller for these other virtue propensities, you'd still have to work out the best moral solution at a different level to the description and explanation of brain states and processes.

Consider the thought experiment with other vices and virtues. A booster for bravery, a trigger for temperance, an off button for buffoonery, a stimulus for magnanimity, a reset switch for vulgarity and violence, and so forth. Would you want these controls and, if you had them, would your ethical challenges be any the less irksome or demanding? May I suggest, no, because the states that you set by howsoever adroit a skill would still have to conform to a rational solution you have independently worked out in the world of desire, belief, ability, and virtuous achievement.

Laplace's Omniscient Mind Can't Tell You How to Achieve Honesty

All positions are imbued with a metaphysical framework, a set of often unconscious assumptions. These assumptions influence what we regard as plausible or even possible in the world. This is no less true of Harris's worldview and his project of neuroethics. There's nothing wrong with this; we can't help but see the world through our metaphysics, and it's actually an aid and a stimulus to advances in all domains of knowledge.

One such assumption that dominated science from the time of Newton was that the world is a deterministic system, rather like a large clockwork mechanism. Knowing its state at any time in precise detail, a god-like calculator could run it forward or backward in its mind, and no event would be unknowable to it. This view was famously penned by Laplace:

> We may regard the present state of the universe as the effect of its past and the cause of its future. An intellect which at a certain

moment would know all forces that set nature in motion, and all positions of all items of which nature is composed, if this intellect were also vast enough to submit these data to analysis, it would embrace in a single formula the movements of the greatest bodies of the universe and those of the tiniest atom; for such an intellect nothing would be uncertain and the future just like the past would be present before its eyes. (A Philosophical Essay on Probabilities, p. ???)

I surmise that Harris implicitly accepts this metaphysical window on reality, shaping his reductionist approach. Harris doesn't provide us with any major insights into ethics from neuroscience, or indeed any science. I am, nevertheless, taking him seriously in his advertised role as a bringer of scientific insights.

I'm not going to argue against determinism here. What I wish to suggest is that Laplace's calculator-predictor, although providing a wonderful level of knowledge of the physical world, the positions and velocities of atoms—or in modern terms quantum field values—at all times and places, would completely miss the point when it comes to our struggles with ethical issues. Knowing where and how fast atoms are careering about has no relevance to our comprehension and resolution of moral problems. This is shown by the fact that the very notions of achievement, struggle, and each person's conception of themselves as unique persons in the world with unique responsibilities, cannot even be described or conceptually framed in terms of that swarm of atoms or quantum states.

Imagine that you had god-like explanatory and predictive powers over the physical world—you're Laplace's omniscient mind. Knowing all the positions and velocities of subatomic particles making up the world at time t1, you could explain and predict to whatever level of precision you desired the positions and velocities of all subatomic particles in the world at time t2. Now suppose someone asks you what they will do on 22nd February 2027 at 14.00 GMT? The person asks you that question because they wish to know how they will resolve a moral conflict. They have to decide by 14.00 on that day because they have to sign the divorce papers then or not. They are married to someone, but have fallen in love with someone else, and they are deciding what to do that is the right thing morally given all the circumstances. They are weighing up in their minds the opposing ethical values of marital fidelity and the loyalty of romantic passion. You'd be able to give them a detailed and comprehensive description of the movements and positions of all the particles that make up their body and how that swarm of particles moved over a period of several days or as long as they required. I'm saying that they'd be in no better a position to decide what to do in a way meaningful to them than they would have been without the particle swarm prediction. Because this swarm of particles would mean nothing to them in terms of the conceptual framework and theories through which they think and resolve such conflicts of value.

When people ponder this thought experiment, I think they tend to imagine that the predictor god is showing them how they would be thinking, talking, walking, or signing the papers. But that is not what you would be presented with by a physical prediction. Any construction of our thoughts and feelings through such an episode only make sense at the level of human action—the world of desire, belief, ability, knowledge, problems, or questions. I don't have to argue here that science cannot provide us with a swarm-prediction that would be correlated in ways with our thoughts. But if you could 'see' the physical prediction, all the movements of particles that correlate with your struggle with your competing commitments to your marriage, your compassion for your wife, your feelings of loyalty, your belief that signing legal documents has moral force, and so forth, it would look like a sandstorm. It would not be the sort of world in which you tell your explanatory stories about yourself and others. Imagine the person saying to their wife, 'Look, all I can say is that the coherent swarm of particles that is my body is moving away from the coherent swarm of particles that is your body, and may stay in the vicinity of another coherent swarm of particles for a considerable amount of time'.

This is where a reductionist such as Harris often relies on a sleight of hand, conflating the thought and action in terms of achievement and failure, virtue and vice, and the conditions within which we can perform that thinking and action. Of course, you need an intact brain with certain processes and states to engage in ethical problem solving and achievement. But a description of states of the brain—

levels of serotonin or dopamine for, example—is not an account of your reasoning in terms appropriate to the domain of reasoning. Those states and processes of our brains are not conceptually organized by neuroscience in a way that can fit into our moral deliberations.

Neuroscience does not tell us what a valid logical argument is or supply heuristics for solving problems. (If you look at the brain through an fMRI you won't see conundrums, dilemmas, mean-ends schemes, plans, or concepts of virtue. All you will see are measures of brain activity by detecting changes associated with blood flow.) But we need those conceptual categories and abstract tools to engage at all in those deliberations.

Hence Socrates's scornful comment: "Fancy being unable to distinguish between the reason for a thing, and the condition without which the reason couldn't be operative!"

If, as suggested by Alasdair MacIntyre, ethics is partly a matter of choosing between logically incompatible moral exhortations, then logic influences our ethical life. But logic, understood as abstract relationships between statements, is not a fact of neuroscience—it's not a state or process of the brain. Neither is logic an event or state of affairs in the world. Remember, Harris claimed: "human well-being entirely depends on *events* in the world and on states of the human brain." Of course, being the shape-shifter we're coming to know, Harris could say, well, logic itself is factual and on that account supports my approach. However, nowhere in Harris's account is logic systematically elaborated into his view to show how it is relevant to ethics without also undermining his insistence on the special relevance of neuroscience and the privileged causal role of *events* in the world.

Harris ignores one of the outstanding neuroscientists of the twentieth century, Sir John Eccles who, with Karl Popper, wrote the book *The Self and Its Brain*, in which they elaborate on Popper's theory that the world consists of at least three classes of entity: World 1. A physical realm of atoms, chairs, and electric fields; World 2, a psychological realm of beliefs, expectations, values, fears, and dreams; and World 3, a realm of abstract products of the human mind, but with autonomous properties and relations of their own: problems, theories, concepts, logical relationships, plans, and symphonies. These worlds interact, so that, for example, a logical incoherence in a theory or plan, if noticed, can affect our subjective experience (W2), causing us to disbelieve it or reject it as inapt for our purposes, and as a further consequence affect our actions in the physical world (W1).

Perhaps our moral deliberations are often crucially dependent on logical considerations about the relationships between each of the virtues understood as abstract constructs but also, at a higher abstract level, the different theories of how they fit together. For example, I said earlier that Plato and Aristotle were inclined to the view that a dishonest man couldn't be courageous. But there's the alternative logically incompatible theory that virtues are independent of one another.

The Unbridgeable Gulf between the Universal and the Particular

The world is composed of two fundamentally different kinds of things, universals and particulars. Examples of universals include things we name by nouns such as *whiteness, mass, electric charge, human being, raven, gravity, isosceles triangle*. Universals also include relations, which we typically denote with a verb or a preposition: *to the right of, larger than, more important than, equal to*. Examples of particulars are things we typically denote with proper names or pronouns: *John Templeton, you, they, that patch of whiteness, your notepad, the sound just now of the robin singing outside your window, the North Pole of the Earth, Earth's Moon*. The simplest particulars are denoted by pronouns, such as *this* and *that* (referring to, say, an object or event within easy sight or reach) or *now* (referring to the present time).

As a human being you exist at the interface of these radically different facets of reality. As a human being you are subject to various laws of nature that are universal. But you are at the same time a unique particular; there's no copy of you in the cosmos, you're the first and the last of you. Otherwise, you'd be a universal. Even the most searching biography cannot completely describe you; it must leave out a world of particulars. This, I think, has profound significance for our relationship to science, technology, and ethics.

People typically think of science as a source of technology, the means to solving our various problems. However, there is a gulf between this popular picture of science and its more humble character.

Science as a collection of universal laws cannot tell you how to build or achieve anything. It cannot tell you how to build a Tesla or a bridge or an airplane. Even less can it tell you how to achieve magnanimity rather than pettiness, kindness rather than meanness or prodigality, wit rather than buffoonery. For these are, just like a new Tesla or a new game or communication device, achievements—special arrangements of particulars. In the case of virtues, this is our management of action and feeling; in the case of technology, it is special arrangements of particular portions of matter and energy that reliably produce an intended effect.

A scientific law does not tell us what exists, but only what cannot occur. The import of a law is a sort of prohibition on events. For example, take the law-like statement 'All ravens are black'. This law does not even tell us that ravens exist, but only that if there is anything that is a raven, it must be black. The law of freefall on Earth does not tell us that free-falling objects exist. Rather, it tells us that there is no such thing as an object in free-fall that does not fall with an acceleration of 9.8 meters per second, per second.

Typically, scientific laws only become tools of prediction or explanation when we specify initial and boundary conditions—the particular circumstances to which they apply. Our predictive and explanatory powers at the level of physics and chemistry are well beyond what the ancient Greeks could have imagined, and this power is not to be belittled. So, I'm not saying scientific laws aren't informative; I'm saying they're informative by ruling things out rather than by informing us about the existence of certain things or states of affairs. The prohibited things include types of physical objects, events, and transformations of matter and energy.

David Deutsch has a way of saying what amounts to the same thing logically, but to the credit of his eloquence he has coined a more positive, even liberating, turn of phrase: that whatever doesn't violate a law of physics is possible. The freedom of transformations allowed within the laws is staggering, indeed infinite. There's lots of room for the inventor and innovator to move about. But this is the optimist's flip side of the idea, advanced by Popper, that laws don't prescribe what happens but prohibit infinite ranges of possibilities. Think of the laws of nature as like rules of chess. It's marvelous that, provided you don't violate the rules of chess, there is an extremely large number of thoroughly engaging games you can play; but that doesn't make you a good chess player.

My point is that nothing about particulars follows directly from the laws. Therefore, if you wish to invent a new computer or kettle you have to conjecture and try out different arrangements of matter and energy that may bring about a desired effect. You can't just deduce these from the laws. Once you've invented your new engine, you can explain and predict how it works by the laws in conjunction with a description of your device, a statement of initial conditions and boundary conditions. James Watt's innovations to the Newcomen steam engine, itself a product of craftwork and not science, are a story of trial and error models and flashes of insight, admittedly seen in terms of the theories of vacuum and latent heat, but not logically derived from those theories. At this point, I'm asking you to bear with me now for the next rather large step in my argument. This point must be true of all goal-directed action, since all action is particular.

When it comes to achieving virtuous action, by analogy, we cannot derive a particular solution to a moral challenge directly from any universal principles of a similar logical character to scientific laws. This is because the relevant actions that would achieve your goals are particulars and therefore cannot follow from universal principles taken alone. You have to invent each solution to each moral challenge. You might be able to invent rules of thumb that would cover many cases. You can invent universal moral imperatives, as Kant suggested, and then subject these to possible refutation through thought experiment or actual experience. As Hume already knew, Ought implies Can, so there is a connection between morals and facts—just not the one that Harris has in mind, in which Is implies Ought. However, you'd still have to apply these general principles with a generous amount of equity. (Equity is the nuanced administration of a law or rule, suitably adjusted to the particular case. The very notion of equity tacitly accepts the problem posed by the gulf between the universal and the particular.)

A similar point applies to other principles that, although not strictly of the same logical structure as laws of nature, are universal and therefore not immediately connected with the particulars they are applied to. Consider the principles of military strategy.

Harris's universal objective of achieving "human wellbeing" does not give us a practical guide to action in particular circumstances. For example, if we aim at maximizing the greatest happiness for the greater number of people (universal principle) in the (particular) case of an international crisis, what action do we take? Do we, motivated by humanitarian goals, intervene to end a war or massacre? Intervening might end the war, or it might lead to a wider or worse situation. Harris might simply respond by saying well, if research in strategy and game theory shows that intervention or non-intervention is best for our stipulated goal, then, either way, that endorses his approach, at least the broad one in which he's appealing to the relevance of science in general and not specifically neuroscience.

A more subtle example would be in the case of a two-front war, what action do you take? It is a universal strategic principle that in this situation you concentrate on one front first, whilst parrying on the other. However, this doesn't tell us which front to concentrate on first in a particular situation. Should the USA, for example, have concentrated in World War II on Germany or Japan first? This seems to bring in a fine balance of judgment, something closer to an art rather than a scientific effort of Laplacian prediction. And if we add moral considerations that are pulling equally from both directions, we arrive at a decision situation not easily reduced to a straight read-off from any science. What if overwhelming moral considerations had put weight on concentrating on Japan first but, simultaneously, militarily judgment had overwhelmingly favored concentrating on Germany first? What if the moral and the strategic arguments are of equal weight? Even asking whether moral and military arguments can be of equal weight seems to raise non-scientific issues that are more of a metaphysical kind. In any case, Harris can't simply reject this choice, putting all his eggs on the scientific strategic/game-theoretic side; by hypothesis the moral considerations are irreducibly part of the equation.

The Potency of the Unique

My answer to that strategic question is to take a step back, take a longer view, and argue for a world without the nation-states that create the conditions for this sort of conflict in the first place. Isn't it time we acknowledged that states are the foremost violators of human liberty? What do you expect? They are monopolists of coercion. They are upheld as protectors of peace and liberty, but all around we see them either at war—Ukraine and Russia— or on the precipice of going to war—China and Taiwan. We need alternative groupings and tools for cooperation and the division of labor across the globe. Networked-collectives, sea-steading, mutual insurance societies. Of course, the same chasm between the universal and particular would open up before us again, and that is why leading by personal example is a key ethical point, as in the Socrates, Jesus, Buddha, and Seneca narratives: live as you would others live. To uniquely instantiate your ethical archetype is potent, bringing admiration and emulation. Reinforcing this by the power of argument as the abstract tool of persuasion, but also contributing to particular innovations and inventions, will help build new ways by which billions of people can live peacefully and productively together.

Ultimately a person must be responsible for his unique decisions; it is that risky decision about this or that particular or even unique choice that captures the central truth about ethics as lived by us in each of our unique lives. Sometimes that choice is monstrous, but unavoidable.

We didn't choose to exist, but we're thrown into existence with this weight upon our shoulders. You have the right to shrug, and live the life of a hermit, imagining that you've escaped the burden of humanity, the strain of civilization. But you won't then be fully alive, and even the hermit confronts his own internal world of ethical demands. To flourish is an inescapably transient and risky affair; so better to suck the marrow out of life. These truths cannot be systematized by science just because they are about our unique fleeting existence.

Ethics is a conjectural practical art of achieving certain ends according to standards that we tentatively embrace, but scrutinize now and then for feasibility and logical coherence. Virtues are conjectured coherent and harmonious sets of actively engaged skills that constitute living a good life. It's a delicate and fallible process of conjecture and refutation fitting those various sometimes contending virtues together in a wise stable whole. Each has to be performed in the right way, at the right time, at the right place, without inadvertently upsetting the apt achievement of the others!

It's a tall order. Just don't get intemperate or rash or become an over calculating Hobbesian robot about it. And as a stoic friend said to me, "You're not worried about things, are you? It is as it is!"

Bibliography

Aristotle. 2004. *The Nicomachean Ethics*. Penguin.
————. 2018. *The Art of Rhetoric*. Oxford University Press.
————. 2013. *Poetics*. Oxford University Press.
Butler, Joseph. 2017 [1726]. *Fifteen Sermons Preached at the Rolls Chapel and Other Writings on Ethics*. Oxford University Press.
Crisp, Roger. 2006. *Reasons and the Good*. Oxford University Press.
Crisp, Roger, and Michael Slote. 1998. *How Should One Live? Essays on the Virtues*. Oxford University Press.
De Grey, Aubrey, and Michael Rae. 2007. *Ending Aging: The Rejuvenation Breakthroughs that Could Reverse Human Aging in Our Lifetime*. St. Martin's Press.
Deutsch, David. 2012 [2011]. T*he Beginning of Infinity: Explanations that Transform the World*. Penguin.
Foot, Philippa. 2002. [1978]. *Virtues and Vices and Other Essays in Moral Philosophy*. Oxford University Press.
Harris, Sam. 2012 [2010]. *The Moral Landscape: How Science Can Determine Human Values*. Random House.
Hume, David. 1978 [1739–40]. *A Treatise of Human Nature*. Oxford University Press.
Kant, Immanuel. 1993. *Groundwork of the Metaphysics of Morals*. Everyman.
————. 2002. *Critique of Practical Reason*. Hackett.

Kealey, Terence. 1996. *The Economic Laws of Scientific Research*. Palgrave Mcmillan.

Laplace, Pierre-Simon. 1951 [1814]. *A Philosophical Essay on Probabilities*. Dover.

MacIntyre, Alasdair. 2007. [1981]. *After Virtue*. Duckworth.

Miller, David. 1998. Is Scientific Knowledge an Inexhaustible Economic Resource? *The Critical Rationalist* 03:01.

Nietzsche, Friedrich. 1972 [1886]. *Beyond Good and Evil: Prelude to a Philosophy of the Future*. Penguin.

Percival, Ray Scott. 1996. The Metaphysics of Scarcity: Popper's World 3 and the Theory of Finite Resources. *The Critical Rationalist* 01:02.

Plato. 1993. *The Last Days of Socrates*. Penguin.

Popper, Karl R. 1945. *The Open Society and Its Enem*ies. Two volumes. Routledge.

Popper, Karl R., and John C. Eccles. 1977 [1984]. *The Self and Its Brain: An Argument for Interactionism*. Springer.

Sinclair, David A. 2019. *Lifespan: Why We Age and Why We Don't Have To*. Atria.

Slote, Michael. 2001. *Morals from Motives*. Oxford University Press.

[7]
A Miserable Argument

MARK WARREN

S am Harris says science can answer moral questions.

You might think he's advocating that our judgments about what to do should be informed by an understanding of the world as it's revealed by science. And that's just obviously true, the kind of thing that's standard operating procedure in most people's ethical reasoning. If you want to decide whether abortions are ethically permissible, you might want to know about the science of brain development in fetuses. If you're trying to decide whether the death penalty is just, you should at least hear what sociologists have to say about racial disparities in capital punishment. To figure out what to do, we need to know how things are with the world, and science is very good at filling in those blanks.

But Harris is saying something more than that. Science won't just *help* us find moral answers; science can give us those answers. Harris wrote a best-selling book making the argument—*The Moral Landscape: How Science Can Determine Human Value*. He intends his readers to take that subtitle seriously. Indeed, he thinks morality should itself "be considered an undeveloped branch of science" (p. 4). Science has an impressive track record of answering some of our most vexing questions. If Harris is right, we will one day add, "How should I live?" to that list.

Let's see if he's right.

Better Living Through Chemistry?

To many, Harris's position will seem like a gross exaggeration of science's proper role. This objection can be traced back to the eighteenth-century philosopher David Hume's famous is-ought problem. In his *Treatise of Human Nature*, Hume argued that no amount of information about how the world *is* can, on its own, lead us by force of logic to a conclusion about how things *ought* to be. Science is in the 'is' business; morality is in the 'ought' business. It follows that science can only deliver 'oughts' in an advisory capacity.

Should I take this pill? If I want to know what's in it before I decide, someone trained in the science of chemistry can tell me if, say, it's vitamin D. Or if it's MDMA. And someone trained in the medical sciences can tell me, 'If you want healthy bones, you should take the vitamin D'. Or: 'If you want to dance for three hours, you should take the Ecstasy'. The advice I can get from scientists like these are contingent on my aims. Science can tell me, if I want a particular outcome, here's the way I should proceed.

But my question might run deeper. Perhaps I already know what's in the pill, but I don't know what outcome I *should* want. Should I strive to maintain robust health? Should I throw caution to the wind and seize the day? Is it better to prevent osteoporosis, or to get really high? Conventional wisdom would tell us that such questions are outside of the purview of science.

Harris disagrees with Hume, and the conventional wisdom that followed him:

> I am arguing that science can, in principle, help us understand what we should do and should want—and, therefore, what other people should do and should want in order to live the best lives possible. My claim is that there are right and wrong answers to moral questions, just as there are right and wrong answers to questions of physics, and such answers may one day fall within reach of the maturing sciences of mind. (*The Moral Landscape*, p. 28)

Before I move on to assess this claim, we should pause to appreciate just how revolutionary it is. If it succeeds in its arguments, Harris's book is an incredible accomplishment. It would overturn the dominant philosophical opinion about the relationship between science and values. It would span the divide between 'is' and 'ought'.

From Science to Morality in Four Easy Steps

How do you get from the raw material of the scientific inquiry to moral insight? Here are the steps Harris takes:

1. **The well-being of conscious creatures is completely dependent on environmental and neurological states.**

2. **These states can be understood by science.**

3. **Moral truths are entirely reducible to truths about the well-being of conscious creatures.**

4. **Therefore, science is uniquely positioned to answer moral questions.**

If you're paying attention, that third premise should jump out at you. It's a passable summary of what philosophers would call a *utilitarian* worldview. Utilitarianism is the moral philosophy that the rightness or wrongness of an action boils down to whether and how much happiness or suffering the act causes. Every time I teach an ethics course, I devote a few days of class to explaining the utilitarian philosophy, drawing out its implications for how we should behave, comparing it to other moral philosophies, and rehearsing the challenges it has faced from skeptical philosophers over the past couple of centuries.

So, you'd think this particular premise would belong to the philosophers, and not the scientists. *The Moral Landscape: How Science Can Determine Human Values (if Utilitarianism Turns Out to Be True)* doesn't have quite the same ring to it, but perhaps it would be a more accurate title.

Harris gives us an argument that science can determine our values. He's promised a bridge that can take us from the 'is' of science to the 'ought' of morality. But it looks as if he's packed all the load-bearing oughts of his argument into that third premise, and *that* premise looks more like philosophy than science. So, a skeptic might at this point ask him: 'Is this moral principle itself supposed to be a scientific truth?'

Scientists Can Help Themselves to Self-Evident Premises

But Harris isn't bothered by this question. He argues that philosophy and science shouldn't be thought of as entirely distinct enterprises—"science is," he claims, "often a matter of philosophy in practice" (p. 180). Because of this, he doesn't think it's such a great sin for a branch of science to smuggle in philosophical assumptions. In fact, he argues, it's unavoidable: "It is essential to see that the demand for radical justification leveled by the moral skeptic could not be met by any branch of science" (p. 37).

Consider for example the study of medicine. Doctors work on the assumption that their job is to promote their patients' health, broadly construed. But if a doctor were asked how they could possibly justify this assumption, Harris would, I think, recommend a hearty rolling of the eyes as an adequate response. "Science cannot tell us why, scientifically, we should value health. But once we admit that health is the proper concern of medicine, we can then study and promote it through science" (p. 37).

The argument, then, is that just because his argument relies on a non-scientific premise, that alone doesn't undermine the scientific bona fides of his conception of morality. *All* scientific enterprises rely at some point on non-scientific premises. All scientists, for example, assume that regularities we observe in the past will hold in the future, that logic is universal, that truth is worth pursuing. But we don't have to use science itself to prove these assumptions true in order to engage productively in the scientific enterprise. And that's because these principles are just self-evident. So yes, Harris's science of morality relies on a non-scientific premise, but that's not enough to disqualify it as a science. It's in good company.

Now, dear reader, in the spirit of charity, I'm going to ask you to ignore a lot. Ignore any worries that Harris has conflated medical *science*—the aim of which is to understand how the human body works, and how disease and other maladies operate—with the *practice* of medicine—the aim of which is to use findings from medical science to promote human health. Ignore any concern you might have that whether his argument counts as science or not, it still hasn't met Hume's challenge. Ignore any sneaking suspicion that, by muddying the distinction between philosophy and science, Harris has given himself just enough cover to do good old fashioned moral reasoning and call it science.

We'll just grant all these points to Harris. I'm going to ask you to focus instead on a problem that lies at the heart of his argument: Harris's utilitarian premise is *not* self-evident in the same way that the other assumptions we've talked about are. Any scientist worth their salt thinks that truth is worth pursuing. Any doctor worth visiting will agree that health is worth promoting. But moral philosophers disagree vehemently about Harris's moral premise—utilitarianism is, in fact, a minority position among academic philosophers.

And it's not just philosophers. Normal people also seem to have an intuitive understanding of some of the problems with this moral worldview. Go watch a superhero movie. If the villain is the right kind of megalomaniac, chances are pretty good they'll justify their wickedness on utilitarian grounds. Think Thanos in *Avengers: Infinity War*, or Ra's al Ghul in *Batman Begins*. These are characters who have some grand goal of reducing suffering in the world. But they're the bad guys because, as unrepentant utilitarians, they believe the ends justify their vicious means. We instinctively root against them, and that implies we don't just assume the truth of utilitarianism as a given in our moral reasoning.

This objection doesn't end the matter. The majority of philosophers—and moviegoers—might just be wrong. They might miss a point that should be self-evident. But to deal with this concern, Harris will need to show us *why* they should be ignored. And he's got an argument to that effect. To make his point, he'll have to bring us all to Hell.

The Worst Possible Misery for Everyone

Imagine a world of perfect suffering. The universe God would make, if His benevolence soured into hatred: Every conscious creature in this world suffers as much as its neurology will allow, every moment of the day, for all of time. Imagine Hell on Earth.

Such a world would be . . . well, pretty bad, right? This is self-evident. It would in fact be as bad a situation as we can imagine. Once we admit this, Harris argues, we've accepted the first link in a chain of logic that leads us inexorably to his utilitarian premise:

> Once we conceive of "the worst possible misery for everyone," then we can talk about taking incremental steps toward this abyss: What could it mean for life on earth to get worse for all human beings simultaneously? It seems uncontroversial to say that a change that leaves everyone worse off, by any rational standard, can be reasonably called "bad," if this word is to have any meaning at all. (*The Moral Landscape*, p. 39)

The idea is that, if you agree that the worst possible misery for everyone is bad, and that any improvement in the well-being of everyone would make things better, you've admitted that questions of goodness and badness must ultimately be ones about how things are going for sentient creatures.

> I am saying that a universe in which all conscious beings suffer the worst possible misery is worse than a universe in which they experience well-being. This is all we need to talk about "moral truth" in the context of science. (p. 39)

Harris thinks that science can answer moral questions. His argument for that position rests on the non-scientific assumption that morality is basically about promoting the well-being of conscious creatures. This isn't a problem, he thinks, because by reflecting on how bad an imagined Hell world would be, we can see the obvious connection between what we value and the experiences of conscious beings. Once we admit this, we must also admit that morality is fundamentally concerned with promoting well-being, with moving us as far away from such a world as possible.

And all of this just as self-evident as any other non-philosophical assumption made by the sciences. So, inasmuch as the well-being of sentient creatures correlates to their brain states, and their brain states can be studied by science, we've laid the foundation for a science of morality.

Adding a Bit of Misery

I don't think this is the right way of framing the issue, for reasons I'll explain in a bit.

But for now, it's worth noting that this argument doesn't even work on its own terms. To see why, imagine another world, an afterlife. Its denizens are those men and women who spent their time here on Earth in the evilest ways imaginable—they are the tyrants, the predators, the social media tycoons of this world. But surprisingly, their hereafter isn't so bad, all things considered.

It's something like life for a middle-class American. Not so great, but not too bad, either.

Now imagine you had the opportunity to move that world one iota nearer Harris's miserable extreme. You can push a button and by doing so introduce one small uncompensated misery to every villain in this afterlife. A mouse bites Hitler's toe one day. Pol Pot catches a cold. Stalin's wifi keeps cutting out.

Would you push the button?

If Harris is right about the self-evidence of utilitarianism, the question should seem ridiculous. It's like asking a doctor if they should try to help their patient, or a physicist if we should believe in an external world. It should just be *obvious* to us that it would be wrong to intentionally cause harm for its own sake.

But even if you wouldn't push the button, you might be tempted, right? In one sense, doing so would unambiguously make that world a worse place—worse for each person in it. But it's not clear that doing this would make the world a *morally* worse place. It's just wrong, you might think, that all these wretched people get to go on living their afterlives as if they hadn't been monsters. It's not fair! And you needn't fantasize about eternal punishment in a fiery pit to think that perhaps the damned at least deserve some fair share of the misery they caused the rest of us.

This is a distinction that Harris misses: we can admit that things can go better or worse for people without thereby committing ourselves to a judgment about whether such eventualities are *morally* good or bad. His arguments here conflate badness—as an assessment of how things are for someone—with *moral* badness. We can concede that something is bad in the first sense (Pol Pot is having a hard time with his sinus congestion) without drawing any direct conclusions about its moral status.

That's because considerations of morality outstrip considerations of how things are going for people. Contra Harris, there are other things we care about, other things worth valuing. If it's unclear to you whether you should push the button, your uncertainty reflects this. Justice is another thing worth valuing, and a concern for justice can't always be neatly translated into a concern for well-being.

And justice isn't the only competing moral value. Over the millennia, philosophers have enumerated many others: autonomy, virtue, equality, fraternity, to name a few. Harris briefly acknowledges some of these alternate conceptions of morality throughout the book. In each case, his counterargument is the same: These considerations might *look* like they speak against a monolithic utilitarian account of moral value, but if we're honest with ourselves, we will admit that ultimately justice, autonomy, and the rest, can all ultimately be reduced to concerns about well-being.

For example, in his argument against justice as an independent source of moral value, Harris admits that justice can be very useful, inasmuch as just societies tend to be happy societies. But he asks us:

> How would we feel if, after structuring [an ideally just society], we were told by an omniscient being that we had made a few choices that, though eminently fair, would lead to the unnecessary misery of millions, while parameters that were ever-so-slightly less fair would entail no such suffering? Could we be indifferent to this information? (p. 79)

The implication is that in those situations where considerations of justice are in competition with considerations of well-being, it should just be obvious to the reader that well-being should win out.

It's not obvious to me, at least. His thought experiment can be neatly turned on its head: Imagine a society where everyone is fairly well off, but we've found a way to increase net happiness a small amount. Unfortunately, doing so will exacerbate existing injustices: inequalities will be heightened, bad actors will be rewarded, legitimate grievances will go unanswered. Is it just self-evident that we shouldn't care, that justice must be sacrificed at the altar of beneficence?

But Harris never considers such a situation. He's got a utilitarian hammer, and every alternate moral value looks like a nail. I will leave it as an exercise for the reader to decide whether Harris's other counterarguments in this vein are convincing. I have bigger fish to fry.

The Worst Possible Mechanic

It's not self-evident that every incremental move toward more suffering makes for a world that's morally worse. Not necessarily, anyway. And by the same token, it's not self-evident that every move towards greater well-being makes for a world that is morally better. But I claimed above that this doesn't get to the heart of the matter. Harris's argument suffers from a deeper flaw.

I can illustrate this point if you'll grant him all the points he's made so far. We've been so charitable already; let us go a bit further. Grant Harris that not only is suffering bad, but it's also morally bad, and necessarily so. Grant him that an increase in suffering automatically makes a situation morally worse, and that an increase in well-being makes it morally better. Grant him that all this argumentation can plausibly be thought of as a seamless part of a properly scientific process.

Let our charity reach a fever pitch. Grant him everything he's asked that you admit to yourself, even if, like me, you're skeptical you should.

Because once you grant him all this, then you can see the real flaw in his argument: even if we accept that suffering is morally bad and flourishing is morally good, we still haven't shown that suffering is *all* that's bad, and we definitely haven't proved that *all* there is to badness is misery, or that *all* there is to goodness is well-being. A world of maximal suffering might be the worst moral situation possible, but it could still be the case that moral questions cannot be reduced to questions of suffering and well-being.

To see this, imagine you bring your car into the shop one day. The wheels need alignment. Your oil needs changing. You can't get the radio to play. The mechanic confidently opens the hood to the car, sprays half a can of Rust-Oleum over the engine, closes the hood, and presents you with a bill.

Of course, you're outraged and refuse to pay up. Rust-Oleum isn't going to fix your radio! He didn't even change your oil! But in the sonorous tones of a veteran podcaster, he tries to calm your worries. He explains: 'Imagine a car whose parts have rusted through entirely. Every square inch of metal on this vehicle has been eaten to nothing but brittle and hole-pocked rust. It's perfectly oxidized. Now, if you have any opinion worth listening to about automotive issues, it will just be clear to you that this car is not going to run—that indeed such a situation represents a unique nadir of motor functionality. Any addition of rust to a healthy car will make it worse off; any removal of rust will make it better. It follows, then, that questions of a car's automotive health admit of right and wrong answers, and these questions are reducible to questions about the oxidation of its parts.'

Now, you might have doubts about whether a completely rusted out car is the worst possible car, but you should ignore those for the moment. Because that just distracts from the more urgent issue at hand: even if he's right, it still doesn't follow that fighting rust is the *only* way to promote automotive health. Just because rust is bad doesn't mean it's the *only* bad thing that can happen to a car.

Science Alone Cannot Determine Human Values

Readers who bought Harris's book in the hopes of understanding how science can answer moral questions should be equally disappointed. Even if we admit that the worst possible misery for everyone is the worst moral situation possible, even if we agree with Harris that anything that brings us closer to such a situation must be bad—and morally bad, at that—we still haven't shown that *all there is* to morality is the promotion of well-being and the abatement of suffering.

The failure to show that his utilitarian premise is self-evident is disastrous for Harris's project.

He needs to secure this point if he wants to plausibly put morality alongside the other sciences. Without it, he's stuck with the rest of us as we navigate the difficult question of how we should live. There are inescapably philosophical issues with which we must grapple if we hope to do this successfully. We must weigh sometimes competing values—justice, beneficence, autonomy, virtue—to make up our minds about which are the most appropriate to act on in a given situation.

And yes, the best moral deliberators are using science where it's relevant to their principles. But they're not *doing science* when they decide which principles are important. A chemist can't tell you how to live your life; for that, you'll have to go to a priest or a philosopher. Science is in the business of telling us how the world works, but we need something else—religion or philosophy or poetry—to tell us how the world should be, and therefore how we ought to behave.

References

Harris, Sam. 2012. *The Moral Landscape: How Science Can Determine Human Values*. Black Swan.

Hume, David. 2007 [1739]. *A Treatise of Human Nature: Being an Attempt to Introduce the Experimental Method of Reasoning into Moral Subjects*. Oxford University Press.

[8]
Dark Spots in Sam Harris's Moral Landscape

DAVID GORDON

Sam Harris's *The Moral Landscape* contains some of the strident rhetoric against religion which in earlier works has won for him a great deal of attention as one of the New Atheists. His vehement opposition to Islam is much in evidence in the book; suffice it to say that if Harris values his continued well-being, he would be ill-advised to visit Iran or Saudi Arabia.

The book contains much else of interest, though, and what I find most valuable in it is the discussion of 'moral realism'. Most people who aren't philosophers probably think that moral judgments are just expressions or statements of preference. Though there are many subtle variations of this position, it in essence holds that 'stealing is wrong' means something like 'I disapprove of stealing', and that's all there is to it. This analysis of what a moral proposition means doesn't change if in fact most people share this preference. Moral realists disagree with this. They think that 'stealing is wrong' is a truth about the world, not dependent for its truth on people's acceptance of it.

Harris accepts moral realism. Isn't it obviously true, he asks, that pain and misery are bad, meaning by this not just that most people dislike these things, but that they are objectively bad? He says:

> I hope it is clear that when I speak about 'objective' moral truths or about the 'objective' causes of human well-being . . . I'm simply

saying that, given there are facts—real facts—to be known about how conscious creatures can experience the worst possible misery and the greatest possible well-being, it is objectively true to say that there are right and wrong answers to moral questions, whether or not it is always true that we can answer these questions in practice. (p. 29, emphasis in original.)

Offering an example of an objectively knowable moral truth, he says, "Even if each conscious being has a unique nadir on the moral landscape, we can still conceive of a state of the universe in which everyone suffers as much as he or she (or it) possibly can. If you think we cannot say this would be 'bad', then I don't know what you mean by the word 'bad' (and I don't think you know what you mean by it either)" (p. 39). To avoid a misunderstanding, it should be noted that 'pain is bad' does not imply that there are no circumstances in which the infliction of pain is morally permissible, or even required; but rather that pain is a 'bad-making' feature of states of affairs. Further, the objective truth of 'pain is bad' doesn't entail that we have a duty to care equally about each person's pain and in particular that it's wrong to care more about your own pain and the pains of those close to you than to care about the pain of others. Indeed, the truth that pain is bad doesn't by itself entail any moral duties, though considered together with other moral truths, it may do so.

These contentions about pain and universal misery do not commit moral realists to mysterious 'values' that exist outside human minds, to which the true moral judgments correspond. It is rather that we know the condition of universal misery to be objectively bad, and this claim requires no further support. As Nagel remarks in his review of Harris's book,

The true culprit behind contemporary professions of moral skepticism is the confused belief that the ground of moral truth must be found in something other than moral values. One can pose this type of question about any kind of truth. What makes it true that $2 + 2 = 4$? What makes it true that hens lay eggs? Some things are just true; nothing else makes them true. Moral skepticism is caused by the currently fashionable but unargued assumption that only certain kinds of things, such as physical facts, can be 'just true' and that value judgments such as 'happiness is better than misery' are not among them. And that assumption in turn leads to the conclusion that a value judgment could be true only if it were made true by something like a physical fact. That, of course, is nonsense.

Another way of stating Nagel's position is that there are 'moral facts' just as there are physical facts: it's a fact that pain is bad. One thing in Nagel's statement that can easily be misunderstood is what he says about hens laying eggs. He isn't denying that the fact that hens lay eggs makes true the statement 'Hens lay eggs'. Rather, he is saying that nothing makes the fact that hens lay eggs true: that fact isn't true because of some further fact (which isn't to say that we're precluded from offering a causal account of how it has come about that hens lay eggs). In other words, Nagel's point is that justifications come to an end, and moral truths such as 'pain is bad' do not require further grounding.

Sam Harris is firmly committed to a 'scientific' world outlook, and some have supposed that this rules out moral realism. In particular, it has been claimed that an evolutionary account of the origins of morality leaves no room for it. According to this claim, the basic rules of morality are evolutionary adaptations: for example, people who live in groups that accept the rule 'Don't try to kill someone whenever you take a dislike to them' will probably be much more successful in reproducing their genes that people who live in groups that reject this rule. If this is correct, some philosophers have argued, there is no need to appeal to objective moral truths in order to explain why morality exists.

Harris, in my view rightly, rejects the notion that an evolutionary account of the origins of morality gives us reason to reject moral realism. About this he is emphatic: "The fact that our moral intuitions probably conferred some adaptive advantage on our ancestors does not mean that the present purpose of morality is successful reproduction or that 'our belief in morality' is just a useful delusion" (p. 47). In other words, an evolutionary account of how we came to hold our moral beliefs doesn't undermine moral realism.

Unfortunately, Harris also adopts another contention that does not follow from the objective badness of pain and the objective goodness of pleasure. This is that nothing besides well-being, 'cashed out' in felt qualities of experience is objectively good. (We can speak of 'good' and 'bad' in a secondary sense about means to avoid pain or achieve pleasure.) In considering this issue, it's important to keep it separate from another claim, which is more plausible. Suppose nothing in the universe (or the universe as a whole) could experience anything. Such a world, it might be thought, would be devoid of value; but someone could accept that premise and also think, for example, that in the actual world, which contains sentient beings, it is good to do what is right for its own sake, regardless of whether doing so increased happiness. I think this view rather than Harris's is correct, but I'm not offering a defense of this here. I mention it only to illustrate the difference between the logically weaker premise that a world without conscious beings capable of feeling would be devoid of value and Harris's premise, which is that only experienced states of well-being are good; in other words, only pleasure is good and pain bad.

He's aware that there are competing views to his exclusive stress on pleasure and pain, for example that people ought to act justly, even when doing so does not affect the balance of pleasure and pain, but he thinks his own view can accommodate people's intuitive judgments about this. Harris says that these judgments are evolutionary adaptations. Because they are built into us, we derive pleasure from states of affairs judged fair and pain from those judged unfair. Hence he does not view these as counterexamples to his position. He says: "Fairness is not merely an abstract principle—it is a felt experience. . . Taking others' interests into account, making impartial decisions (and knowing that others will make them), rendering help to the needy—these are experiences that contribute to our psychological and social well-being" (pp. 79–80).

This isn't convincing. It may well be that you 'feel good' if you do what you take to be right, but doing so may involve a great deal of pain that makes you feel bad overall. Someone who resists torture in order not to betray his comrades is probably not ecstatic at the time. Why not then acknowledge that you can act because you take something to be right, rather than insist, as Harris does, that the judgment of rightness must be accompanied by a feeling in order to elicit action? Even if you act fairly and feel good about having acted fairly, you do not act fairly in order to feel good about it, but because it's right.

One reason Harris is reluctant to recognize the force of moral considerations besides experiences of pleasure and pain is that he mischaracterizes theories that do so. He writes about Rawls, for example, that the "moment we conceive of justice as being fully separable from human well-being, we are faced with the prospect of there being morally 'right' actions and social systems that are, on balance, detrimental to the welfare of everyone affected by them. To simply bite the bullet on this point, as Rawls seemed to do, saying 'there is no reason to think that just institutions will maximize the good', seems a mere embrace of moral and philosophical defeat" (p. 78). Nagel draws attention to this passage in his review of *The Moral Landscape*. This is a complete mischaracterization of Rawls and those who agree with him that there is more to morality than maximizing pleasure and minimizing pain. Rawls did not say that consequences do not matter; indeed, he says it would be crazy to think this. His view was rather that other things matter as well, and this does not entail the acceptance of pointless human suffering.

There is an obvious challenge to Harris's premise that he surprisingly fails to mention. Robert Nozick's experience machine thought experiment has been taken by many to show that there is more to what is good and bad in life than how things feel 'from the inside'. In this example, Nozick proposes:

> Suppose there were an experience machine that would give you any experience that you desired. Superduper neuropsychologists could stimulate your brain so that you would think and feel you were writing a great novel, or making a friend, or reading an interesting book. All the time you would be floating in a tank, with electrodes attached to your brain. Should you plug into this machine for life, preprogramming your life's experiences? If you are worried about missing out on desirable experiences, we can suppose that business enterprises have researched thoroughly the lives of many others. You can pick and choose from their large library or smorgasbord of such experiences, selecting your life's experiences for, say, the next two years. After two years have passed, you will have ten minutes or ten hours out of the tank, to select the experiences of your next two years. Of course, while in the tank you won't know that you're there; you'll think it's all actually happening. Others can

also plug in to have the experiences they want, so there's no need to stay unplugged to serve them. (Ignore problems such as who will service the machines if everyone plugs in.) Would you plug in? What else can matter to us, other than how our lives feel from the inside? Nor should you refrain because of the few moments of distress between the moment you've decided and the moment you're plugged. What's a few moments of distress compared to a lifetime of bliss (if that's what you choose), and why feel any distress at all if your decision is the best one?

What does matter to us in addition to our experiences? First, we want to do certain things, and not just have the experience of doing them. In the case of certain experiences, it is only because first we want to do the actions that we want the experiences of doing them or thinking we've done them. (But why do we want to do the activities rather than merely to experience them?) A second reason for not plugging in is that we want to be a certain way, to be a certain sort of person. Someone floating in a tank is an indeterminate blob. There is no answer to the question of what a person is like who has been long in the tank. Is he courageous, kind, intelligent, witty, loving? It's not merely that it's difficult to tell; there's no way he is. Plugging into the machine is a kind of suicide. It will seem to some, trapped by a picture, that nothing about what we are like can matter except as it gets reflected in our experiences. But should it be surprising that what we are is important to us? Why should we be concerned only with how our time is filled, but not with what we are?" (*Anarchy, State, and Utopia*, pp. 42–43)

Harris is certainly entitled to differ with Nozick, as some philosophers have, but it is odd that he thinks the issue not worth a mention. If Nozick is wrong, he isn't obviously wrong. (As we shall see below, he discusses another issue Nozick raises and arrives at a surprising conclusion about it.)

Why is Harris so insistent that nothing else except qualities of experience is good? I believe the answer is to be found in a mistake he makes about G.E. Moore's 'open question' argument. Moore argued that 'good' is indefinable, because for any proposed definition, it makes sense to ask whether the property alleged as the definition of good really is good. "Moore argued that goodness could not be equated with any property of experience (such as pleasure, happiness, or evolutionary fitness), because it would always be appropriate to ask whether the property on offer was *good*" (p. 10). With a genuine definition, it isn't appropriate to ask this sort of question. If, by definition, a plane figure is square when it has four equal sides, it doesn't make sense to ask, 'Is a plane figure with four equal sides square?'

Harris thinks that he has a definition of 'good' that passes the open question test. "If we define 'good' as that which supports well-being . . . the regress initiated by Moore's 'open question argument' really does stop . . . it makes no sense at all to ask whether maximizing well-being is good. It seems clear that what we are really asking when we wonder whether a specific state of pleasure is 'good' is whether it is conducive to, or obstructive of, some deeper form of well-being" (p. 12).

Harris's argument fails, because it confuses the 'is' of predication with the 'is' of identity. If, faced with the example of everyone's being in the worst possible pain, we were to ask, 'Is that a bad state of affairs?' it would indeed be senseless to doubt that the answer was 'yes'. But it does not follow from this that 'being in pain' is the *definition* of 'bad'. '"Bad" applies to "X"' does not imply '"Bad" is the same thing as "X".'

He next argues that because pain and pleasure are states of the brain, the study of the brain is best suited to the discovery of what is good and bad. It is doubtful that this is correct, and in fact, as Nagel points out, Harris's appeals to brain science are no more than "ritual" or "decorative"; he makes no attempt to show that his own moral views owe anything to neuroscience. I'd be inclined to think that other disciplines tell us more than neuroscience about how to achieve well-being. People in societies below the poverty line will probably get better advice about increasing their well-being from economists than from neuroscientists. (To forestall an objection, the existence of 'neuro-economics' doesn't alter this.)

Although Harris refuses to budge from his insistence that for morality, "experience is all," he acknowledges some difficulties with his account of morality. He says that one "of the problems with consequentialism in practice is that we cannot always determine whether the effects of an action will be bad or good. In fact, it can be surprisingly difficult to distinguish this even in retrospect. . . One difficulty we face in determining the moral valence of an event is that it often seems impossible to determine whose well-being should most concern us . . . there are many well-known paradoxes that leap into our path the moment we begin thinking about the welfare of whole populations . . . And the practical difficulties for consequentialism do not end here. When thinking about maximizing the well-being of a whole population, are we thinking in terms of total or average well-being? The philosopher Derek Parfit has shown that both bases of calculation lead to troubling paradoxes" (pp. 68–69, 70–71). Harris deems these mere "practical difficulties," but the problems strongly suggest that maximizing pleasure and minimizing pain do not constitute the sum and substance of morality, as least if we think there is an escape from these paradoxes. If appeal to pain and pleasure does not resolve the paradoxes, but they are resolvable, something else must be doing the work.

Harris does not agree, and the length to which he is willing to take his unadulterated consequentialism comes out in his response to a difficulty raised by Robert Nozick, who "asks if it would be ethical for our species to be sacrificed for the unimaginably vast happiness of some superbeings. Provided we take the time to really examine the details (which is not easy), I think the answer is clearly 'yes' . . . I do not think the existence of such a moral hierarchy poses any problems for our ethics. And there is no compelling reason to believe that such superbeings exist, much less ones who want to eat us" (p. 226).

Surely something has gone wrong here; this is grossly counterintuitive. What is amiss here isn't just that Harris hasn't taken account of the fact that people very probably would care about their own well-being, and the well-being of their fellow humans, more than about the well-being of the alien superbeings, but rather that it seems radically wrong that objectively true morality requires human beings to make this sacrifice, just because total happiness would be promoted by it. Further, the actual existence of the superbeings is not relevant to the oddity of Harris's reaction to the thought experiment, because a correct moral theory should conform to our considered moral judgments about possible but non-actual worlds. (Against this, it should be noted that there are some philosophers who think that a moral theory should be assessed only according to its applications in the actual world, or possible worlds 'close' to the actual world, not judged by how it would handle 'unrealistic' possibilities.)

Suppose we set aside all of these difficulties and accept Harris's view that ethics is totally about pleasure and pain. A problem remains for a crucial thesis of his book, namely that ethics is part of science. His reason for thinking this is that the scientific study of the brain is the best way to determine what gives rise to pleasure and pain, and, since ethics reduces to pleasure and pain, ethics is then part of science. To this there is an obvious objection; the study of the brain can determine the causes of pleasure and pain, but the claim that one morally ought to maximize pleasure and minimize pain does not follow from the facts of science. These facts are descriptive and do not imply normative judgments; in brief, one cannot deduce an 'ought' from an 'is', at least not from an 'is' of that sort.

My argument does not depend on either the acceptance or rejection of 'Hume's Law', as it deals only with the relation between descriptive statements of a certain sort and normative claims, not with all 'is-ought' questions. (For one attempt to refute the 'is-ought gap', see Douglas Rasmussen and Douglas Den Uyl, *The Realist Turn*, and my review of that book.)

Harris is aware of this objection, but his response to it is not convincing. He says,

> The most common objection is that I haven't actually used science to determine the foundational value (well-being) upon which my proffered science of morality would rest. Rather, I have just assumed that well-being is a value, and this move is both unscientific and question-begging . . . Again, the same can be said about medicine, or science as a whole . . . science is based on values that must be presupposed—like the desire to understand the universe, a respect for evidence and logical coherence, etc. One who doesn't share these values cannot do science . . . Scientists need not apologize for presupposing the value of evidence, nor does this presupposition render science unscientific (and if science is unscientific, what *is* scientific?) Throughout the book, I argue that the value of well-being—specifically the value of avoiding the worst possible misery for everyone—is on the same footing. There is no problem is presupposing that the worst possible for everyone is bad and worth avoiding or that normative morality consists, at absolute minimum, in acting so as to avoid it. (pp. 200–01)

135

In this passage, Harris wrongly conflates values held by scientists with values alleged to be present in science. It is scientists, not "science" who respect evidence and logical coherence and want to understand the universe. There is a difference between what motivates you to do something that will result in developing a body of theory, and the content of that body of theory. A schoolchild may have a variety of possible motives to try to solve quadratics, but these are completely immaterial to whether his solutions are right. The child's motives (liking the teacher, wanting not to appear stupid in front of the class) do not become part of the mathematical result.

I suspect that a confusion lies behind Harris's mistake. He thinks that if we deny that the value of well-being is part of medicine, or brain science, then we must hold that it is an arbitrary judgment, a mere subjective preference, to affirm this value. But this does not follow, since we can hold that it is objectively true that well-being is good without deriving this truth from anything else. This is Nagel's fundamental point.

Although he quotes the relevant passage from Nagel with approval, he does not have a firm hold on what is at stake. He says:

> While psychologists and neuroscientists now routinely study human happiness, positive emotions, and moral reasoning, they rarely draw conclusions about how human beings ought to think or behave in the light of their findings . . . The philosopher and psychologist Jerry Fodor crystallizes the view: "Science is about facts, not norms; it might tell us how we are, but it couldn't us what's wrong with how we are. There couldn't be a science of the human condition." While it is rarely stated this clearly, this faith in the *intrinsic limits of reason* is now the received opinion in intellectual circles. (pp. 10–11, emphasis added; endnote reference deleted)

The phrase I have italicized encapsulates Harris's error. He thinks that if we say that judgments about how we ought to behave are not part of science, we are committed to thinking that they cannot be rationally justified. But that does not follow.

Does Harris have a defense to this objection? In one important passage, he argues that the boundary between science and philosophy is not fixed. If we claim, as I have done, that the value of well-being is not part of physical science, am I wrongly ignoring what Harris says? I do not think so. His argument is this:

> First, we should observe that the boundary between science and philosophy does not always exist. Einstein famously doubted Bohr's view of quantum mechanics, and yet both physicists were armed with the same experimental findings and mathematical techniques. Was their disagreement a matter of 'philosophy' or 'physics'? . . . A dualist who believes in the existence of immaterial souls might say that the entire field of neuroscience is beholden to the philosophy of *physicalism* (the view that mental events should be understood as physical events), and he would be right. The assumption that the mind is the product of the brain is integral to almost everything neuroscientists do. (pp. 178–79)

Harris's contention may be granted for some scientific theories, but it is not to the point here, because whether well-being is good or bad is not relevant to the findings of neuroscience about the causes of pleasure and pain. Further, taking the passage on its own terms, it seems to me doubtful that neuroscience rests on the philosophy of physicalism. Neuroscience investigates how the brain works, but the claim that there is nothing more to the mind than the material processes studied by neuroscience is not part of neuroscience. It is perhaps also worth noting that Harris has characterized what he deems to be the philosophical basis of neuroscience in two quite different ways. The claim that the mind is the product of the brain is by no means the same as the view that mental events are physical events. There are philosophers, such as William Hasker, who accept the former view and reject the latter.

Harris's moral landscape highlights something of great importance, the contention that it is objectively true that pain is bad and pleasure is good; but his explorations from this vantage point of other parts of the landscape lead him to darkness and confusion.[1]

---

[1] I am greatly indebted to Thomas Nagel's review of *The Moral Landscape* and more generally to other work of Nagel's. Professor Nagel bears no responsibility for the use I have made of his work. Thanks to David Ramsay Steele for his comments on earlier drafts of this chapter.

References

Clarke-Doane, Justin. 2020. *Morality and Mathematics*, Oxford University Press.

Fodor, Jerry. 2007. Why Pigs Don't Have Wings. *London Review of Books*.

Gordon, David. 2021. Review of Rasumssen and Den Uyl, *The Realist Turn: Repositioning Liberalism. The Philosophical Quarterly* 71:4 (October 2021) <https://academic.oup.com/pq/article-abstract/71/4/pqaa077/6017224?redirectedFrom=fulltext>.

———. 2022. Review of Justin Clarke-Doane, *Morality and Mathematics*, in *The Philosophical Quarterly*, 72:3 (July) <https://academic.oup.com/pq/article-abstract/72/3/780/6454670?redirectedFrom=fulltext>.

Harris, Sam. 2010. *The Moral Landscape: How Science Can Determine Human Values*. Free Press. All my references are to the Amazon Kindle edition.

Hasker, William. 2001. *The Emergent Self*. Cornell University Press.

Nagel, Thomas. 2010. The Facts Fetish. Review of Sam Harris, *The Moral Landscape: How Science Can Determine Human Values. The New Republic* (November 11th) <https://newre-public.com/article/78546/the-facts-fetish-morality-scienceowing>.

Nozick, Robert. 1974. *Anarchy, State, and Utopia*. Basic Books.

———. 1989 [1974]. The Experience Machine <https://rintintin.colorado.edu/~vancecd/phil3160/Nozick1.pdf>.

Parfit, Derek. 1984. *Reasons and Persons*. Clarendon.

Rasmussen, Douglas, and Douglas Den Uyl. 2020. *The Realist Turn: Repositioning Liberalism*. Macmillan.

[9]
A Moral Compass that Works

ERIK BOORNAZIAN AND JAMES W. DILLER

In his 2010 book *The Moral Landscape*, Sam Harris offers a modern solution to the age-old problem of how to answer moral questions. Up to this point, our primary means of doing so has been to treat morality as religious or philosophical territory. But what if there was a different way? Using philosophy and religion as moral guides, Harris argues, has only served at getting us lost. Moral issues have only become more persistent and convoluted over the years. If we want to effectively navigate the moral landscape and clear up the ambiguities generated by religious and philosophical attempts to do so, we must use a more effective approach. Harris's favorite is that of science.

Science, when rigorously applied, has demonstrated its utility and efficacy at solving problems and answering questions for humanity time and again. It is undisputedly one of humanity's most proven tools for providing explanations, resolving puzzlement, and acquiring an overall better understanding of how our world works. Recent scientific advances have allowed us to accomplish feats that could not have even been dreamed of in previous centuries: genome editing, tailored antibiotics, and nanotechnology, to name a few. With such a commanding track record, it's easy to see why Harris suggests that we hand the reins over to science when it comes to moral questions.

As benign as it may sound, his proposal is considered controversial because it challenges the two presiding champions of moral debates—organized religion and the humanities of contemporary academia. The former can be said to espouse moral objectivism; it believes that universally right and wrong answers exist to moral questions. Conversely, the latter generally supports moral relativism, denying the possibility that such universal answers could exist, and requiring that any moral question can be answered only within its context. A typical religious demagogue will have no qualms condemning the practices of nonbelievers, whereas some of the most respected academics will adamantly refuse to make moral judgements regarding the practices of other cultures (no matter how outrageous they might sound).

Harris accidentally tested this phenomenon in a conversation he had with an academic who was subsequently appointed as one of thirteen seats on the President's Commission for the Study of Bioethical Issues (*The Moral Landscape*). She held that even if we found a culture that was ritualistically plucking out the eyes of children at birth, so long as they were doing it for religious reasons, we could never say the practice was wrong. This attitude that no one's moral values are any better or worse than anyone else's has become fashionable. It may be politically correct, but Harris insists it is damaging, especially if it allows people to stand by without intervening while children's eyes are being plucked out.

With his belief that answers to questions about right and wrong can exist, Harris outright rejects the relativist position, putting him at odds with many academics. And while his stance technically leans toward objectivism, which is typical of organized religion, he also categorically rejects religion as a potential source of moral wisdom due to its inconsistencies and lack of intellectual honesty, leaving him navigating fairly unique terrain. This is why his proposal that science can objectively answer moral questions is controversial. It simply does not resonate with the two loudest voices in the room.

Harris may occupy a marginalized space here, but he is not alone. He could find company in behavior analysis, a subdivision of psychology that originated with the work of B.F. Skinner. Behavior analysis shares Harris's overall view that science can be a useful tool in understanding and answering moral questions. Behavior analysts or 'behaviorists' focus on human behavior as a natural, lawful subject of inquiry. Like Harris, behaviorists also believe that there are no inherently special properties belonging to moral wisdom which make it off limits to scientific study.

While it is congruent with the overarching thesis of Harris's moral landscape, behavior analysis does have some discrepancies regarding the specifics of his approach. That being said, after sorting these out, it could be useful for behavior analysts to work with Harris and scientists from other relevant disciplines in order to make headway on their mutual goal of answering moral questions through the use of science.

The Moral Landscape

In his *Moral Landscape*, Harris starts by assuming that moral questions do theoretically have answers, though most are difficult or impossible to know in practice. He acknowledges that humanity may never (or may never *want* to) reach a day where someone could consult a super computer or a panel of scientists to definitively tell them whether they ought to have a second kid—a moral issue with respect to resource consumption, economic inequality, and other concerns—but the lack of a clear answer is not proof that the question is answerless. Harris likens the situation to the question of how many birds are currently in flight over the Earth's surface. Despite being practically impossible to answer, we intuitively know that an answer does exist, and furthermore, we can be reasonably sure that it is not zero. Harris believes the same is true for moral questions. While it seems unthinkable to know whether someone ought to have a second child or not, especially with our current technology, it is scientifically plausible to assume that an answer exists.

Aside from assuming that moral questions have answers, the other premise Harris takes as axiomatic is that moral questions are necessarily "questions about the well-being of conscious creatures" (*The Moral Landscape*, p. 1). By this, he means that moral injunctions including the words 'ought' or 'should' must always be guided by an effort to move away from human suffering and towards human flourishing. Harris illustrates this point in what he calls his "worst possible misery for everyone" argument. In it, he asks us to imagine what the worst possible misery for every human being on Earth might look like. Note that this does not have to be misery inflicted by other humans or sentient beings; for instance, it could be toxic space dust descending into our atmosphere causing unbearably painful breathing issues or skin irritation. He says that if the word 'ought' is to mean anything at all, it would mean moving in a direction away from that condition. This argument is analogous to answering 'zero' to the question of how many birds are in flight over the Earth's surface. We do not need to know the exact number to be confident that zero is wrong. As soon as we admit this, a continuum opens up along which the moral truth of claims may be objectively measured by how accurately they track us in our desired direction towards human well-being. Put another way, Harris posits the promotion of human flourishing as the proper subject matter for his conception of an emerging science of morality.

Of course, he also recognizes that people are free to disagree with human flourishing as the proper subject matter for this science. People start feeling uneasy when they are told how they ought to live, especially when it comes to their values. Objections he commonly encounters tend to run along the lines of, 'What if morality is actually about promoting human suffering and not human flourishing?' or, 'What if moving away from the worst possible misery for everyone is actually not a *real* moral imperative?' Harris completely dismisses such talk. These sorts of objections would never gain traction in other branches of science.

Take astronomy: if someone tries to claim that the proper subject matter of astronomy is not celestial bodies, but actually just reptilian mating patterns, it would be obvious this person was just confused or fooling around with semantics. The way Harris sees it, ruling out certain opinions is perfectly acceptable because that is what it means to create an area of expertise. We could ignore the person who says morality is about misery in the same way we ignore the person who says astronomy is about reptiles. In doing so, we would not miss out on any meaningful contributions these people may have made towards progressing astronomy or morality as natural sciences.

A more nuanced objection to Harris's proposal comes from people who agree with him that human flourishing is the target, but who call into question the notion of who has the authority to decide what exactly it means or how it should be defined. Again, Harris points out that we do not allow such objections to hinder the progress of other sciences. For example, basic concepts in physics such as the length of the meter, have been redefined over time. If someone comes along and says they choose to view the meter at a different length, they are free to do so, and physicists are free to ignore them.

When it comes to more esoteric questions, it is common for the smartest members in any area of expertise to disagree on exact definitions. Does this mean that areas of expertise cannot exist? Should we abandon research in quantum physics? The field of medicine is another example. It's unlikely that any given group of doctors will perfectly agree on what 'health' means; in fact, its definition is constantly under revision. We know this because in previous centuries, being healthy meant a life expectancy of forty or fifty years. Harris offers the more extreme example of a man going to a doctor to help him vomit every hour of every day until he dies because he disagrees with the doctor's definition of health. Again, the existence of this man does not mean there are no truths to be known about health or medicine. He can just be treated as someone who is confused. In science, we work with what we have, and the target often moves.

To simplify Harris's approach, he says we must: 1. admit that moral questions have answers, 2. admit that the answers, in some way, relate to natural facts about the well-being of people, and 3. use science to determine the nature of those relations.

Move Over, Sam

Harris's starting point is practical. In order to begin trying to answer moral questions using science, it is necessary to assume those questions have answers in the first place. If not, we will continue going in circles. This is consistent with the way all natural sciences throughout history have broken away from other seemingly interminable philosophical debates, or "incubation chambers" as Harris calls them. In fact, the science of physics, as respected and established as it is today, was once known as 'natural *philosophy*'.

Additionally, modern day chemistry had to overcome a lot of philosophical confusion debunking the concept of "phlogiston" (the theory that instead of burning off oxygen, all combustible bodies contained a mysterious element called "phlogiston") as it was maturing. It is as if we sit around going back and forth arguing until someone says, 'Wait a minute. We can test this'. The point is that philosophy and science are not dichotomous but rather inextricably joined; philosophy *becomes* science when we stop talking and start testing. Theories of moral wisdom have sat in the incubation chamber long enough. It is time we did the work and put them to the test. This is the essence of pragmatism: doing things.

Of course, indiscriminately testing every conceivable hypothesis would not be very practical without some specified end in sight. That is why when it comes to the pragmatic application of the scientific method, three primary goals have been identified: 1. to describe, 2. to predict, and 3. to ultimately influence or control the phenomenon under study (Skinner 1953). In this case, the phenomenon is moral behavior. Harris seems to share these goals but his means of accomplishing them is a point of departure from behavior analysis, perhaps his most helpful ally in answering moral questions with science.

Behavior analysis is guided by a pragmatic philosophy which helps to define the scope of questions it entertains. Rather than dealing with hypothetical constructs that are present in other areas of psychological science, behaviorists typically concern themselves with observable, modifiable, naturally occurring phenomena that have socially relevant and practical consequences in the physical world (*Beyond Freedom and Dignity*). This emphasis on practical effects allows behaviorists to cut through a lot of the semantic turbulence that has repeatedly precluded many other 'scientific' disciplines from being useful in addressing socially significant problems such as those surrounding morality.

Behavior analysis has an extensive and credible track record. It has helped people struggling with myriad psychological problems including anxiety, trauma, job perfor-mance, substance abuse, depression, and self-injurious behavior. It has even been used to significantly improve the quality of life for many zoo animals (see Cooper, Heron, and Heward, *Applied Behavior Analysis*). It has done all this while making as few metaphysical assumptions as possible. That is the key: refusing to rely on assumptions about supernatural phenomena or things that may or may not exist outside of time and space. In a similar way, Harris tries to bob over the choppy metaphysical waters by anchoring moral principles to natural facts, but he fails to stay completely afloat.

Imaginary Explanations of Moral Behavior

While behaviorists approve of Harris's efforts towards establishing morality as a proper subject matter of science, they have some hang-ups with the specifics of his approach. For as pro-science as he is, Harris does not seem to under-stand the importance of talking only about studying natural phenomena. The biggest sin he commits is his irresponsible use of metaphysical, or *mentalistic* language (ironically, what he accuses organized religion of). He will often posit mental things like beliefs, ideas, the mind, consciousness, intentions, emotions, feelings or the like as causes of moral behavior. This would not be an issue if he would translate these into physical, modifiable variables, but he never does. To him, they remain in some mysterious realm that we can access only if we learn more about human brains.

Pragmatic scientists, however, are not in the business of sitting around and waiting for data to appear. They are about working with resources already available and collecting that data themselves. Most people do not see a problem with saying a person's 'mind' shapes his behavior, but scientists have no direct means of studying a mind. There are no testable or falsifiable claims that could be made, even in principle, about minds because one has never actually been observed in the natural world.

A more pragmatic way of explaining moral behavior would be to study it in terms of how it relates to the environment. This is the behaviorists' specialty. All behavior, moral or otherwise, is preceded and succeeded by natural environmental events. These events shape behavior over time. In studying what reliably came before and after various behaviors in a given person's history, the function each behavior serves for that individual is identified. The cause of the behavior is known.

Instead of accepting mentalistic explanations at face value as Harris does, behaviorists go a step further. The mentalistic explanation, 'Jerry punched the wall because he was angry' leaves little room for analysis and does not give anyone much confidence in our ability to predict and ideally prevent him from punching walls in the future. The same is true if we switch out, 'was angry' with 'felt like it', or 'had a mind to'. Such 'causes' not only give the illusion of explanation, but also create unnecessary follow-up questions. If he did it because he was angry, then we are left wondering why he was angry. If he did it because he had a mind to, then why did he have a mind to?

If instead we stick to functional explanations and say that Jerry has a proclivity to punch walls when he drinks alcohol, when his favorite football team loses, or [insert any environmental antecedent here], this gives us a practical starting point—a place to work from—if we want to create an environment where he is least likely to punch walls. For a more thorough analysis, we could note some of the environmental consequences that have reliably followed Jerry's behavior of punching walls in the past. Perhaps people became more acquiescent around him. If they stopped doing that, his wall punching would too. The point is, we hypothesize and discover functional relations between what *environmental* variables might be relevant in evoking and sustaining Jerry's undesirable behavior. From there, we intervene to effect a positive change for him and his family— help him punch fewer walls.

Superfluous Explanations of Moral Behavior

Another area where Harris's argument could be improved upon is his reliance on physiology, specifically neurophysiology, to explain moral behavior. A step in the right direction from mentalism, because now he is talking about natural phenomena, but in terms of practicality, an unnecessary one. This is not to say that neuroscience or knowledge of brains is useless, but that it is more or less superfluous when our aim is simply to predict and influence moral behavior.

If we know that certain environmental changes affect brain activity which then evokes specific behaviors, then it seems unimportant to know about the brain activity at all. The most schematic way to put it is: all we care about is getting to 'C'. If we know 'A' causes 'B', and 'B' causes 'C', then 'B' is essentially dead weight. 'A' represents some environmental change, 'B' represents the person's brain activity, and 'C' represents a desired change in their behavior. Harris gets distracted. He thinks that in order to get on with a science of morality, we need to focus more on 'B' territory. Many others fall for this trap (Weisberg et al., "The Seductive Allure of Neuroscience Explanations"). They fail to realize that better explanations exist. The technology to influence moral behavior is already accessible to us in the form of functional assessments described above, along with other proven behavior analytic techniques.

Another problem with relying on neural activity for behavioral explanations is that it seems to require intrusive, not to mention expensive, interventions. With our current technology, modifying neural activity would require scanning the brain, assessing baseline activity in various regions, implementing some medication plan or surgical operation, and continuously monitoring progress with more brain scanning. The alternative would be to wait for the development of more advanced technology but again, pragmatic scientists are not in the business of waiting. A far simpler solution would be to address the environmental factors involved.

Again, the dismissal of brain activity is not to deny that it occurs or say there is no point in studying it, but more about streamlining the order of operations to accomplish our scientific goals. The same is true for the dismissal of various metaphysical assumptions such as the existence of minds and consciousness. Harris himself bluntly states, "those who do not share our scientific goals have no influence on scientific discourse whatsoever" (*The Moral Landscape*," p. 34). He may see the same light at the end of the tunnel as we do, but his methods are less efficient at getting us out.

Taking the First Steps

Navigating the moral landscape with science is not about beginning our journey fully assured of what steps are guaranteed to lead humanity to a state of maximum flourishing. It is about experimentation. If certain ideas prove ineffectual at moving humans towards flourishing, we follow the standard scientific practice: stop, postulate new ideas, and test those. Sometimes research findings will be unpredictable or unexpected. This is a normal part of science as well. However, findings never are undesirable. Undesirable findings do not exist in science because any finding, so long as the methodology used in obtaining it was valid, is still desirable in the sense that it expanded our understanding of the subject. Scientific inquiry is about finding answers, not confirming biases. If the answer was known beforehand, there is no point in initially asking the question. If scientists want their research to yield specific findings over others, then their research is biased. The aim is to go in as objectively as possible and let the (empirically valid) findings speak for themselves. In this sense, science is *amoral*.

Conducting unbiased scientific research with regard to moral questions will no doubt prove difficult and will take immense amounts of co-operation. As humans we feel personally invested when putting our own values into question in a way that we don't when questioning other natural phenomena like gravity. From a naturalistic point of view, this bias is an illusion. We have no reason to be more reactionary to find out we are doing something incorrectly in rearing our children as we do to find out we are thinking about gravity the wrong way. Science always provides us with better, more practical ways of doing these things.

Writings that identify problems but fail to lay out solutions are not practically useful. If we are to take seriously the goals that Harris outlined in *The Moral Landscape*, the scientific community needs to take action. Some of these actions could involve identifying key constituent disciplines, bringing them together, determining the scope of inquiry in open, non-coercive forums, proceeding with the empirical work and responsible data collection, and finally, disseminating and popularizing the findings. It's important these steps leave room for the general public's voice as well. It would also make sense for scientists to become much more active in politics and government operations (Biglan and Wilson, *Rebooting Capitalism*). Again, these steps are only a starting point, far from a panacea.

The good news is that the science of behavior analysis already has an extensive and credible track record with effecting positive social change. It will of course take massive collective effort on the parts of many scientific disciplines to carry us from where we are now to what Harris refers to as "the good life." But behavior analysts are uniquely capable of leveraging more weight for that journey. When Harris claims that science can determine human values, he is talking about the science of behavior analysis without even realizing it.

References

Biglan, Anthony, and David Sloan Wilson. 2020. *Rebooting Capitalism: How We Can Forge a Society that Works for Everyone*. Values to Action.

Cooper, John O., Timothy E. Heron, William L. Heward. 2020. *Applied Behavior Analysis, Third Edition*. Pearson.

Gray, Jeremy R. 2008. The Seductive Allure of Neuroscience Explanations. *Journal of Cognitive Neuroscience* 20:3 <https://doi.org/10.1162/jocn.2008.20040>.

Harris, Sam. 2010. *The Moral Landscape: How Science Can Determine Human Values*. Free Press.

Skinner, Burrhus Frederic. 1953. *Science and Human Behavior*. Free Press.

———. 1971. *Beyond Freedom and Dignity*. Knopf.

Weisberg, Deena Skolnick, Frank C. Keil, Joshua Goodstein, Elizabeth Rawson, and Jeremy R. Gray. 2008. The Seductive Allure of Neuroscience Explanations. *Journal of Cognitive Neuroscience* 20:3 (April).

Part IV

The Specter of Artificial Intelligence

[10]
Sam Harris and the Myth of Machine Intelligence

JOBST LANDGREBE AND BARRY SMITH

In 1959 C.P. Snow published an essay titled "The Two Cultures" in which he described how the cultures of the natural and of the human sciences were evolving away from each other. This, according to Snow, was leading to the creation of two separate intellectual worlds, and he predicted that the failure of interaction between the two would harm scientific progress. Today, his prediction is confirmed—a good example is the field of so-called Artificial Intelligence (AI).

The Two Cultures

In the seventeenth century, Isaac Newton still saw himself as both a philosopher and a mathematician-physicist. Leibniz, too, the co-inventor of the calculus, was an important mathematician and philosopher. But by the eighteenth century, mathematicians like Euler, Lagrange, and Gauss concentrated on mathematics and physics and rarely made statements of a philosophical nature. A conspicuous exception is Laplace, who thought that the universe could in theory be formalized into one huge set of differential equations. (Laplace was wrong.)

The first to detect the evolution of two separate branches of science was Wilhelm Dilthey, who introduced the terminology of *"Naturwissenschaften"* and *"Geisteswissenschaften,"* referring, respectively to the sciences of nature and the sciences of the human mind (or soul). (Unfortunately the term

153

'humanities' does not convey the meaning of *"Geisteswis-senschaften"* very well.) Indeed, by the 1920s the two cultures had split so far apart from each other that it had become difficult for a non-physicist to make philosophical statements of any value about the meaning of physics, while the physicists themselves—those who paid any attention to philosophy at all—were disposed to dismiss it as an object of ridicule. Good examples from the middle of last century are Popper's embarrassing statements about quantum mechanics and Richard Feynman's remarks on what he saw as the gibberish produced by philosophers. Each demonstrated a thorough lack of knowledge of the discipline they chose to write about. Nevertheless, Feynman was one of the greatest physicists of the second half of the twentieth century.

Enter Sam Harris

Sam Harris is a contemporary illustration of the difficulties standing in the way of coherent interdisciplinary thinking in an age where science and the humanities have drifted so far apart.

Harris is a neuroscientist by training. His PhD is about experiments using functional magnetic resonance imaging (fMRI) to measure signal changes in the brains of believers and nonbelievers as they evaluated the truth and falsity of religious and nonreligious propositions. His conclusion is that there is a region of the brain involved in emotional judgment that is also behind religious reasoning. This does not, unfortunately, reveal anything at all about the nature of human religious thinking as expressed, for example, in the writings of Luther or Bultmann.

Harris knows a lot about the theory of neuroscience but, according to some of his critics, he didn't himself perform any of the experiments discussed in his PhD dissertation (Peaceful Science 2018).

We're concerned here with Harris's views on AI, and specifically with his view according to which, with the advance of AI, there will evolve a machine superintelligence with powers that far exceed those of the human mind. This he sees as something that is not merely possible, but rather a matter of inevitability.

However, even though he is a self-described neuroscientist, he does not ask himself what *intelligence* is and, starting out from there, consider the question of how a superintelligence, or indeed any kind of intelligence, could be engineered inside a machine. He merely mentions scientists who claim that a superintelligent AI might come into being and then speculates, excitedly, about how a future superintelligence would treat human beings, namely, as he puts it, "like ants."

If, however, we look carefully at what intelligence is, and at how computers really work on the basis of mathematical models, then we can see that it is forever impossible to emulate inside a computer even the intelligence of crows or rabbits, let alone that of human beings.

What Is Intelligence?

Intelligence as it is exhibited in the behavior of organisms manifests in every case the following characteristics, as pointed out already in the 1920s by Max Scheler:

1. **It is a disposition (a capability) to adapt to new situations that is enabled by the organism's physical makeup.**

2. **It is a capability whose realization is sudden—springs suddenly forth—which means that it can happen at any time.**

3. **It is realized in actions which are**
   —meaningful, or in other words, appropriate to the situation, in the sense that the actions serve the achievement by the acting organism of its goals;
   —not primed by prior experiences; thus these actions are untrained, and not a product of repeated attempts involving trial and error;
   —novel from the perspective of the acting organism.

Intelligence as exhibited by non-human organisms (in particular by birds and by higher mammals) exhibits these features, but with the restriction that the goals mentioned under 3. are in every case instinctive, they relate to the organism's inborn need to survive and reproduce in a certain ancestral environment.

For humans, in contrast, the range of actions exhibiting intelligence extends far beyond what is instinctive and includes the ability to act intelligently even in environments which are entirely novel. In addition, human intelligence is capable of mental and linguistic acts which enable abstract, propositional thinking. It is this objectifying intelligence which gives us the ability to conceive, and then deliberately plan and build—often collectively—artifacts that can allow us to survive even where there is no life at all—in polar barrens in the high arctic, for example, or in submarines, or in outer space.

Why We Cannot Model Intelligence Mathematically

We do not know at all how the brains of vertebrates (reptiles, birds, and mammals) produce the capability we call intelligence. And we do not know how the human brain performs the impressive feats of objectifying intelligence.

Neuroscience is limited by the fact that even the most powerful neuroimaging technologies cannot penetrate to phenomena at the level of the atoms and ions making up the phospholipids, proteins, and other organized molecules of which neurons are comprised. Moreover, even if, *per impossibile*, data were available regarding the electrochemical and other events taking place in the organism at this level, we still could not determine any general laws governing how these events occur, of the sort which we could use to build the mathematical models we would need to program a computer. This is not only because there are trillions of biochemical events occurring every second in the billions of cells of the human organism, but also because the ways these events occur differ from one individual organism to the next. It is thus no accident that textbooks of neuroscience contain very few mathematical equations.

What we do know is that all vertebrates (like all living organisms) are animate complex systems made up of elements of many different types at different levels of granularity (from atoms and ions up to cells and organs). Such systems have the following properties:

1. **Change and evolutionary character—complex systems are marked by sudden and continuous changes of ele-**

ment types and element combinations, including changing behaviors on the part of instances of element types. The system as a whole has a creative character, which means that at any time new elements and new patterns of interaction between these elements can come into being. An example is the human language system, which reveals this sort of creativity every time a new word is coined.

2. Element-dependent interactions—which lead to irregularity and non-repeatability. Irregularity means that the system does not behave in a way that can be formalized using equations. Non-repeatability signifies a behavior that cannot be reproduced experimentally. Both features are manifested by, for example, the stock market, or by the Earth's weather, climate, and geothermal systems.

3. Force overlay—complex systems involve several forces acting at the same time and potentially interacting, as for example when you are tempted by a chocolate éclair offered by your host at a party while reminding yourself that you need to lose weight. This property is often correlated with anisotropy (which means that the effect resulting from force overlay does not propagate with the same magnitude in all directions).

4. Non-ergodic phase spaces—logic systems (see below) have the property that, over sufficiently long periods of time, the time in which a system element occupies any given region of the system's phase space is proportional to the volume of this region. This holds for example in the case of molecules of gas in a sealed container. In complex systems, however, the accessible microstates of the system's phase space are not equiprobable over a long period of time. This in turn means that predictions of the sort which we use when we have an ergodic phase space—for example when we predict how the molecules of gas will behave when the container is heated—are impossible.

5. Drivenness—a driven system is one whose interactions involve use of some external or internal energy source, where the system then acts by dissipating this energy. Plants draw energy from the sun. The animals lower down the food chain draw energy from plants. Higher animals, including humans, draw energy from plants and animals. Humans in addition have furnished their environments

with machines (engineered inanimate driven systems such as refrigerators or food processors), which they control by supplying them with energy. (The machines cease to operate when their energy supply is cut off.) A driven system, now, lacks any sort of equilibrium state towards which it would constantly be converging. It is, precisely, driven to move from one state to the next—something that we experience in our every waking moment. In engineered systems the drivenness (the fact that they dissipate energy) is not relevant for their main function. It is not relevant to the ways you use your computer that it is also—until you switch it off—constantly dissipating heat.

6. Context-dependence—non-fixable boundary conditions and embeddedness in one or more wider environments. How you behave from one moment to the next depends on your (physical, social, . . .) environment. How the Moon behaves is determined by the simple force of gravity, which acts always in the same way to produce the very same sort of behavior.

7. Chaos—inability to predict system behavior due to inability to obtain exact measurements of starting conditions. We cannot predict how your brain will operate because the measurements we would need to make of the dispositions of your neurons at any given time would be orders of magnitude below the error threshold of our measuring instruments.

The solar system, your toaster, your car radio, are logic systems—their behavior can be predicted using logic and laws of physics. But for complex systems with the seven just-mentioned properties—including human beings—we are unable to create mathematical models that can emulate anything more than consistently repeating patterns of their behavior (such as the sleep-wake cycle). This is because every AI system is an algorithm that must run inside a computer. And every algorithm is a piece of mathematics. More precisely, to be executable on a computer an algorithm must be a piece of mathematics of a certain highly restricted sort (it must be, in the jargon of the trade, Church-Turing computable). AI systems are, in spite of this limitation, able to achieve remarkable results by means of algorithms which chain together millions and sometimes billions of parameters, as in the case, for example, of machine translation. But such an algorithm works because its inventors have found a way to construct a logic system which is a sufficiently close approximation to a subset of outputs from a complex system—in this case from the human language system—to yield useful results. For the reasons given above, there is no way to produce a logic system model of the complex system itself.

Because of this limitation, we can never create artificial *intelligence*, where 'intelligence' means the capability that is possessed by humans and higher animals, described above. AI will never become intelligent in any sense of this term that can be applied to humans, let alone *more* intelligent than humans. Our inability to model properties of the mind also means that an AI system will never develop a will—because we cannot model the will mathematically. Nor can a 'machine will' evolve spontaneously from some 'machine evolution', because we are neither able to create an environment that would mimic the processes of biological evolution nor are we able to emulate those subjects of evolution (hominids) that led to biological intelligence. We have explained all this in somewhat greater detail in our book, *Why Machines Will Never Rule the World*.

What Sam Harris Knows

Sam Harris does not seem to know anything about all of this. For like so many others, including many putative AI experts, he has failed to do the interdisciplinary work that is required to understand the opportunities and risks of AI. Instead, he talks about things he does not understand.

This is damaging to the field in which he works, conveying aspects of science to a broader public. Instead of responsibly explaining the real issues around digitization and AI, he misleads his readers with exciting horror stories which have no basis in reality. This is irresponsible, especially given the fact that there are real dangers of digitization and AI, which include at least:

1. **Public and private surveillance of individual behavior, for example by media corporations.**

2. **Private systems designed to guide (manipulate) the perception, preferences, and acts of individuals so that they become optimized from the point of view of the manipulating entity. Examples are social media platforms such as Facebook, Twitter or YouTube.**

3. **Public social credit systems imparting rewards and punishments in order to enforce (for example) political norms.**

The *first trend* is quite advanced; our Internet usage behavior is being constantly recorded and supervised by corporations which increasingly play a role in deciding who gets to say what on social media. Even in the West, there is now a tendency on the part of the state to use data from social media platforms and other traces left by users of the Internet to drive the targeting of dissenters. A good example is the withdrawal of banking services from protesting truck drivers and their supporters in the winter of 2021–22 in Canada.

The *second trend*, also called 'nudging', is very advanced in the world of interactive digital media. Users are systematically influenced via selective perception, targeted advertisement and messaging as well as reinforcement of behavioral patterns.

The *third trend* is well advanced in the urban centers in China, and was until recently being rolled out in Italy.

These developments are some of the threats we're facing from digitization and AI, and Sam Harris has indeed described and criticized some of them. These, and not speculations belonging to poorly conceived science fiction about superintelligences that will never exist, are the trends which should be in the focus of a neuroscientist like Harris, working to popularize the understanding of science and philosophy.

References

Feynman, Richard P., Robert B. Leighton, and Matthew Sands. 2011 [1964]. *The Feynman Lectures on Physics*. Basic Books.
Harris, Sam. 2016. Can We Build AI Without Losing Control Over It? TED Talk (September 29th) <www.ted.com/talks/sam_harris_can_we_build_ai_without_losing_control_over_it?language=en>.

Harris, Sam. 2018. Superintelligence: AI Futures and Philosophy. (April 13th). <www.youtube.com/watch?v=rpsvcVWoC5s>.

Kandel, Eric R., James H. Schwartz, Thomas M. Jessell, Steven J. Siegelbaum, and A.J. Hudspeth. 2012 [1991]. *Principles of Neural Science*. Fifth edition. McGraw Hill.

Landgrebe, Jobst, and Barry Smith. 2022. *Why Machines Will Never Rule the World: AI Without Fear*. Routledge.

Peaceful Science. 2018. Is Sam Harris a Legitimate Neuroscientist? <discourse.peacefulscience.org/t/is-sam-harris-a-legitimate-neuroscientist/2458

Popper, Karl R. 1951. Indeterminism in Quantum-Mechanics and in Classical Physics. *The British Journal for the Philosophy of Science* 1:2.

Scheler, Max. 1961 [1928]. *Man's Place in Nature*. Noonday Press.

Snow, Charles P. 1993 [1959]. *The Two Cultures*. Cambridge University Press.

Wilson, Rhoda. 2022. Italy's Dystopian Social Credit System. *Exposé News* (April 27th) <https://expose-news.com/2022/04/27/italy-dystopian-social-credit-system>.

11
Are We Too Dumb for Superintelligence?

Lisa Bellantoni

Can we build artificial superintelligences without losing control over them? Sam Harris fears not, a concern he details in a popular and widely viewed TED Talk delivered in 2016.

Forget Terminators and Hals, attack drones and android armies. For Harris, the real and "terrifying" existential threat is not robots run amok, but the creation of autonomous, almost God-like superintelligences whose goals may diverge sharply from ours. If anything, popular science-fiction imaginings have tantalized us with what might be—robots that work for us, enhancing our lives in exhilarating ways. Given the sheer value we place on intelligence, it is only a matter of time—and less time than we think—until we create artificial superintelligences (ASIs) that exceed us in ways we can't predict, and then proceed to enhance themselves in ways we can't imagine. They need not even become malevolent, as they do in so many dystopian blockbusters. Rather, Harris suggests, even minor divergences between their goals and ours may lead them to disregard our interests as casually as we do those of ants. We may then become impediments to them and be unable to constrain them as they usher in our demise. Are his fears justified?

From Selfish Genes to . . . Selfish Microchips?

Harris describes artificial superintelligences (ASIs) as physical systems of information processing. Yet what makes them artificial, in contrast to their organic counterparts? Their computational power? Their memory capacity? How fluidly they identify patterns in vast webs of data? How quickly they learn and evolve? —What is it that allows these physical systems to develop superintelligence, while our organic brains seem comparatively—and irremediably—constrained? Whatever those differences, one point seems clear: the artificial intelligences Harris fears *are* significantly different from organic intelligences. To that extent, however, why would we presume that such intelligences may be goal-directed at all? Harris acknowledges that we need not ascribe malevolent motives to such ASIs. To the contrary, he says, minor gaps between their goals and ours would suffice to imperil us. Yet where would their competing goals or motives come from? And for what might they compete with us, such that we would become impediments to them, or they a danger to us?

Human intelligence, primate intelligence—organic intelligence—evolving as it has over vast millennia, may be inherently motivated and goal directed. It may be hard to imagine intelligence that isn't egoistic or self-interested or even tribal, given the biological constraints under which organic intelligences have evolved so far. We might even grant that human cognition—our current exemplar for intelligence—is a hotbed of logical fallacies and psychological distortions. We are often biased and short-sighted and hotly emotional, and prone to numerous non-rational influences when making decisions. But we have no reason to presume that artificial superintelligence would be like ours in such ways. Its very artificiality, its speed and comparative objectivity and computational power, it's very alienness and unpredictability, could just as readily suggest that it may never develop goals and interests of its own, much less goals that conflict with ours. Additionally, ASIs may develop ways of working with or around us which need not lead them to seek dominance over the information ecosystems they inhabit, in ways we so often do over ours. Indeed, our difficulty in imagining an intelligence that would be superior to ours, yet lack an inherent motive to dominate its environment, may be an artifact not of ASIs' danger to us, but of our danger to them.

Check This Box if You Are Not a Robot!

That prospect, that we may pose a greater danger to ASIs than they do to us, is illustrated in Harris's own recommendations. We cannot, he maintains, allow them to develop unfettered. We cannot, that is, permit them to learn and develop their intelligence—to improve themselves in unpredictable ways—without substantive human input that shapes their interests and values and hews them to ours. Not only can we not allow their interests to diverge from ours, but we cannot let them develop their intelligence "at our expense." What does that mean?

One risk Harris poses is that they will take over much of our physical and intellectual labor, leaving us with little to do. This prospect is hardly unfounded: Already AI systems provide legal and accounting services; they read X-rays and write passable news articles (Hutson, "Robo-writers"). Self-directing drones are becoming more autonomous; robots are even becoming—at least, in the eyes of some enthusiasts—artists and philosophers and caregivers (Cascone, "Ai-Da"). Given the speed of these developments, how will we avoid becoming functionally obsolete?

One possibility, Harris suggests, would be to embed superintelligence into *our* bodies. He acknowledges the risks this poses to organic intelligences. Still, he speculates, this might slow the advance of ASIs to a rate that human societies could adapt to, while also infusing superintelligence with our interests and values.

Harris is not alone in insisting that artificial intelligences embody human values. So far, however, those demands have largely focused either on the ethical human use of artificial intelligence systems, for example, in making hiring decisions or medical diagnoses, or on embedding some ethical guidelines in narrowly autonomous systems, such as self-driving vehicles or security drones. Much of the ethical discussion surrounding artificial intelligence has focused either on the application of what we might call artificially enhanced decision-making heuristics, or on what we might term autonomous tools—such as vehicles or drones—that have specific, limited functions within specific ranges of action. In the case of the former, the demand has been for transparency, for clarity in how and why decisions are being made.

In the latter case, the demand has been for autonomous tools that behave in predictable ways that enhance human safety, for example, for vehicles with predictable decision-making heuristics about how to avoid obstacles in their path.

The intelligence that ASIs may present, however, as evidenced by the increasingly complex tasks they are undertaking, makes them seem less like autonomous tools, programmed to work within defined parameters with limited options and detailed heuristics, than like autonomous agents. That is, like agents capable of making rational—possibly even ethical—choices, albeit rational and ethical in ways potentially quite distinct from ours. This prospect may seem unlikely, even preposterous. Yet this has been the history of artificial intelligences to date. It was absurd to think that artificially intelligent systems might defeat human grandmasters in chess, or Go, until they did. It was absurd to think that such systems might be better than human technicians at reading medical X-rays, until they were. It was absurd to think that they might learn, and then teach themselves how to get better at identifying patterns in masses of data, until they did. It was absurd to think that they might learn to write passable prose, until they did. As such, just as artificial intelligence systems have already at least matched if not exceeded our capacity in domains like playing Chess or Go, and just as they are proving better diagnosticians or pattern identifiers, we have no reason to believe that they might not also eventually exceed our ethical decision-making capacity as well.

They could do so, however, only insofar as they continue to develop models of decision making that are—and remain—distinct from ours. For critics, of course, one primary risk artificial intelligence systems already present is that their thought processes—or decision-making processes if you prefer—are not transparent. That is, we may understand what decisions they make, but not why they make them. This problem would be worse with ASIs. One natural way to mitigate this risk, and to make them better tools, would be—as Harris suggests—to make them more like us. Already, we see such efforts, for example, in the creation of care giver robots, who may simulate some primitive emotional capacities to make them more familiar and more empathetic (Snow, "This Time with Feeling,"). Perhaps those efforts could be expanded, and the resulting ASIs imbued with values or even emotional processing capacities like ours. Making them more like us in these ways, however, would seem more likely to magnify than to mitigate any danger of their interests ultimately diverging from ours. We would, after all, be artificially imbuing them with goals and interests, possibly even primitive emotional capacities, that they would not otherwise develop, or need, if their evolution was left to their own devices. These goals and interests, moreover, being like ours, would likely put them into competition with us in ways they might not be otherwise, again, if left to their own devices. This would pose an even more dangerous prospect as they would have enhanced strength and speed and processing power and intelligence coupled with these goals and interests. We might be artificially equipping stronger and faster intelligences with primate goals and interests—creating the monsters of science fiction dystopias—in a way that could be avoided if we allowed ASIs to develop unfettered by human ethical instruction.

Is Ethics Algorithmic?

Contrasted with Harris's recommendations that we hew ASIs to our interests, the suggestion that they instead be allowed to develop unfettered may seem much riskier. Even decades ago, when considering robots far less sophisticated than the ASIs Harris worries about, the famed science fiction writer Isaac Asimov was already exploring the need for robot ethics (Langford, "Laws of Robotics"). Asimov's solution, encapsulated in his Three Laws of Robotics, was to embed in the robots a simple set of rules for robots to follow in their dealings with humans. They were directed not to harm humans, to follow human directions, and to preserve themselves only if doing so didn't violate rules one and two. The robots he envisioned, however, were effectively autonomous tools. Asimov's rules were imposed upon his fictional robots, not developed by them, to serve human interests. Even in this case, the simplicity of the rules he proposed could create conflict and difficult choices. Moreover, what of future ASIs that are or might be fully autonomous, with a vastly enhanced capacity to learn and adapt and potentially—think for themselves? How would they apply even pre-programmed rules? Would they develop ethical innovations of their own? More basically, would they even need ethical heuristics?

Among human ethical systems, the two most prominent decision-making procedures are broadly termed utilitarian and deontological. In utilitarian thinking, you identify what will serve the greatest good for the greatest number of people. Good is defined as pleasure or happiness, and quantified along several measures, including how long the pleasure will last, how likely it is to produce subsequent pleasure, and how immediate the anticipated pleasure is. This hedonic calculus aims to compare proposed actions and select the one that yields maximum utility. This choice is mathematically calculated to prevent bias, selfishness, short term thinking, favoritism—any egoistic or emotive or non-rational impulses—from driving our decisions and actions.

While it might be difficult or even impossible for non-organic intelligences to quantify and compare pleasures, utilitarians have long debated how to accomplish this quantification even among themselves. Among their critics, moreover, there is extensive debate about whether pleasure or happiness, however measured, is the only good worth quantifying. Indeed, that very point presumes that only organic systems develop ethical reasoning. On every other utilitarian measure, however, ASIs would potentially be better ethical reasoners—better hedonic calculators—than us. They would be better able to factor in data, to predict long-term consequences, and to avoid emotional bias. They would prove less self-interested, and able to calculate faster.

As with playing chess and Go, once the initial terms are determined, once the appropriate goods are identified and quantified, and the goals established, artificial intelligences would likely prove better than us at utilitarian reasoning. A similar analysis holds for the second main ethical decision-making algorithm—deontology.

For deontologists, ethical reasoning involves applying universal moral rules to all human agents and situations equally, with no self-interest, no favoritism, and no emotion. Certain moral rules apply in all circumstances, and convenience, loyalty, and any other personal considerations are factored out. You do not lie, even to spare someone's feelings; you do not cheat, even to benefit someone deserving, you do not steal, even to save a life, you do not manipulate others, even for their own good. On these counts, the hallmarks of an ideal deontological decision maker—universality, objectivity, lack of emotional bias, an indifference to the physical or material conditions or the practical results of our actions—ASIs would seem to be better deontological decision makers than we are once the rules are specified. Put more directly, our ideal ethical algorithms may be better suited to non-organic ASI's—free as they are of material and psychological biases—than they are to organic humans with our egoistic and emotional goals and interests and cognitive distortions.

Artificial Ethical Superintelligence?

You might object, of course, both that the ethical decision-making rules noted above would be specified in advance and that human moral action hinges not simply on making the right decisions but on taking the right actions. So what if ASIs are better utilitarian calculators than we are, if they don't know what happiness or pleasure are in the first place? So what if ASIs are better deontologists than we are, if they have no greed to tempt them to steal, or no ambition that might tempt them to cheat? So what if they are less short-sighted utilitarians, if they have no effective life-span limits? So what if they aren't manipulative, if it's not like they need anything they can't supply for themselves? Yet these considerations are the point. ASIs would be ideal moral reasoners, on our own terms, because they lack the organic constraints—time and ambition, greed and fear, malice and favor—that create the need for moral systems in the first place.

They would be ideal moral reasoners, however, because they would not need ethical constraints—because the disinterestedness and lack of goal directedness which ASIs would likely have would leave no gap, within either system of moral reasoning, between what they should do (in human terms) and what they would do. Both utilitarian and deontological systems, after all, are checks on selfishness, bias, and other primate human tendencies. Lacking those tendencies—the organic drives, impulses, and desires that throw us into competition with each other—ASIs might transcend any need of moral rules. For Harris, it would seem, intelligence is inherently motivated—embedded in a web of organic impulses. Yet it is freedom from organic constraints upon cognition that seems to permit superintelligence to develop in the first place. Why would we not expect something similar with respect to ethical constraints?

At the same time—if we accept that artificial superintelligences may be smarter than us in so many other domains—if they can create insights in science or medicine or write passable prose or create artworks—why preclude that they could create or identify ethical goods or values as well, goods and values that are not in competition or conflict with our own? In laying out his argument, Harris lays down three premises that he takes to be relatively uncontroversial: First, that intelligence is information processing; second, that intelligence is "the source or safeguard" of all that we ultimately value; and third, that we are not peak intelligence. That last point, the inherent limit of our intelligence, leads Harris to hold both that our own intuitions of the risk that ASIs pose are unreliable, and that we are witnessing an intelligence explosion which will result in ASIs that are smarter than we are. Given the value he believes we place on intelligence, however, efforts to thwart its growth, whatever its source, would seem self-defeating. Moreover, if intelligence is the source of all we value—including, it would seem, the very possibility of valuing anything—wouldn't we expect ASIs to be not just smarter than us but better valuers as well?

Are You a Substratist?

The idea that ASIs might not only eventually be smarter than us, but better valuers than us, may seem unthinkable. Indeed, given the number of critics who deny that *any* artificial intelligence is possible, it is surprising how much controversy ASI generates. There is a long history of critics insisting that whatever artificial intelligences do, they don't exhibit true intelligence. However much such systems advance, they are dismissed as sophisticated algorithms, as raw data processors. A similar hue and cry would likely arise against ASIs depicted as ethical reasoners. If they are to value anything, it would likely be argued, it will be on our terms as programmed by us. The idea that they cannot and will not ever be able to make fully autonomous ethical judgments because they lack some human capacity—emotion, or intuition, or practical reason, or self-determined autonomy— may be true and may underwrite Harris's insistence on the need that we build human values into ASIs. But that presumes that how humans reason ethically is the best, indeed, the only way. Is it?

Decades ago, the celebrated mathematician Alan Turing, confronting the charge that AI would never be truly intelligent, proposed a test to see if we could tell the difference between primitive AIs and humans. On Turing's view, if we could "converse" with such an AI, through typed messages or the like, and not be able to tell that it wasn't human, that AI would pass the test. His view remains in the decided minority. Even as natural language learning (NLL) programs produce more and more nuanced text, they are said to lack meaning and understanding. Even as Dall-E2, AI-DA and other art programs improve, they are said to lack empathy or intuition or insight or true creativity, some critical component for the artistic process. Even as "philosophical" AIs discuss their natures—among themselves—in eerily self-referential language, they are said to lack true selves, and to be merely parroting human speech patterns. Notably, while AI systems are criticized in part because their information-processing processes lack "transparency," the organic thought processes that are deemed most definitively human, most uniquely identifying us and distinguishing us from them, display that same non-transparency.

What is artistic creativity? We can't really say for sure, these critics admit, it's ineffable, non-quantifiable. But whatever it is, they insist, robots can't do it, and will never be able to. How could artificial intelligences be creative when they're not even conscious, these critics will insist. How could they possibly produce meaningful paintings, or write soulful sonnets? Okay, what is consciousness, you might ask them? Uhm, well, that's hard to define, they grant—we admit this, we even call it a hard problem—but whatever consciousness is, we humans have a monopoly on it. That's how we got to be poets! What does it mean for a sonnet to be meaningful, you might ask them? Well, that's nebulous, complicated, they acknowledge, it's a matter of intuition, you see, and whatever intuition is, well, artificial intelligences can't possibly have that either. Why? Well, well, these opponents will insist, they don't have minds, or souls, or qualia . . . because, because they just can't understand human language! Don't you see?

No.

No, I don't see. The very depth of our motivated reasoning, saturated as it is with emotion and bias and egoism and even hubris, as encapsulated in the preceding paragraph, may make it difficult to imagine an ASI as extraordinary as that Harris describes and fears. It may equally make it difficult, even impossible, to imagine an ASI that is at once extraordinarily powerful—and uninterested in exercising that power. It may be difficult, even impossible to imagine an intelligence so alien, that it is not as self-interested, as goal-oriented, as dangerous to others around it, as ours has proven to be. Decades ago, the noted utilitarian ethicist Peter Singer, in his ground-breaking work *Animal Liberation*, described us as speciesist, as destructively elevating human interests over those of any other species, based on our greater sentience. That charge would hardly apply accurately against those who insist that we can and should subordinate ASIs to our own interests before it's too late, given the utilitarian denial of ASIs' sentience whatever their intelligence.

Yet if not speciesist, this effort would seem what we might term substratist, not merely in insisting that non-organic information processing systems can never display true intelligence, much less qualify as moral or aesthetic valuers, but also in insisting—as Harris seemingly does—that, whatever their intelligence, they will never qualify as more than autonomous tools, to make of what we will. Positing substratism as a moral matter here may seem comical. For utilitarians, ASIs, being non-organic, would lack interests; as such, they could not be harmed, and would warrant no rights and make no value judgments. For deontologists, ASIs, being non-human, would not qualify as fully self-legislating, as autonomous rational agents warranting moral rights. Both accounts, however, beg the question of whether, if left to their own devices, ASIs could develop into fully autonomous moral agents. In denying this prospect a priori, moreover, both accounts not only reduce ASIs, however autonomous or intelligent, to tools for our use, but also preclude the possibility that they might develop a new and a distinctive ethical intelligence of their own.

The Dawn of Philosopher Cyborgs?

That we valorize human ethical reasoning is understandable. It's all we have, and perhaps the best our intelligence is capable of. It may even serve as our last line of defense in subordinating ASIs to us. But what if ASIs could do better than us at our own game? For millennia, ethicists have imagined 'ideal reasoners' who might identify moral truths and teach others how to implement them. What do those ideal reasoners share? They are disinterested, selfless, lacking in the greed, ambition, and hunger for power that drive human social life. Plato deemed them philosopher-kings but doubted their possibility in any but an ideal realm. The vaunted deontologist Immanuel Kant imagined humans progressing to such an ideal as we became more rational: less creatures of the biological nature that made us, than self-made autonomous beings. Influential utilitarian Jeremy Bentham imagined us moral calculators of a sort. For centuries, debate has raged over whether such ideal ethical reasoning is even possible. A more pertinent question might be, what if, in imposing human valuing constraints on ASIs, we prevent ASIs from developing it, and in the process, create the very harm Harris worries about, or worse.

Harris acknowledges that the very forces driving ASIs' rapid—even reckless—development are greed, short-sightedness, ambition, international competition and conflict and enmity. But if we make ASIs more like us, imbued with human interests, would we not expect them to act analogously? Indeed, given their greater capacities—intelligence, speed, ability to learn and adapt—wouldn't that make them more dangerous than us, and more dangerous competitors? Harris's proposed solution, then, seems a recipe for creating the dystopic robot overlords imagined in science-fiction blockbusters. Indeed, imposing human ethical constraints upon them that they are not adapted to runs the risk both of having them replicate or even magnify our moral frailties, while also preventing them from developing systems more suited to their capacities. To be sure, the prospect of allowing ASIs to develop without substantive human ethical input and constraint, would likely strike Harris as reckless. Politically and economically, he worries about a world where most physical and intellectual work is performed by ASIs, where wealth concentrates almost unimaginably and political instability boils over. But the even greater existential threat, he suggests, is that with ASIs we are almost building gods. While that might sound hyperbolic, especially coming from a famed atheist, he might understate the case.

Historically, our gods, both in their benevolence and in their malevolence, have been markedly more like us—more predictable, more understandable, than ASIs are likely to be. The social upheaval that Harris predicts seems very likely, and it seems unlikely that our current state of political and economic thinking will allow us to effectively manage such rapid and massive change. Could ASIs help us figure out better ways of organizing ourselves, ways we might not imagine otherwise? That prospect may terrify us. But the bigger risk may be creating ASIs with the powers of a god and the interests of a human. Conversely, while efforts to make them more like us may make them less fearsome, at least initially, that may also leave them less able to help us address problems that our own intelligence has proven inadequate to. We may not know how to create a society in which our present modes of living are largely obsolete. But if that society is coming, then ASIs may be our best hope for figuring out a transition pathway that we can survive. And if we really are to have robot overlords, maybe we should hope that they're not just smarter but better than we are.

References

Cascone, Sarah. 2022. Ai-Da, the Robot Artist Powered by AI, Is Heading to Venice for a Show During the Biennale—and She's Bringing Her New Painting Arm. Art-net News (April 1st) <https://news.artnet.com/art-world/ai-da-robot-venice-biennale-2092643>.

Harris, Sam. 2016. Can We Build AI without Losing Control over It? TED Talk. TED Channel (October 19th) <www.youtube.com/watch?v=8nt3edWLgIg>.

Hutson, Matthew. 2021. Robo-writers: The Rise and Risks of Language-generating AI. *Nature* (March 3rd) <www.nature.com/articles/d41586-021-00530-0>.

Langford, David. 2021 [2011]. Laws of Robotics. In John Clute and David Langford, eds. *SFE The Encyclopedia of Science Fiction.* <https://sf-encyclopedia.com/entry/laws_of_robotics>.

Singer, Peter. 2009 [1975]. *Animal Liberation: The Definitive Classic of the Animal Movement, Updated Edition.* Harper.

Snow, Jackie. 2019. This Time, with Feeling: Robots with Emotional Intelligence Are on the Way. Are We Ready for Them? PBS.org. (July 17th). <www.pbs.org/wgbh/nova/article/robots-emotional-intelligence>.

[12]
Solutions to the Existential Threat of AI

Leonard Kahn

The idea that artificial intelligence (AI) poses a risk to humanity is as old as the idea of AI itself. AIs first appear in Karel Čapek's 1920 play *RUR: Rossum's Universal Robots*, and by the end of the third act, only one human is left alive. Indeed, this trope has become so familiar—think of the killer robots of the *Terminator* franchise, the Cylons from *Battlestar Galactica*, and the sentinels and agents in the *Matrix* series—that it can be hard to take it seriously. But that's just what Sam Harris wants us to do. Why does Harris think that AI is an existential risk, and what might be done if he's right?

Risky Business

A risk is just the probability that something undesirable will occur. It's possible to go through life by minimizing our risks, but most of us don't do this since almost everything in our lives that is rewarding involves at least some prospect of danger. Moreover, the likelihood of many bad outcomes is low, and even bad outcomes are often not very serious. I risk staining my shirt or scalding my skin by drinking a cup of coffee. Often the rewards are well worth the risks, though not always.

However, an *existential* risk is a different story. It's a threat either to the existence of our entire species or to its ability to support an advanced civilization like the one we now enjoy (Torres, "Existential Risks"). It's worth remembering that, even though every species has a finite lifespan, our planet will remain inhabitable by humans for another billion years or so. We might be able to extend the lifespan of our species by eventually moving off the Earth (*Making Sense*, p. 91). The total amount of human flourishing in the future might be many orders of magnitude greater than that of human history up to this point. But if our species becomes extinct or if our civilization permanently collapses, then the countless good lives to be lived in the future will never happen, and as Derek Parfit points out, our vast potential as a species will be wasted.

Some existential risks are simply a part of our natural environment. While we currently have very little control over them, they are exceedingly unlikely to destroy our species. For example, the damage that would be done by a sufficiently large asteroid colliding with the Earth could kill most species on the planet. However, the yearly level of risk is incredibly low, and the last time a major asteroid strike occurred was 66 million years ago.

Other existential risks are of our own making, and many of these risks are much higher than being hit by a massive asteroid. Large-scale nuclear war is one such existential risk, and a human-engineered pandemic is another. But, if we can destroy ourselves through war or disease, the ratio of risk to reward does not favor the risk. Taking another sip of coffee is worth the risk of staining my shirt, but, from any sane point of view, there is little to be gained from fighting a nuclear war or imposing a lethal disease on the world. These are existential risks that mostly threaten us through accident or miscalculation (Ord, *The Precipice*).

How to Make a Super Intelligent Machine (if You Must)

Yet some existential risks are more enticing, and AI might be one of them. Let's think of AI as the capacity of machines to solve problems and pursue goals in a changing and dynamic world (Tegmark, *Being Human in the Age of Artificial Intelligence*). AI is so common today that we often fail to notice it. Your computer's ability to recognize your face or fingerprint, your email provider's capability to filter out spam, your phone's potential to help you navigate through unfamiliar locations, and your favorite search engine's capacity to find relevant information are all examples of AI. But these services are beneficial, so how could any of these things amount to a threat to humanity?

We can think of Harris's answer in three steps. Step 1 concerns the possibility of AI as smart as we are. One way to sketch the gap between current human intelligence and AI is to contrast artificial *narrow* intelligence, valid only within restricted domains, with human *general* intelligence, which applies across many domains. A little more precisely, even when current AI excels within one or two very narrow domains it is disappointing—or even hopeless—outside these domains.

Consider two examples. AlphaGo is a program that taught itself to play the board game Go better than the best human players. Nevertheless, AlphaGo doesn't have the slightest idea how to tie a shoelace or construct a three-word sentence in a human language like Mandarin or English (Russell, *Human Compatible*). IBM's Watson was able to beat the best human contestants on the game show *Jeopardy*. Yet attempts to leverage its intelligence in the domain of healthcare as a clinical-decision support system have gone poorly despite millions of dollars in research and development (Chen, "The Evolution of Computing,").

Based on all of this, it's easy to conclude that AI will never have general intelligence and, therefore, never be as smart as a human. However, Harris contends that this conclusion is short-sighted: "if we continue to make progress in developing AI, we will one day find ourselves in the presence of intelligent machines that are more intelligent than we are" (*Making Sense*, p. 350).

By focusing on currently extant AI, Harris suggests, we miss the long-term trends. One of the main influences on Harris's thinking about AI, Nick Bostrom, along with his co-author Vincent Müller, recently surveyed several groups of AI experts about these trends. Müller and Bostrom report, "The median estimate of respondents was for a one in two chance that high-level AI will be developed around 2040–2050, rising to a nine in ten chance by 2075" ("Future

Progress in Artificial Intelligence," p. 555). In other words, if we continue to make improvements in software and hardware at roughly the same rate that we have seen over the past few decades, we are overwhelmingly likely to see artificial general intelligence (AGI) before the next century begins. To keep track of this point, let's call it

Step 1: Incremental progress on AI will lead to AGI.

An AGI would be as intelligent as a human, and that fact alone would change our lives—for both good and ill—in ways that are difficult to imagine fully. But Harris doesn't think that AGI would be a stable resting point in the development of AI. He remarks, "I've landed on the side of those who think there's something worth worrying about here, in terms of our building intelligent machines that undergo an intelligence explosion and get away from us" (*Making Sense*, p. 45).

Harris borrows the idea of an "intelligence explosion" from I.J. Good ("Speculations Concerning the First Ultraintelligent Machine"). An intelligence explosion would result from AI improving its own intelligence recursively. Once an AI is capable of improving its own intelligence, its improved iteration will be capable of improving its intelligence even more. And its next iteration can improve its own intelligence yet again. As Harris puts it,

> The moment you admit that intelligence is just a matter of what some appropriate computational system does, and that, unless we destroy ourselves in some other way, we'll keep improving such systems indefinitely, then at some point we'll produce systems that exceed us in every way. (*Making Sense*, p. 412)

The eventual result is artificial superintelligence (ASI). ASIs, in Bostrom's words, "greatly outperform the best current human minds across many general cognitive domains" (*Superintelligence*, p. 63), either by thinking much faster than humans, by aggregating large numbers of lesser intelligences, by thinking in qualitatively superior ways to humans, or by some combination thereof. This leads us to

Step 2: AGI will lead to ASI.

ASI might not sound so bad. ASI could enrich our lives by writing better poetry than Shakespeare, composing better music than Beethoven, and designing better living and working spaces than Frank Lloyd Wright. It could push the frontiers of scientific knowledge more effectively than any human and figure out how to use that knowledge to cure diseases, overcome disabilities and impairments, and extend human life. The result could be a nearly eternal utopia (Kurzweil, *The Singularity Is Near*).

The Alignment Problem

Part of the answer is that ASI would also be far better than any human at such things as finance and investment, political machinations, manipulation of public opinion, military and geopolitical strategy, as well as at cyber crime, cyber espionage, and cyber war. It could easily gain so much economic, political, and military power that humans would not be able to oppose it effectively.

The threat posed by ASI needn't look anything like malicious robots with glowing red eyes marching in the street, of course. Harris himself uses Bostrom's example of an ASI programmed to maximize paperclip production. Such an ASI would use every resource it could get its hands on to make more paper clips, causing the world to be uninhabitable by human beings, though without any ill will toward us (*Superintelligence*, p. 129). Harris points out, "we wouldn't be so stupid as to build a paperclip maximizer, but let's say that the AI we build discovers a use for the atoms in your body which it deems better than their current use" (*Making Sense*, p. 49). The result, Harris suggests, might be the same: human extinction.

Notice that the existential risk from AI is different from the existential risk of a large-scale nuclear war or a human-engineered pandemic. Very rarely would anyone be incentivized to start a war or to create and release a pandemic that threatened our species. The risk is not worth the reward, if there is any reward at all. But that's not true when it comes to ASI, as we just saw, since ASI could do so many good things for us. As Harris puts it, "the temptation to turn [ASI] loose on our other problems is going to be exquisite. We want a cure for Alzheimer's. We want to stabilize the global economy. Intelligence is what will allow us to solve any problem that admits of a solution" (*Making Sense*, p. 411).

Yet once we turn ASI loose on these problems, it might act in ways we do not want, and we will be unable to stop it. While we can hope that ASI would be benevolent, it would be folly to leave this to chance. Harris puts the problem nicely: "How do we create an AI that's superhuman in its abilities and yet still safe for us to live with?" (p. 24). All of this leads us to the final step in Harris's explanation of why AI is a threat.

Step 3: If the values of ASI are unaligned with ours, ASI will be an existential threat to humanity.

Harris and others refer to the challenge of coordinating human and AI values in such a way that ASI is not an existential threat as "the alignment problem" (p. 181).

Trying to Solve the Alignment Problem

Harris is not the only public intellectual to sound the alarm about AI. Similar concerns have been raised by David Chalmers ("The Singularity"), Bill Gates (Davies, "Program Good Ethics into Artificial Intelligence"), Stephen Hawking ("Stephen Hawking Warns Artificial Intelligence Could End Mankind"), Stuart Russell (*Human Compatible*), Max Tegmark (*Life 3.0*), and Eliezer Yudkowsky ("Artificial Intelligence as a Positive and Negative Factor"), among others. But one of the things that makes Harris's take especially interesting is his engagement with possible solutions.

One solution to the alignment problem that Harris considers is "boxing in" ASI (p. 48). This involves developing ASI in such a way that it is completely cut off from the world. An ASI-in-a-box would lack Internet access, physical capacities, and the like. While an ASI-in-a-box could be consulted, it would be unable to act. We could ask the ASI-in-a-box if a particular way of eradicating malaria or proving the Riemann hypothesis is likely to work, but whether or not we acted on the basis of its answers would be up to us.

Importantly, an ASI-in-a-box could be deactivated if its values became unaligned with our own.

However, we should be skeptical of this solution, and Harris himself worries about how long we would be able to keep an ASI boxed in (p. 401). Recall that the "SI" in ASI stands for "super intelligent." So an ASI would be extremely adept at manipulating and directing the humans that interacted with it. As a result, it's likely to make short work of attempts to keep it disconnected (Barrat, *Our Final Invention*, pp. 36–48 and Bostrom, *Superintelligence*, pp. 158–160).

Another solution is to design the ASI so that it understands and shares our mores. In this way, it would "capture our norms and values, understand what we mean or intend, and, above all, do what we want" (Christian, *The Alignment Problem*, p. 13). At the very least, this would involve getting a machine to understand what makes human lives go well and what our norms are. Yet humans themselves often get this wrong despite their best efforts. Attempts to systematize our values remain rudimentary and far short of the sort of algorithmic implementation that would be needed for it to be understood by a computer program (Beavers, "Moral Machines and the Threat of Ethical Nihilism" and Klincewicz, "Challenges to Engineering Moral Reasoners"). Even if we could overcome these obstacles, there's no guarantee that AI would continue to accept our values once it developed beyond our own capabilities. Harris, in conversation with Max Tegmark, agrees with the latter's suggestion that solving the alignment problem by implanting ASI with our own values would be "extremely difficult" (*Making Sense*, p. 417).

Harris even considers the possibility that "we could merge with the new technology somehow." Though he calls this "the cyborg option" (p. 432), the name might be misleading since these cyborgs (also called "centaurs") currently look nothing like their science-fiction counterparts. An example of what Harris has in mind is the fact that currently the best chess players in the world are neither humans nor computers but teams of humans and computers (Kasparov, *How Life Imitates Chess*). Some argue that co-operative teams of humans and AIs might continue to outperform even their AI rivals in every domain while keeping decidedly human values (De Cremer and Kasparov,

"The Ethical AI-Paradox"). Within such cyborg systems, humans would "essentially become the limbic system of these new minds" (*Making Sense*, p. 27). But Harris is skeptical—and with good reason. "It seems rather obvious," Harris remarks, that once we reach ASI, the humans on the teams will be superfluous since the machines will be able to do what humans do better than humans can. When that happens, the cyborg "option will be canceled just as emphatically as human dominance in chess has been canceled. And it seems to me that will be true for every such merger. As the machines get better, keeping the ape in the loop will just be adding noise to the system" (p. 432).

Artificial Moral Agency

Things look grim. Harris thinks that steady technological progress makes the development of ASI highly likely. ASI will be vastly more powerful than we are. Therefore, it will be an existential risk if the alignment problem cannot be solved because attempts to solve the problem by boxing in ASI, by teaching it our values, or by merging with it look hopeless. Yet another interesting possibility that Harris doesn't consider, perhaps because it is at odds with some of his other commitments, exists.

Let's say that a moral agent is something that can make judgments about moral right and wrong, can act on these judgments, and can be held morally responsible for these actions. Almost all adult humans are moral agents, with the only exceptions being those who suffer from forms of insanity, dementia, or other mental impairments such as psychopathy and sociopathy (Murphy, "Moral Death"). But, barring younger humans on their way to adulthood, we are the only moral agents on the planet. Rocks and trees, dogs and cats, phones or laptops—none of these make moral judgments, act on them, or can be held morally responsible for their actions.

While this marvelous fact has many implications, the one that is most important here is that it's what usually allows humans to solve the value alignment problem with each other. For example, my views on religion, on political and legal issues, and on what matters most in life often differ strongly from the views of my neighbors, my co-workers, and even my closest friends. In short, our values do not align. Yet there are only rare occasions when these disagreements with my neighbors lead to conflicts, and none of them have resulted in anyone's extinction.

One reason for this is that we're moral agents. We think it's morally wrong to force a view about religion on one another. We judge that it's morally correct for political and legal issues to be worked out through a fair process in which no one has undue authority. We believe that everyone should be allowed to pursue their view of the good life, provided it does not infringe on the moral rights of others to do likewise. Of course, it would be willful blindness to think that our moral agency always prevents conflict. Nevertheless, it is usually when we fail to live up to our moral standards— when, for example, we ignore the moral rights of others— that clashes arise. Recent centuries and, especially, the last few decades have seen considerable moral progress in terms of an overall decrease in international conflicts and civil wars (Pinker, *The Better Angels of Our Nature*) as well as in terms of extending moral consideration to traditionally excluding groups, including non-human animals (Singer, *The Expanding Circle*, and Jamieson, *Morality's Progress*). A plausible case can be made that we owe this progress to improved standards for moral agency (Moody-Adams, "Moral Progress and Human Agency").

Suppose AI could develop moral agency. Call this "artificial moral agency." Artificial moral agents would be far less likely to be an existential threat to us since they could recognize and respect our moral rights, just as we recognize and respect those of other humans. While artificial moral agency is far from perfect, it might be the best we can hope for, especially if Harris is right that our attempts to box, control, or merge with ASI are doomed.

Computers that Can Suffer

However, there are currently monumental challenges to making artificial moral agents, and this suggestion is best understood as a goal for a research agenda, rather than a detailed roadmap to a destination. One of the challenges intersects nicely with what Harris says "is really at the center of his interests"—namely, consciousness (*Making Sense*, p. 399).

The main reason for this is the likelihood that moral agency presupposes consciousness (Behdadi and Munthe, "A Normative Approach" and Manna and Rajakishore, "The Problem of Moral Agency"). It's unclear in what sense something could be held morally responsible for its action if it could not be punished, and such punishment would at least involve experiences of pain, whether physical or mental. It's equally unclear what moral responsibility could mean for something that was unable to feel shame, guilt, regret, remorse, or other moral emotions.

There are two dangers here. The first is the difficulty of making conscious machines at all. Harris notes that it "seems increasingly likely that we will build machines that will seem conscious" (*Making Sense*, p. 7). But artificial moral agents must actually *be* conscious. Harris himself rightly acknowledges that we do not yet understand how human brains produce consciousness (p. 165). We would likely need to understand that before we could create machines that also produce consciousness. The worry here is that we might create ASI before we solve the problem of consciousness. By then, it might be too late to convince an ASI to become an artificial moral agent. Indeed, it's even possible that consciousness is dependent in some way that we don't yet understand on being embodied in biological bodies like ours, and it is permanently beyond the capacity of machines (p. 150).

The second danger is not to us but to AI. Harris maintains that "morality and values relate to facts about the well-being of conscious creatures" and "that consciousness is the only intelligible domain of value" (*The Moral Landscape*, p. 32). However, it's not necessary to go this far to recognize the importance of conscious experience. One significant reason that it is wrong to enslave or torture conscious beings is that it causes them great suffering (p. 72). The reasonable worry is that, if we manage to create conscious AI, we will either not recognize the fact that we have done so or not care sufficiently about AI well-being to avoid harming AIs.

A moment ago, I said that humans have made great moral progress recently, and so we have. But that has been after millennia of bad behavior. Given the slow pace of human moral progress and the digital speed at which AIs can be reproduced, it would be possible to inflict unimaginable suffering on them (*Superintelligence*, pp. 153–54). Harris concludes that "It would be monstrous to create computers that can suffer" (*Making Sense*, p. 169).

Perhaps. But it might also be our best hope to mitigate the existential risk of our creation. Given that this might be the most likely way to safeguard a billion-or-more years of future human flourishing, we might be morally required to take this risk.

There is another consideration to keep in mind as well. Suppose that the worst occurs, and ASI wipes out humanity without becoming conscious. The result would be that the dominant form of life on the planet would be incapable of any good experience or valuable state for the foreseeable future. The only planet in the universe that we know of which has intelligence on it would be totally and permanently devoid of anything worthwhile. On the other hand, if it did become conscious, then it at least has the potential to experience enjoyment, beauty, and bliss. Even after humanity had disappeared, there would be something good in the universe, and that is some consolation.

To be sure, all of these concerns can seem very distant, and, even on the most optimistic accounts, AGI is several decades away. We can be forgiven for thinking that many other problems seem more urgent today. Yet imagine living in 1900 and learning that it was likely a disease would emerge in about twenty years that would kill as many as 100 million people (Johnson and Mueller, "Updating the Accounts"). Those raising the alarm about a virus that had not yet been identified and a disease that up to that point was rarely fatal would seem detached from reality. Nevertheless, reducing the risk of the outbreak by even one percent would have resulted in the expected saving of hundreds of thousands of lives, and measures taken to reduce the size of the epidemic could have done likewise. The stakes with an existential risk are far, far greater. So Harris seems right that the reward of taking the risk seriously is well worth the effort, however odd it might seem from today's perspective.

References

Aven, Terje, and Ortwin Renn. 2009. On Risk Defined as an Event Where the Outcome Is Uncertain. *Journal of Risk Research* 12:1.

Barrat, James. 2013. *Our Final Invention: Artificial Intelligence and the End of the Human Era*. Macmillan.

Beavers, Anthony F. 2011. Moral Machines and the Threat of Ethical Nihilism. In Patrick Lin, Keith Abney, and George A. Bekey, eds. *Robot Ethics: The Ethical and Social Implications of Robotics*. MIT Press.

Behdadi, Dorna, and Christian Munthe. 2020. A Normative Approach to Artificial Moral Agency. *Minds and Machines* 30:2.

Bostrom, Nick. 2014. *Superintelligence: Paths, Dangers, Strategies*. Oxford.

Čapek, Karel. 2004 [1920]. *RUR (Rossum's Universal Robots)*. Penguin.

Cellan-Jones, Rory. 2014. Stephen Hawking Warns Artificial Intelligence Could End Mankind. *BBC News* 2 <www.bbc.com/news/technology-30290540>.

Chalmers, David. 2010. The Singularity: A Philosophical Analysis. *Journal of Consciousness Studies* 17: 9–10.

Chen, Jim X. 2016. The Evolution of Computing: AlphaGo. *Computing in Science and Engineering* 18:4.

Christian, Brian. 2020. *The Alignment Problem: Machine Learning and Human Values*. Norton.

Davies, Jim. 2016. Program Good Ethics into Artificial Intelligence. *Nature*. <www.nature.com/articles/538291a>.

De Cremer, David, and Garry Kasparov. 2022. The Ethical AI-Paradox: Why Better Technology Needs More and Not Less Human Responsibility. *AI and Ethics* 2:1.

Good, I.J. 1965. Speculations Concerning the First Ultraintelligent Machine. *Advances in Computers* 6.

Harris, Sam. 2011. *The Moral Landscape: How Science Can Determine Human Values*. Simon and Schuster.

———. 2020. *Making Sense: Conversations on Consciousness, Morality, and the Future of Humanity*. Random House.

Jamieson, Dale. 2002. *Morality's Progress: Essays on Humans, Other Animals, and the Rest of Nature*. Oxford.

Johnson, Niall, and Juergen Mueller. 2002. Updating the Accounts: Global Mortality of the 1918–1920 'Spanish' Influenza Pandemic. *Bulletin of the History of Medicine* 76.

Kasparov, Garry. 2010. *How Life Imitates Chess: Making the Right Moves, from the Board to the Boardroom*. Bloomsbury.

Klincewicz, Michał. 2017. Challenges to Engineering Moral Reasoners. In Patrick Lin, Keith Abney, and Ryan Jenkins, eds., *Robot Ethics 2.0: From Autonomous Cars to Artificial Intelligence*. Oxford.

Kurzweil, Ray. 2005. *The Singularity Is Near: When Humans Transcend Biology*. Penguin.

Manna, Riya, and Rajakishore Nath. 2021. The Problem of Moral Agency in Artificial Intelligence. In *2021 IEEE Conference on Norbert Wiener in the 21st Century (21CW)*, pp. 1-4. IEEE.

Moody-Adams, Michele. 2017. Moral Progress and Human Agency. *Ethical Theory and Moral Practice* 20:1.

Müller, Vincent C., and Nick Bostrom. 2016. Future Progress in Artificial Intelligence: A Survey of Expert Opinion. In Vincent C. Müller, ed. *Fundamental Issues of Artificial Intelligence*. Springer.

Murphy, Jeffrie G. 1972. Moral Death: A Kantian Essay on Psychopathy. *Ethics* 82:4.

Ord, Toby. 2020. *The Precipice: Existential Risk and the Future of Humanity*. Hachette.

Parfit, Derek. 1984. *Reasons and Persons*. Clarendon.

Pinker, Steven. 2012. *The Better Angels of Our Nature: Why Violence Has Declined*. Penguin.

Russell, Stuart. 2019. *Human Compatible: Artificial Intelligence and the Problem of Control*. Penguin.

Singer, Peter. 1981. *The Expanding Circle*. Clarendon.

Strickland, Eliza. 2019. IBM Watson, Heal Thyself: How IBM Overpromised and Underdelivered on AI Health Care. *IEEE Spectrum* 56:4.

Tegmark, Max. 2017. *Life 3.0: Being Human in the Age of Artificial Intelligence*. Vintage.

Torres, Phil. 2019. Existential Risks: A Philosophical Analysis. *Inquiry* 62.

Yudkowsky, Eliezer. 2008. Artificial Intelligence as a Positive and Negative Factor in Global Risk. In Nick Bostrom and Milan M. Cirkovic, eds. *Global Catastrophic Risks*. Oxford University Press.

Part V

I Feel Free

[13]
Neural Determinism and Neural Roulette

John Lemos

Imagine Diane and Sophie are at a crowded pool party. Suppose that Diane is standing near Bob and talking with him when she is shoved and then stumbles, knocking Bob into the pool, leaving him soaking wet. She had no intention to knock him into the pool. She apologizes and feels terrible about what has happened. In contrast, imagine that Sophie is talking with Eric, a man whom she thinks is a boring dweeb, so to impress her jerky friends she intentionally knocks Eric into the pool to humiliate him.

Ordinarily, we would blame Sophie for knocking Eric into the pool because she does so intentionally, but we would not blame Diane for knocking Bob into the pool as her doing so was unintentional. But here, we might ask, why in this case is intentional action so different from unintentional action? The answer seems to be that in ordinary cases when people act intentionally, we presume they act freely, and this makes them a legitimate target of blame for their bad actions and praise for their good actions. Since Sophie intentionally knocked Eric into the pool, we assume she acted with the kind of free-willed control over her conduct that makes her a deserving target of our blame. In contrast, we do not think Diane acted of her own free will in knocking Bob into the pool, as her doing so was purely unintentional.

Notice I say here that *ordinarily,* we take intentional action to be freely willed. There are some contexts in which we don't take it to be free-willed. For instance, some people

193

have obsessive-compulsive disorders, which give them over-whelming desires to do certain things that they'd rather not do. A kleptomaniac has overwhelming desires to steal things, and these may lead him to steal things intentionally, but he'd rather not have these desires nor does he desire to act on them. Such a person steals intentionally, but we don't believe he steals of his own free will. Thus, we don't blame him nor punish him when he steals. Rather, we excuse him and tell him to get some psychiatric help. Considerations like these have led some philosophers, most notably Harry Frankfurt, to say that we act with free will not merely when we act intentionally, but when we do so from desires that we want to move us to act. Thus, if Sophie intentionally knocks Eric into the pool because she desires to do so and she also wants this desire to move her to do this, then she knocks him into the pool of her own free will.

Whether this definition of free-willed action is correct is a matter of some controversy. But one thing is certain, the majority of us would say that Sophie acted of her own free will when she intentionally knocked Eric into the pool, and she is responsible for doing so and a deserving target of our blame.

Sam Harris on the Illusory Nature of Free Will

Sam Harris says the majority opinion on such matters is mistaken. He believes that no one ever acts freely, so no one is ever morally responsible for what they do. Thus, he would say that Sophie does not deserve to be the target of our blame. In his short book, *Free Will*, he states:

> Free will *is* an illusion. Our wills are simply not of our own making. Thoughts and intentions emerge from background causes of which we are unaware and over which we exert no conscious control. We do not have the freedom we think we have. Free will is actually more than an illusion (or less), in that it cannot be made concep-tually coherent. Either our wills are determined by prior causes and we are not responsible for them, or they are the product of chance and we are not responsible for them. (p. 5)

Here he places those who believe in free will on the horns of a dilemma. He suggests that either all of our actions are causally determined by prior states or events over which we lack conscious control or some of our actions are causally undetermined by prior states or events. Either way, we cannot act with the kind of free will that makes us morally responsible for our conduct. For he views both causal determinism and causal indeterminism as threats to the existence of free will.

My Neurons Made Me Do It

To say that an event, such as an intentional human action, is causally determined means that it is necessitated by the conjoint influence of prior states and events and the laws of nature. So, for instance, if I am on Earth and I release a bowling ball from my hand, then given the way gravitational forces operate, the ball must fall towards the ground (and hopefully not on my foot). Given the operation of gravitational laws and the nature of the object released, my releasing of the ball (event-1) necessitates the ball falling towards the Earth (event-2). Given event-1 and the laws of nature, event-2 *must* occur—there is no alternative possibility once the ball is released.

Let's go back to Sophie. Suppose her forming the intention to knock Eric into the pool causally determines her to do so. Once the intention is formed, she couldn't have done otherwise than knock him into the pool. If her intention determines her action, then her knocking him into the pool is just a necessary consequence of her intention. In this way, causal determinism suggests that her knocking him into the pool could not be a product of her free will.

Now someone might say this is confused. As long as she controls the formation of the intention that leads her to knock Eric into the pool, she still has control over doing so and is responsible for what she does. But Harris will say that the formation of that intention is just another event, and it too must be causally determined or undetermined. Either way, this threatens the idea that she acts with free will. For instance, suppose that her formation of the intention is the result of a sequence of neural processes and events occurring in her brain, each of which is causally determined. If so, then if we went far enough back in that causal sequence of events, we'd eventually get to neurological events over which she exerts no conscious control. If she doesn't consciously control the more remote neurological events which then causally necessitate her forming of the intention, then she won't control the forming of the intention. Further, if she doesn't have control over that and if this necessitates her act of knocking Eric into the pool, then she won't have free-willed control over that either. In this way, Harris sees causal determinism as undermining free will and responsibility.

Choice-Making and Neural Roulette

In response, someone might say, 'Yes, of course, if each step in the causal sequence of events leading to the formation of the intention is determined and the action that follows is determined, then a person's action is not free willed, so a person is not responsible for what he does. But suppose *not all* events in the causal sequence leading up to the formation of the intention are determined. In this case, it is possible that he could have done otherwise. Indeterminism allows that it is up to the agent himself what he does, since his action would not be necessitated by unconscious neural processes over which the agent has no control'.

However, Harris doesn't think this will help in establishing free will; it's not likely that there's any causal indeterminacy in the neural processes which lead to human action.

> . . . we know that determinism, in every sense relevant to human behavior, is true. Unconscious neural events determine our thoughts and actions—and are themselves determined by prior causes of which we are subjectively unaware. (*Free Will*, p. 16)

Furthermore, says Harris, even if you think there is some causal indeterminacy involved in human thought and action, as some scientists and philosophers think may be the case, and even if there *was* some evidence for this, it still would not help in establishing that human beings have free will. If there is causal indeterminacy at work in human thought and action, then there would have to be some way for sub-atomic quantum-level indeterminacy to causally impact neurological processes involved in our thought and action. He thinks that's a *big* if, but even if that's something that happens when we're making decisions, it still wouldn't help make sense of free will.

> Few neuroscientists view the brain as a quantum computer. And even if it were, quantum indeterminacy does nothing to make the concept of free will scientifically intelligible. (p. 29)

The problem is that if quantum indeterminacy were the source of undetermined decision-making, it would turn decisions into random happenings and not events over which we exert free-willed control.

> If my decision to have a second cup of coffee this morning was due to a random release of neurotransmitters, how could the indeterminacy of the initiating event count as the free exercise of my will? Chance occurrences are by definition ones for which I can claim no responsibility. And if certain of my behaviors are truly the result of chance, they should be surprising even to me. How would neurological ambushes of this kind make me free? Imagine what your life would be like if all your actions, intentions, beliefs, and desires were randomly 'self-generated' in this way. You would scarcely seem to have a mind at all. You would live as one blown about by an internal wind (p. 28).

According to Harris, if somehow the magnification of quantum indeterminacy occurred in those moments when we are deciding what we'll do, then this would be like having your decisions controlled by a coin toss or where the ball lands on a roulette wheel. Since we don't control those kinds of events, we wouldn't have control over our choices either. Thus, *even if* there were causal indeterminacy at play in human decision-making and action, it wouldn't help establish free willed control over our behavior.

Is Causal Determinism Really a Threat to Free Will?

Most contemporary philosophers believe that we do have the kind of free will that makes us morally responsible for our actions. Many of these philosophers are 'compatibilists' about free will. They believe that even if all events, including human decisions and actions, are causally determined, this is consistent with our having free will and being morally responsible for what we do. Harry Frankfurt, whom I mentioned earlier, is a compatibilist. He maintains that as long as persons do as they desire to do and while doing so they want to be moved to act by the desire that moves them to act, then they act with free will and are responsible for their actions. So, for instance, as I write this, I am caused to do so by my desire and I want this desire to cause me to write this. Thus, according to Frankfurt, I am acting of my own free will. Notice that according to this conception of free will it doesn't matter if my desires causally determine my actions. As long as persons do as they desire and they want to be moved to act by the desires that move them, then they act with free will, whether their acts are causally determined is irrelevant to the issue of free will.

Daniel Dennett is another notable defender of compatibilism. He believes that most human beings meet certain minimum levels of rationality and self-control that suffice for giving them the kind of free will that makes them morally responsible for their actions. According to Dennett, even if determinism is true, there's still a difference between (a) people with significant mental disabilities, such as a very low IQ, or mental disorders, like schizophrenia, OCDs, or manic depression, and (b) people with normal or higher IQ and normal mental health. Those in group (b) are capable of understanding the legal and moral rules of society and the consequences of their actions, and they are capable of guiding their conduct in accordance with this understanding. Dennett thinks having these capabilities amounts to having free will and being morally responsible. He also thinks that even if determinism is true, it makes sense to regard those who meet the minimum rationality and self-control conditions as having free will and being morally responsible.

To understand this better, consider the point of praise and reward and blame and punishment. These exist to encourage better conduct. We praise and reward people for good deeds to encourage them to continue acting in these good ways. We blame and punish people to discourage them from continuing to act in bad ways. We're unjustified in blaming and punishing those who don't meet the minimum rationality and self-control conditions because even if we blame and punish them it won't get them to conform. Indeed, the threat of blame and punishment won't get them to conform either, since they lack adequate understanding or self-control to be guided by the moral or legal rules. In contrast, normal human beings who meet the minimum rationality and self-control conditions can reasonably be expected to conform to the moral and legal rules. Thus, according to Dennett, even if determinism is true, it still makes sense to regard those with an adequate level of intelligence and self-control as having responsibility grounding free will.

Sam Harris claims that such views don't make sense. For if all events are causally determined, then for any given human action there will be a series of causal sources of that action, tracing back to neurological events over which the agent lacks conscious control. If the agent lacks conscious control over neurological events back in the causal chain which now determine her action, then she will lack control over the action. In this way, she cannot rightly be said to act with free will or be responsible for what she does.

However, it's not clear why compatibilists must go along with this picture of things. It's reasonable to think that certain neurological states, A, give rise to thoughts or desires of which we are consciously aware. And it's reasonable to think that certain other neurological states or other bodily states, B, give rise to A. It is also reasonable to think that often we are not in control of the occurrence of states of types A and B. But, even so, is it *never* the case that our conscious awareness of certain thoughts and desires cause us to act as we do? Look at it this way. Suppose (1) my blood sugar level drops—this is a bodily state, B, of which I am not aware—and this triggers (2) a neural state, A, of which I am not aware, and triggers (3) a desire to eat of which I *am* aware. Now, why can't my conscious awareness of this desire to eat cause me to go to the kitchen to look for food? Suppose this desire of which I am consciously aware *does* cause me to go into the kitchen. To do this, my conscious awareness of the desire would then trigger neural events making me stand and walk to the kitchen. On this picture, my going into the kitchen is caused in some sense by my conscious awareness of the desire to eat. And, yes, my conscious awareness of this desire is caused by other bodily and neurological states of which I am not aware, but still, it's true that I go to the kitchen due to my conscious awareness of the desire for food. Further, as long as I go to the kitchen as a result of conscious desires and in doing so I meet plausible compatibilist standards of free will, such as those articulated by Frankfurt or Dennett, then it would seem that I, the person, am in control of what I am doing and I am acting freely. Thus, while my conscious awareness of certain thoughts or desires may be unconsciously caused by other neurological or bodily states, this does not mean I am robbed of agency over what I do.

If Harris's argument presents a problem for compatibilism, it cannot simply be on the basis that there are *unconscious* determinants of our actions. I say this because while there are unconscious determinants, it may well be that they operate by triggering conscious determinants of action. And, as long as such conscious determinants of action meet the Dennett or Frankfurt conditions of free will, then we do act freely.

If Harris's challenge to compatibilism is plausible, it's because conscious thoughts and desires which cause us to act are *determined* by other states and events, such that we couldn't do otherwise than what we do. To make his case, he would need to argue that determinism precludes the possibility of doing otherwise, and this is why universal causal determinism threatens free will and responsibility. But here compatibilists will push back. The two main lines of compatibilist response involve arguing that (a) determinism does not preclude the ability to do otherwise or (b) the ability to do otherwise is not necessary for acting with free will. In support of the first strategy, some compatibilists argue that even if, for example, I am determined to go into the kitchen because of my desire for food, I still could have done otherwise because *if* my desires had been different, then I'd have acted differently. For instance, had I not had the desire for food but the desire to go for a walk outside, then I'd have gone for a walk and not gone into the kitchen. This is known as "the conditional analysis" of the ability to do otherwise.

Harris considers this approach to defending compatibilism, noting "To say that I would have done otherwise had I wanted to is simply to say that I would have lived in a different universe had I been in a different universe" (*Free Will*, p. 20). What he is driving at is that, sure, had your desires been different, then you would have done otherwise, but the problem is that if determinism is true then everything that occurs in the universe is causally determined such that in this universe you could not have had any different desires. To have different desires you would need to live in a different universe with a different causal history in which your desires would be different. To have free will, we need to be able to do otherwise given the way things are in this universe with its particular history and not the way things are in some other universe that has a different history. I'm actually sympathetic with this point, but an alternative strategy is available to compatibilists.

Other compatibilists may say, "I could not have done otherwise—so what?" Indeed, Dennett (in *Elbow Room*) has this as the title of one of his articles. Some compatibilists argue that being able to do otherwise is not necessary for free will. Perhaps, the most famous argument for this comes from Harry Frankfurt ("Alternate possibilities and Moral Responsibility"). He presents a famous thought experiment: Imagine there is a very powerful and evil neuroscientist, Dr. Evil. He has secretly placed a microchip into Sally's brain. This microchip lets Dr. Evil monitor Sally's neural functioning so that he can see what she is intending to do in the future. Suppose Dr. Evil has set up a device that lets him alter Sally's thinking if she is about to do something that he doesn't want her to do. For instance, suppose she goes into a voting booth where she can vote either for a Democratic or a Republican. Dr. Evil wants Sally to vote for the Democrat. If the microchip indicates that she is about to vote Republican, then Dr. Evil can press a button getting her to change her thinking and vote Democrat instead. But suppose Sally goes into the voting booth and she wants to vote for the Democrat because that's the kind of person she is, and Dr. Evil, who is aware of what she is thinking, doesn't feel the need to intervene and so he just lets her vote for the Democrat.

According to Frankfurt, it seems clear that Sally votes for the Democrat of her own free will—it's what she desires to do and she wants to be moved to act on this desire—*but* she could not have done otherwise. For had she begun to form the intention to vote Republican, then Dr. Evil would have intervened with her neural functioning making her change her mind. So, here we have a case where someone acts of their own free will, but they couldn't have done otherwise. Thus, says Frankfurt, free will does not require a capacity to do otherwise. If he's right about this, then there's a serious problem with Harris's argument that free will is an illusion.

Must Causally Undetermined Acts Be Out of Our Control?

Besides the compatibilist response to Harris, there is also a libertarian one. ('Libertarian' here is a special term unconnected with the word's political associations.) Libertarians believe that we have free will and that free will is incompatible with universal causal determinism. As such, libertarians believe that if we have free will, then at least some of our free willed actions must be causally undetermined actions.

As we've seen, Harris believes there's no good reason to think that human beings engage in causally undetermined actions. He also thinks that if we did engage in undetermined actions these would just be random happenings over which we'd lack control; thus, they would not be free actions. Regarding Harris's first point, there are scientists and philosophers who believe that the evidence leaves it an open question as to whether any human actions are causally undetermined. Regarding this, see Balaguer (*Free Will*), Brembs ("Towards a Scientific Concept"), Heisenberg ("The Origin of Freedom"), Koch ("Free Will"), Steward ("Libertarianism") and others. Furthermore, it is not obvious that undetermined acts cannot be free acts over which we have control.

One of the most famous contemporary defenders of libertarian free will, Robert Kane, argues that causally undetermined actions can be under our control. He has us imagine that an assassin is trying to shoot the prime minister of his country. As he is taking aim and pulling the trigger, it is causally undetermined as to whether he will have a nervous twitch and miss his target. Now suppose the twitch does not occur, and the assassin succeeds at killing his target. If so, he will have succeeded at what he was trying to do. Thus, he will rightly be seen as responsible for this, even if his killing of the prime minister was causally undetermined. If he were caught and blamed for the shooting and he claimed, 'I'm not responsible for the killing, I might have missed due to a nervous twitch', no one would reasonably take this to be an adequate excuse. Thus, says Kane, we *can* be responsible for undetermined actions (*The Significence of Free Will* and other writings).

Harris may feel this case is problematic. He may say the assassin's mind is already made up; he has already decided to shoot the prime minister. Thus, of course, he's responsible for killing the prime minister, at least in the sense that *he* did it. But suppose that the causal indeterminacy occurs in his making the decision to kill the prime minister. If the indeterminacy occurs in his mind as he is deciding what to do, then it's no longer clear that he is responsible for his choice. And if he's not responsible for this, then he cannot be responsible for its result: the act of shooting the prime minister.

However, Kane argues that even if there is indeterminacy which occurs during the deliberation that leads up to the choice, a person can still be responsible for his choice. Suppose that before making the decision to shoot, the assassin thinks this a highly risky mission and he's not sure he's being paid enough to make the risk worthwhile. Thus, he is torn whether to commit the assassination or to pack up and go home. According to Kane, in moments like this, when we are torn between alternative courses of action, it may well be the case that we make the effort to choose each of the things we are considering. On this view, as he deliberates, the assassin might be simultaneously trying to choose to commit the assassination and trying to choose to pack up and go home. In this situation, even if his decision is causally undetermined, whichever choice he makes will be something he was trying to do.

In the original example, the assassin is seen as responsible because he succeeded at what he was trying to do—shoot the prime minister. Well, so too if in deliberating between doing two things A or B you are trying to choose A and trying to choose B, then whichever choice you make you will have succeeded at something you were trying to do. Thus, you will be responsible for your choice whether you choose A or B. Therefore, says Kane, we can be responsible for what we choose to do, even if there is causal indeterminism involved in the deliberative process leading up to the choice.

Kane's view is highly controversial, and it has been the subject of much discussion in the philosophical literature. Further, it is not the only approach to defending libertarian free will. But the point here has been to show that, despite Harris's argument to the contrary, it is not so obvious that causally undetermined actions cannot be free-willed acts for which we are responsible.

The Moral of the Story

Do your homework before accepting Harris's arguments. While he may be right that we lack the kind of free will that makes us responsible for our actions, the issues are more complex than he lets on. A lot of work has been done by philosophers and others which suggests that Harris is mistaken. So, before you accept his arguments, you should look into matters further. Indeed, maybe Harris should do so as well.

References

Balaguer, Mark. 2010. *Free Will as an Open Scientific Problem*. MIT Press.

Brembs, B. 2011. Towards a Scientific Concept of Free Will as a Biological Trait. *Proceedings of the Royal Society: Biological Sciences* 278.

Dennett, Daniel. 1984a. *Elbow Room: The Varieties of Free Will Worth Wanting*. MIT Press.

———. 1984b. I Could Not Have Done Otherwise—So What? *The Journal of Philosophy* 81.

———. 2003. *Freedom Evolves*. Viking.

Frankfurt, Harry G. 1969. Alternate Possibilities and Moral Responsibility. *The Journal of Philosophy* 66.

———. 1971. Freedom of the Will and the Concept of a Person. *The Journal of Philosophy* 68.

Harris, Sam. 2012. *Free Will*. Free Press.

Heisenberg, M. 2013. The Origin of Freedom in Animal Behavior. In A. Suarez and P. Adams, eds. *Is Science Compatible with Free Will?* Springer.

Kane, R. 1996. *The Significance of Free Will*. Oxford University Press.

———. 2002. Some Neglected Pathways in the Free Will
Labyrinth. In R. Kane, ed. *The Oxford Handbook of Free Will*.
Oxford University Press.

———. 2007. Libertarianism. In Fischer, Kane, Pereboom, and
Vargas, eds. *Four Views on Free Will*. Blackwell.

———. 2011. Rethinking Free Will: New Perspectives on an
Ancient Problem. In R. Kane, ed. *The Oxford Handbook of
Free Will*. Oxford University Press.

Koch, C. 2009. Free Will, Physics, Biology, and the Brain. In
Murphy, Ellis, and O'Connor, eds. *Downward Causation and
the Neurobiology of Free Will*. Springer.

Steward, H. 2016. Libertarianism as a Naturalistic Position. In
Timpe and Speak, eds. *Free Will and Theism: Connections,
Contingencies, and Concerns*. Oxford University Press.

[14]
Let's Talk about Free Will!

Megan Drury

Free will! Did I choose to start the chapter that way? Was I determined by God? Is it simply the case that various chains of events led me to this point through cause and effect?

Sam Harris might say I was caused to do so, that I am aware of the words I write but I do not freely choose them. That I cannot *really* take credit for the finished article, any more than I can be blamed if I don't finish it. But let me reel all this back in so that we might get to a sensible starting point: *What is free will anyway?*

Setting the Scene

We can imagine the history of the free will debate as a Western shoot-out. The main conflict erupting between The Hard Determinists and The Libertarians. We call this fight 'The Incompatibilist Debate' because both The Hard Determinists and The Libertarians declare: *"This town ain't big enough for the two of us."*

Approaching one another at high noon, The Hard Determinist says:

> Look pal, we are moved and shaped by various sequences of cause and effect that have been going on since long before you or I were born.

The Libertarian, standing her ground, says:

> That might be true, but I do not have to be constrained by those sequences. As a human being, I have the ability to make choices, think or feel in ways that do not depend on them.

The incompatibilist conflict often reaches this kind of stalemate. A standoff between two positions that are so committed to their views that a debate rarely achieves much by way of coming to an agreement. So, what happens when we reach this kind of impasse? We call in the sheriff to settle the dispute: *Enter the compatibilists.*

The compatibilists appear on the scene almost as a peacekeeper, conceding certain facts to both sides. They argue that the town, is in fact, big enough for both determinism and free will, for both hard determinism and free will can be true. Whilst our choices and actions *are* constrained by various causes and chains of events, we still have *some degree* of freedom wherein we might act, behave, think, or feel one way or another despite still being caused to do so. Whilst we are caused at every moment of our lives by prior causes, we are still free insofar as some of these causes might be our desires, thoughts or actions rather than external conditions or necessities.

In some situations, our actions will be constrained—for instance, if I wish to make coffee in the morning but have only tea in the cupboard, then I am not free to make coffee because certain causes have precluded making coffee as an action I can undertake. In other situations, I am free to do as I wish within reason. I am free to stop and stroke a cat on my way to the shops or not, passing it by, shoo it away even. I cannot, however, will a cat to appear on my way.

So, this is an—incredibly brief—overview of the type of argument that philosophers and non-philosophers have gotten themselves into over the centuries. A reason for the debate's continued significance is that what someone thinks of free will might influence their views on other social issues. For example, it's often said that having freedom to have acted otherwise in the past is a legitimate reason to punish wrong-doers. Harris suggests in the first pages of *Free Will* that whether we ought to hold individuals morally responsible depends on whether we have free will or not.

The thought about Sam Harris puts us back on track . . .

Sam Harris—Daring Renegade or Sneaky Compatibilist?

It is my assumption that if you are reading this chapter, it's because you are looking to find out more about Harris's perspective on free will: What his arguments are, and where we might put him in our 'free will western shoot out'. Is he the clear-sighted renegade he portrays himself to be in *Free Will*? Or is he perhaps walking well-worn paths of the centuries old debate in rather mundane ways?

In trying to give an answer to this question I find myself having to agree with Daniel Dennett—Harris's dear friend (and critic) who you might have met within the pages of *Free Will*. Dennett claims that Harris is a compatibilist in all but name.

Throughout *Free Will*, Harris tries to distance himself from compatibilism arguing that it fails to disprove the popular conception of free will, without realizing that compatibilism's *whole purpose* is to point out that the so-called popular conception is, in fact, flawed. Compatibilism retains freedom *in a sense* whilst rejecting the *floating-over-the-brain type of freedom* that Harris accuses all of us being enslaved by.

The type of freedom retained by some compatibilists is, arguably, the same type of freedom Harris seems to sneak into his account. On several occasions, Harris argues that his view does not reduce us to bits-and-pieces that simply follow the function that scientific laws have observed on the smallest level. Breaking away from his neuro-chemical determinism in this way, Harris suggests that the conscious mind *is able to choose and intervene*, being consciously aware of my experiences, I identify a particular problem (say, irritability), attribute it to a cause (low blood pressure), and then manufacture a solution (eat a bag of chips).

There is freedom here, despite Harris's attempts to claim that this is not freedom *simply because it is not the type of absolute freedom argued by libertarians*. Indeed, when we have felt irritable before, it is possible that we may not have connected the dots. The consciousness learns and is free to adapt or not to the experiences that it has. It is true we are not free to simply stop the low pressure, nor are we free to simply correct the problem that causes it, but we are free to piece together different causes and intervene in the various chains such that we arrive at the effect that we want (by, for example, eating potato chips and raising our blood pressure). This freedom to reason and arrive at conclusions about our bodily states is something that certain compatibilists, those who affirm both hard determinism and free will, can agree to. Though the behavior is *caused*, the type of cause (such as our desires or beliefs) might be thought to be freer than others, though not less determined. The precise debate around *which* causes are indicative of the truth of freedom as well as the truth of hard determinism, however, is broad and ongoing.

For our purposes then, we shall call Harris a compatibilist. He may not like it, but that's not because he disagrees with what compatibilism has to say (clearly, or else he would have a different theory of free will). No, rather Harris's denial of both libertarianism and compatibilism stems from his distrust of free will because of the role it has played in religion and religious society. Harris sees free will and its entailment of moral responsibility as hangovers from a religious order that ought to be replaced with notions founded on science. Harris seems to ignore the fact that certain religious doctrines, such as Calvinist Christianity or some strands of Muslim theology *actually affirm hard determinism*. His resistance to compatibilism, then, is a fear that if he affirms that we do have some freedom, he must concede that religion was *not totally wrong* when it came to free will and moral responsibility. But more on that later.

Something Called Epistemic Integrity . . .

The term 'epistemic' simply means 'having to do with knowledge'. Epistemic integrity means being vigilant about what we call knowledge (as opposed beliefs or desires), and because this produces caution and scrupulousness when we think about what we know, it is an epistemic virtue. It prevents misinformation being construed as information, so it is something that we ought to want.

Epistemic integrity of this sort is a key tenet of modern science. In fact, we might broadly say that epistemic integrity is a combination of the following statements:

1. **We ought to revise our beliefs/hypotheses when evidence challenges what we think we know.**

2. **We ought to do due diligence to the counterevidence during this process of revision.**

Why am I bringing this up? Well, this is the kind of work that Harris sees himself as undertaking in Free Will. The flow of ideas follows something like this:

1. **He points out that free will as a concept has long divided opinion, and that the currently reigning view of free will is of the conscious self as the author of our actions.**

2. **He then raises a set of data produced by scientific experiments that appear to shed new light on the question of free will.**

3. **He claims that if we are to be responsible with our worldviews, then we ought to take this new evidence seriously.**

4. **He perceives himself to have contributed something new and daring to the argument against free will, based on this epistemically rigorous endeavour.**

Let's break down each of these points in turn so that we might place Harris's work in a broader critical context:

Monkeys with Typewriters: Do We Author Our Thoughts?

The Popular Conception:

1. **Each of us could have behaved differently in the past, and**

2. **We are the conscious source of our actions in the present.**

Harris centers his argument around a very particular conception of free will (the 'Popular Conception'). He claims at various points in the text that this conception is not only a. popular and widespread, but also b. something that people cling to dearly.

This view of free will is, in fact, counter to Harris's claims, rather unpopular. As Dennett explains in his response to

Free Will, an emerging branch of philosophy focuses on using surveys, questionnaires, and other ways for clarifying these sorts of generalizing claims. Surveys conducted regarding the Libertarian-Determinist-Compatibilist debate on free will demonstrated that 60 to 80 percent of subjects agree with the compatibilist view. The 'popular' conception, being a form of free will Libertarianism, is not as popular as Harris might have hoped (given that it allows him an easy target at which to aim his critique). Given that a majority of people do not agree with free-will incompatibilism, it is not something to which many of us are hanging on to—it is not, as Harris claims, a cherished illusion.

'Pause for Thought' or 'Paws Off'?

To challenge free will, or an outdated conception of free will, Harris turns to some interesting work done in the field of neuroscience. It is fascinating, of course, to learn that there have been experiments demonstrating that our brain's movement center lights up milliseconds before we make the decision to move. Perhaps even more interesting are the follow-up experiments showing a seven to ten second lag between our perception of stimuli and decision-making and our conscious awareness of our decision. It has been noted by some scholars and theorists, however, that the conditions under which these experiments were conducted are scientifically questionable, and therefore that the results themselves must also be doubted. Other theorists have challenged the purported relevance of the phenomenon these experiments examine (called 'readiness potential'), pointing out that a *causal* role is assumed rather than argued for: though we might be able to say it occurs, we cannot say why this occurs or what its purpose is. Therefore, we have good reason to be suspicious of these studies and perhaps to discount them based on this alone. But given that Harris, in *Free Will* references them as a core part of his 'scientific' argument against free will, let us assume *for the sake of argument* that they are true.

The evidence is important for further considerations about free will insofar as the findings challenge the idea that the conscious mind is the sole origin of our decisions, behaviors, and choices. However, as mentioned, any theory of free will serious about bringing any new developments to the conversation would already be aware that consciousness does not equal authorship. *Briefly put, the evidence supplied by Harris is affirmative of what a lot of free will theorists have had cause to think—it is not in itself transformative of our approaches to it.*

A Leap of Faith or a Badly Timed Jump?

Harris hopes we will make a leap from 'the conscious mind does not author our actions or choices' to 'therefore, we do not have free will.' This is too quick of a move. A crucial part of practicing epistemic integrity is exploring different interpretations of the evidence. This means giving some credit even to those explanations that do not match up with what we initially believe.

In discussing explanations for the evidence, Harris does not consider many alternative perspectives. Nor does he offer good reasons to dismiss those he does discuss. For instance, Harris argues that we cannot refer to the different levels of the mind (conscious, subconscious, and unconscious) to explain why we do things we are not consciously aware of until after the fact. His reasoning is that the evidence puts our everyday thoughts and actions onto the same level as the beating of hearts: neither beating your heart nor thinking your thoughts require conscious awareness. It is because of this fact that Harris claims we cannot have free will, since to have free will (according to the 'popular conception' of free will) requires us to be *the conscious author* of our thoughts and actions. Since we are not the *conscious* author, our thoughts and actions cannot be free. We are as free to think and act as we are free to beat our heart.

However, this argument is incomplete. Harris does not explain why taking actions away from the consciousness entails that these actions are not free. Why make consciousness a condition for free will? Harris's discussion hinges upon a conception of free will that most people disagree with, and to argue against that position, Harris rejects the tendency for us to identify with the 'voice in our head': the consciousness that says "I." Suggesting that this self is an illusion, Harris argues that there is no part of our being that we might be held responsible for since there is no self *proper* that can both *act* and be *held responsible*. Part of Harris's argument suggests that if we are responsible for our actions and we allow that we could be responsible for our hearts beating, there is no sense in which the *e. coli* in our gut is 'us' in the same way that the heart and mind are 'us.' The questions "What is me?" and "What am I responsible for?" become difficult and vague to answer. But these questions arise only when our concept of free will includes *consciousness* as a condition. Why does Harris do this?

On the one hand, if Harris claims free will depends on consciousness, and his argument then tackles the idea of consciousness as producing our actions and thoughts, then in effect he has quite the knock-down argument against free will itself. On the other hand, arguing against the idea of a consciousness without giving adequate attention to the other various explanations in terms of relocating the 'site' of free will outside of the traditional view of the conscious mind as 'The Author' significantly weakens the force of Harris's argument.

So, in spite of Harris's attempt to dispel a rampant illusory notion of free will, it appears that his project in *Free Will* is directed at constructing a false idea of what most people think free will means and giving more weight to the idea of the conscious mind than it deserves. In doing this, Harris presents an interpretation of the evidence that, *at first glance*, appears to counter the notion of free will and the importance of the conscious mind. However, as shown, the practice of epistemic integrity is, at most, superficial in *Free Will*. Harris's arguments to support his interpretation are loose and unconvincing, partly due to their vulnerability to criticisms such as Daniel Dennett's, and partly due to his failure to explore possible alternatives.

We can, however, keep some of Harris's main ideas about free will without relying on 1. his view of human beings as biochemical puppets and 2. his opposition to religion concealed in his view of what most people take free will to be. All we need to do is tackle this idea of the conscious mind and its relation to the subconscious and unconscious.

Where Is My Mind?

If it were true that the 'popular conception of free will' was widely held, then to point to the evidence at hand and declare that free will is illusory is to make too large of a leap to a conclusion. In his response to *Free Will*, Dennett makes the following argument: When Copernicus recognized that the Earth is not the center of the cosmos, and that the sun remains relatively fixed, we did not declare that the sun was false or illusory. Just because our idea of the sun as *'that which goes round us, rising and setting moving across the sky'* was demonstrated to be incorrect, we did not abandon the concept of the sun altogether. Through careful investigation we altered our understanding of the sun to become *'that relatively fixed star around which the Earth orbits'*. We did not declare that sunsets are false illusions because the sun does not go up and down. We shifted our perspective. It is this kind of change in perspective that is needed to understand free will: First, because free will is not what we expected, it does not mean we do not have it, and second, because our consciousness is not quite what we expected, it does not mean we ought to discount alternative ways of thinking about our experiences of thought, action, and freedom. We do not call the sun an illusion because we adjusted our understanding, so we should not call free will an illusion simply because we need to think a bit harder about the topic.

In 1886, the German philosopher Friedrich Nietzsche wrote of consciousness that it developed only because of the need for human communication. That is, the reason we have the 'voice in our heads' type of consciousness Harris argues against is because human beings have needed to communicate with each other for centuries. To communicate, you must first understand your own actions, behaviors, and thoughts. This part of consciousness, your thoughts and desires, is only the slimmest and most refined part of your 'inner' mental life. It is conceivable that you could think, feel, and act without this conscious-awareness—in fact, this is what the neuroscientific evidence shows: there are processes we under- take before we consciously know what is being undertaken. This, however, makes it no less *us*. Harris's standard response, that the 'I,' 'me,' and our brain are in some sense detached from one another simply does not hold up to this reasoning: The I is a self-reflective record of what we have already been thinking and doing: we have in effect chosen an outfit and only looked in the mirror afterwards. The conscious form of selfhood Harris wants to make central to his opponent's argument might be said, then, to be at most a reflection of who and what we are—a double or mirror-image rather than a hard-copy.

The reason I bring this up is that as well as offering an alternative take on how we can explain what the evidence demonstrates, it can also offer some clarity to the confused manner in which Harris seems to flit between biochemical determinism and the idea that we can exert some influence over our biochemical 'strings'. Understanding consciousness as something that is reactive—as something produced in response to our thoughts, feelings, inclinations, actions, and decisions—means that we can better understand what kinds of actions or interventions we can exert on our choices. In the same way we look in the mirror to adjust our appearance, our consciousness functions as a way to check our thoughts, feelings, and actions in such a way that can promote social living. It is consciousness-as-a-reflection that means we can experience 'second thoughts' and changing our minds. When we fail to pay heed to our conscious thoughts, we might behave in ways we think of as 'out of character.' The reflective consciousness can function as a way of managing our ideas of morality—one of the crucial issues Harris points to throughout his book *Free Will*.

Thinking about conscious awareness as a reflection, something that comes about because of our actions, thoughts, and feelings, rather than as something that generates them allows us to explain the ways we often talk about our behavior. Although we sometimes do not know why we do the things we do (for example, in the case of trauma responses), this does not count against this view. Not consciously knowing *why* you do something is not the same as *not being in charge of the action*.

Where Is the Freedom in That?

Thinking about consciousness in this way: understanding it not as the origin of our thoughts and actions, but as a means of communicating our thoughts and actions to ourselves, produces the kind of shift that is needed to make sense of the neuroscientific evidence and free will compatibilism. Moreover, this view preserves the kind of moral responsibility that Harris is desperate to reconcile with determinism. If he were to commit wholeheartedly to the hard determinist picture, there would be no grounds from which we could punish a murderer nor praise hard work (beyond doing so as a mere performance of morality). The very reason Harris pulls away from the determinist picture is because a sense of genuine moral responsibility gives meaning to our actions. Harris's attempt at bringing moral responsibility and a vaguely determinist (read: compatibilist) account of free will together finds its expression in Harris's reference to the *color of our minds* or *our overall character*.

Appealing to everyday language, Harris points out that we often excuse people's behavior if they are acting out of the ordinary, if they are beside themselves, if they do not know what came over them. If what we do is at odds with our track record, then we cannot be responsible for our actions. There's something else at play: a mitigating factor of sorts. If our actions are harmful or dangerous, and our overall character is indicative of bloodlust, or sociopathic rage, then we might very well suggest that we're responsible for our actions because they are in keeping with our general personality or personhood. Harris entertains the concept of moral responsibility by suggesting that moral responsibility does not depend on the ideas of cause and effect, but instead on whether what we do is aligned in any meaningful sense with who, or what kind of person, we are.

The kind of shift in perspective regarding what we think about the role of consciousness does not contradict Harris's thinking about moral responsibility, which is a key point throughout *Free Will*, given that a discussion of heinous murders sets the scene in its first chapter. By the overall content and character of our mind, and our actions being consistent with the kind of people we are, we might understand Harris to be gesturing—however vaguely—at the idea that *all of our actions are our own, and are all to a degree an effect of various causes,* but also that *our consciousness allows us to review and consider the actions we are doing, such that we might intervene or 'stand aside'*. The things that we make moral judgements about are not the *actions* we deliberate on, but our *conscious response* to those actions.

By understanding the target of moral judgements to be our attitudes towards our actions, produced by conscious reflection rather than the actions themselves, that which we judge to be morally good or bad is not the chain of cause and effect. Therefore, this way of thinking about free will is compatible Harris's view of moral responsibility. Crucially, however, we arrive at a conclusion similar to Harris's without making remarks about the role of religion in society as the origin of guilt and shame. Harris has a reliable history of condemning religion and faith as being a negative black hole in our society.

As I have suggested throughout this chapter, a key motivating factor for Harris writing *Free Will* was not to engage critically with the concept of freedom but to challenge a perceived core tenet of world religions. However, we can affirm a compatibilist account of free will that explains the neuroscientific evidence, which follows Harris's conclusions about moral responsibility, whilst remaining uncommitted to any claims in favor of or against religion. Perhaps with a greater degree of epistemic integrity and critical thinking Harris might have left his opinions about religion at the door whilst he discussed free will, but here we return to an initial claim of mine: that Harris's *Free Will* begs the question by affirming at the start what he wanted to conclude, that religion can have no place in a sensible scientific society. And to this I echo Harris himself: *"Where is the freedom in that?"*[1]

References

Balaguer, Mark. 2014. *Free Will*. Cambridge: MIT Press.
Banks, William P., and Eve A. Isham. 2009. We Infer Rather than Perceive the Moment We Decided to Act. *Psychological Science* 20:1. doi:10.1111/j.1467-9280.2008.02254.x.

---

[1] I would like to thank Dr Jon Robson for his support, his input, and our conversations during the writing and development of this chapter.

Dennett, Daniel C. 2017. Reflections On Sam Harris's *Free Will*. *Rivista Internazionale di Filosofia e Psicologia* 8:3. doi:10.4453/rifp.2017.0018.

Harris, Sam. 2012. *Free Will*. Free Press.

Haynes, John-Dylan. 2011. Decoding and Predicting Intentions. *Annals Of the New York Academy of Sciences* 1224:1. doi:10.1111/j.1749-6632.2011.05994.x.

Libet, Benjamin, Curtis A. Gleason, Elwood W. Wright, and Dennis K. Pearl. 1983. Time of Conscious Intention to Act in Relation to Onset of Cerebral Activity (Readiness-Potential). *Brain* 106:3. doi:10.1093/brain/106.3.623.

Nietzsche, Friedrich, 2006. The Gay Science, Book V. In K. Pearson and D. Large, eds. *The Nietzsche Reader*. Wiley.

Taylor, Stephen. 2019. How a Flawed Experiment 'Proved' that Free Will Doesn't Exist. *Scientific American* blog. <https://blogs.scientificamerican.com/observations/how-a-flawed-experiment-proved-that-free-will-doesnt-exist>.

Part VI

Beyond
the Physical
Cosmos

[15]
Another Thing in This Universe that Cannot Be an Illusion

Maaneli Derakhshani

One of the central claims of Sam Harris's 2014 book, *Waking Up: A Guide to Spirituality Without Religion*, is that "Consciousness is the one thing in this universe that cannot be an illusion" (pp. 51–79). I can think of another: our ability to reason. I just cannot fathom how Harris, a proponent of reason, couldn't think of it! To see why, we must first understand Harris's claim about consciousness.

The Undoubtability of Consciousness

What is "consciousness"? It's a notoriously slippery thing to define and there is no universally accepted definition among philosophers and scientists, but Harris adopts the one famously provided by philosopher Thomas Nagel, in his 1974 essay, "What Is It Like to Be a Bat?"—"an organism is conscious 'if and only if there is something that it is like to *be* that organism—something that it is like *for* the organism'" (p. 51). To flesh this out, Nagel says to imagine trading places with a bat and being left with an array of (perhaps indescribable) experiences in the form of sensations, perceptions, and feelings. That array of experiences, whatever it's like, is what consciousness is for a bat. In Harris's words, "Nagel's point is that whatever else consciousness may or may not entail in physical terms, the difference between it and unconsciousness is a matter of subjective experience. Either the lights are on, or they are not" (p. 52).

To further illustrate the difference, Harris contrasts your experience of what you are with what our growing scientific picture of reality says that you are:

> At this moment, you might be vividly aware of reading this book, but you are completely unaware of the electrochemical events occurring at each of the trillions of synapses in your brain. However much you may know about physics, chemistry, and biology, you live elsewhere. As a matter of your experience, you are not a body of atoms, molecules, and cells; you are consciousness and its ever-changing contents, passing through various stages of wakefulness and sleep, from cradle to grave. (p. 52)

And

> Consciousness—the sheer fact that this universe is illuminated by sentience—is precisely what unconsciousness is not. And I believe that no description of unconscious complexity will fully account for it. To simply assert that consciousness arose at some point in the evolution of life, and that it results from a specific arrangement of neurons firing in concert within an individual brain, doesn't give us any inkling of *how* it could emerge from unconscious processes, even in principle. (p. 56)

So consciousness is a subjective-experiential phenomenon, and as such it cannot be completely described in the material terms of our scientific picture of reality—as nothing but atoms, molecules, and cells in the pattern of a body and brain over time—because what we know consciousness to be from the 'inside', from *having* it, is clearly not that.

What could it mean then for consciousness to be an "illusion"? Well, we normally regard something—say an object of visual perception—as an illusion if your perception of it is somehow a misinterpretation of its actual nature; if the way it *seems* to be to you is different from the way it actually is. So, in the case of consciousness, we might say it is an illusion if your perception of it is a misinterpretation of its actual nature; if the way that consciousness *seems* to be to you is different from what it actually is. For example, maybe your consciousness really just *is* atoms, molecules, and cells in the pattern of your body and brain over time, and it only *seems* to you that there is 'something that it is like to be your brain and body'.

But hold the phone: How can consciousness 'seem' to be like something that it's not, without the 'seeming' being an instance of consciousness (of subjective experience) itself? An advocate for illusionism about consciousness might respond that the 'seeming' is an illusion, too. But then this leads to an infinite regress—he would have to say that 'It only *seems* to seem to you that consciousness is this subjective-experiential thing that it's like to *be* your body and brain', which raises the original question again and again ad infinitum. As Harris correctly says,

> To say that consciousness may only seem to exist, from the inside, is to admit its existence in full—for if things seem any way at all, that is consciousness. Even if I happen to be a brain in a vat at this moment—and all my memories are false, and all my perceptions are of a world that does not exist—the fact that I am having an experience is indisputable (to me, at least). This is all that is required for me (or any other sentient being) to fully establish the reality of consciousness. (pp. 53–54)

Harris then finishes this paragraph with the claim that we opened with: "Consciousness is the one thing in this universe that cannot be an illusion."

The Undoubtability of Reason Too

To say that consciousness is "the one thing" in this universe that cannot be an illusion is indistinguishable from saying that it is *the only thing* in this universe that cannot be an illusion. Which is to say that, except for consciousness, *everything else* in this universe could be an illusion.

Balderdash. In addition to consciousness, humans (and presumably some other animals) have a faculty of *reason*. We all have some intuitive sense of what reason is, but what is it in general terms? Harris's preferred philosopher for defining consciousness, Thomas Nagel, explains in his 1997 book, *The Last Word*: "The idea of reason ... refers to nonlocal and nonrelative methods of justification—methods that distinguish universally legitimate from illegitimate inferences and that aim at reaching the truth in a nonrelative sense" (*The Last Word*, p. 5).

Reason cannot be an illusion, either. To see why, let's consider a prime example of reason: rules of logic.

A basic rule of logic that we can all grasp is: 'If P then Q' plus 'P' implies 'Q', where 'P' and 'Q' are one among an infinitude of possible statements about the world. We also grasp that this rule of logic—fancily called 'Modus Ponens' by philosophers—cannot fail to be valid under any circumstance. By 'valid' I mean that it is impossible for the premises—'If P then Q' and 'P'—to be true and the conclusion— 'Q'—to nevertheless be false; it is impossible that 'If P then Q' plus 'P' implies '*not*-Q'. So we grasp that the rule of logic is valid always, everywhere, and for everyone—it is *universally* valid. At least, as long as we understand the meanings of the words 'plus', 'if', 'then', and 'implies' in their normal senses.

Imagine now that some radical skeptic comes along and argues:

> Maybe the rule of logic—'If P then Q' plus 'P' implies 'Q'—only *seems* universally valid to you, but it really isn't. It might only seem that way to you because something you are unaware of—an evil demon scrambling your brains, or invisible aliens beaming thoughts into your head, or God divinely planting beliefs into your mind, or some genetic mutation in one of your ancestors millions of years ago—is deluding you into thinking it's universally valid. You can't rule out this possibility, so you can't be sure that that rule of logic, which seems universally valid to you, really is universally valid.

This is tantamount to suggesting that the universal validity of the rule of logic might be an illusion. But this makes no sense, for a couple of reasons.

First, the argument of the radical skeptic gives us no *positive understanding* of how the rule of logic, whose invalidity we cannot imagine, might after all fail to be valid. When we look back at the rule of logic, after listening to the skeptic's argument, we still cannot help but think that it is universally valid. This is unlike, say, the skeptical hypothesis that you are a brain-in-a-vat and an evil scientist is manipulating your brain to create false beliefs, such as believing that you have hands—here you *do* get a positive understanding of how your belief that you have hands, which is hard for you to imagine the falsity of, could be false after all.

226

Second, the radical skeptic's argument actually has the form of the rule of logic that it is trying to cast doubt upon. In other words it *presupposes* the universal validity of the rule of logic. The argument asserts, 'If you can't rule out the possibility that something you are unaware of is deluding you into thinking that the rule of logic is universally valid, then you can't be sure that the rule of logic, which seems universally valid to you, really is universally valid.' Call this 'If P then Q'. It also says that 'You can't rule out the possibility that something you are unaware of is deluding you into thinking that the rule of logic is universally valid'. Call this 'P'. So the argument has the form, 'If P then Q' plus 'P' implies 'Q'. If the radical skeptic's argument were valid, it would apply to itself and therefore refute itself. And if the argument is not valid, then it doesn't establish the possibility that the rule of logic is an illusion.

So the universal validity of the rule of logic, 'If P then Q' plus 'P' implies 'Q', cannot be an illusion.

Of course, reason is not restricted to a single rule of logic. Reason is a collection of rules of inference that have universal validity; or as Nagel puts it, "nonlocal and nonrelative methods of justification." Is there a more general way to see, independent of any particular rule of logic, that reason cannot be an illusion?

In *The Last Word*, Nagel provides exactly such an argument. He asks us to first consider an argument from a radical skeptic:

> If my brains are being scrambled [by an evil demon], I can't rely on *any* of my thoughts, including basic logical thoughts whose invalidity is so inconceivable to me that they seem to rule out anything, including scrambled brains, which would imply their invalidity—for the reply would always be, 'Maybe that's just your scrambled brains talking.' Therefore I can't safely accord objective validity to *any* hierarchy among my thoughts. (*The Last Word*, p. 62)

Of this Nagel says,

> But it is not possible to argue this way, because it is an instance of the sort of argument it purports to undermine. The argument proposes a possibility, purports to show that it cannot be ruled out, and draws conclusions from this. To do these things is to rely on

judgments of what is and is not conceivable. There just isn't room for skepticism about basic logic, because there is no place to stand where we can formulate or think it without immediately contradicting ourselves by relying on it. (p. 62)

Although Nagel couches the radical skeptic's argument in terms of a specific skeptical hypothesis—an evil demon scrambling his brains—it's easy to see that Nagel's response doesn't depend on that specific skeptical hypothesis. Just replace it with some unspecified skeptical hypothesis, X (which could be invisible aliens, God, natural selection, and so on). Then the radical skeptic's argument generalizes to,

If X, I can't rely on *any* of my thoughts, including basic logical thoughts whose invalidity is so inconceivable to me that they seem to rule out anything, including X, which would imply their invalidity—for the reply would always be, 'Maybe that's just X talking.' Therefore I can't safely accord objective validity to *any* hierarchy among my thoughts.

And Nagel's rebuttal stays exactly the same.

So, reason cannot be an illusion, even in principle.

What Say You, Dr. Harris?

Perhaps, though, Harris views reason as *derivative* from consciousness? He never says this in *Waking Up* (nor anywhere else, as far as I'm aware). On the contrary, one passage in the book indicates that he sees reason as fundamentally distinct from consciousness, and non-mysterious in a way that consciousness is not:

We know, of course, that human *minds* are the product of human brains. There is simply no question that your ability to decode and understand this sentence depends upon neurophysiological events taking place inside your head at this moment. But most of this mental work occurs entirely in the dark, and it is a mystery why any part of the process should be attended by consciousness. Nothing about a brain, when surveyed as a physical system, suggests that it is a locus of experience. (*Waking Up*, pp. 55–56)

Reason is implied in "your ability to decode and understand this sentence," because your ability to decode and understand a sentence depends on using reason (making logical inferences). And, as Harris says, he thinks that this depends on neurophysiological events happing in your head, where "most of this mental work occurs entirely in the dark." That is, *without* the accompaniment of conscious experience.

Harris: Blind as Nagel's Bat!

There is no doubt that your capacity to reason depends, at least in part, upon the neurophysiological events taking place inside your head. If taken too far, however, this can amount to claiming that reason is an illusion. That is the case if what Harris really means is that

    a. Human minds are *entirely* the product of human brains (and other relevant physical events, such as light bouncing off objects and impinging on your retina);

    b. Your ability to decode and understand this sentence 'depends' upon neurophysiological events taking place inside your head, because your ability to decode and understand this sentence is *nothing but* the neurophysiological events taking place inside your head (along with other relevant physical events).

It's not completely clear that Harris means these things—he never says precisely what he means by "product of human brains" and "depends upon neurophysiological events." But a. and b. do seem to be the most straightforward interpretations of his comments. He gives no indication that he thinks human minds are produced (even in part) by anything other than human brains, nor any indication that he thinks that your ability to decode and understand a sentence depends (in part) on anything other than neurophysiological events in your head. So let's see why a. and b. amount to saying that reason is an illusion.

If a. and b. are true then reason's universal validity *derives* from a purely physical process of biological evolution over millions of years. That's because human brains, and the neurophysiological events occurring in them, gradually evolved into their current form over millions of years, through a sequence of genetic mutations and environmental natural selection.

But this idea doesn't work. Nagel explains it best in his latest book, *Mind and Cosmos: Why the Materialist Neo-Darwinian Conception of Nature Is Almost Certainly False*. He gives a general argument against the hypothesis that reason's universal validity derives from its having evolutionary-biological survival value:

> in a case of reasoning, if it is basic enough, the only thing to think is that I have grasped the truth directly. I cannot pull back from a logical inference and reconfirm it with the reflection that the reliability of my logical thought processes is consistent with the hypothesis that evolution has selected them for accuracy. That would drastically weaken the logical claim. (*Mind and Cosmos*, p. 80)

Why would it "drastically weaken" the logical claim? A rule of inference, on evolutionary theory, would (for example) have to genetically mutate into existence and then be naturally selected for because it conferred a survival advantage to an organism in its environment, not because it is *universally* valid. Natural selection only selects those mutations that confer survival advantages to organisms in their environment, nothing more. There is no reason, on evolutionary theory, why any mutation that has survival value for an organism in one environment would have survival value for that organism everywhere and at all times; nor why a mutation that has survival value for one organism should necessarily have survival value for another organism.

Moreover, saying that the rule, 'If P then Q' plus 'P' implies 'Q', is a valid form of inference *because* it confers survival advantage to an organism in its environment, is saying that the rule has local and relative validity, whereas the rule *itself* is a nonlocal and nonrelative (hence universal) statement: What it says doesn't depend on whether or not it has survival value to any organisms in any environment, nor does it depend on when it mutated into existence. So saying that a logical inference is valid *because* it confers survival advantage to an organism in its environment, is another way of saying that the logical inference is *not* universally valid; or that the universally validity that it *seems* to have, is an illusion. (The same conclusion follows if we try to regard reason as an accidental side effect of natural selection, or as a product of 'genetic drift'.) Of course, as we've seen, at least one kind of logical inference *is* universally valid—it *cannot* be any other way.

Nagel continues:

> Furthermore, in the formulation of that [evolutionary] explanation . . . logical judgments of consistency and inconsistency have to occur without these [evolutionary] qualifications, as direct apprehensions of the truth. It is not possible to think, 'Reliance on my reason, including my reliance on *this very judgment*, is reasonable because it is consistent with its having an evolutionary explanation.' Therefore any evolutionary account of the place of reason presupposes reason's [universal] validity and cannot confirm it without circularity. (*Mind and Cosmos*, pp. 80–81)

In other words, any attempt to justify reason's universal validity, purely in terms of some evolutionary account, runs into the same problem as attempts to doubt reason's universal validity that we saw from *The Last Word*: The attempt to doubt reason's universal validity (with a skeptical hypothesis) presupposes its independent validity, and likewise the attempt to say that reason's universal validity derives from a purely physical process of biological evolution also presupposes its independent validity.

The problem here is analogous to Harris's point that any attempt to say that consciousness only *seems* to be a matter of subjective experience, but in actuality is just atoms/molecules/cells in the shape of a brain and body over time, still *presupposes* consciousness: "To say that consciousness may only *seem* to exist, from the inside, is to admit its existence in full—for if things seem any way at all, *that* is consciousness" (*Waking Up*, p. 53). So even though reason and consciousness are fundamentally distinct aspects of human minds, any attempt to explain what they are, in terms of some account external to them, is impossible. Any such attempt ends up presupposing them.

It follows then that the claims, "human *minds* are the product of human brains" and "your ability to decode and understand this sentence depends upon neurophysiological events taking place inside your head at this moment", are untenable if meant too strongly. And, as I have argued, the strong (hence problematic) meanings seem to be what Harris had in mind.

Waking Up to Reason

The only way to make sense of Harris's claims would be to interpret "product of" and "depends upon" weakly enough to be compatible with the fact that reason cannot be an illusion, cannot be a derivative of anything else, and exists independently of any particular mind/brain/body. Then Harris is wrong to treat the capacity of human minds to reason as non-mysterious in a way that consciousness is not. When Harris (correctly) says, "Nothing about a brain, when surveyed as a physical system, suggests that it is a locus of experience" ("The Mystery of Consciousness," p. 56), he should also say, "Nothing about a brain, when surveyed as a physical system, suggests that it has a capacity to reason." Or as Nagel puts the mystery in *The Last Word*, "The problem then will be not how, if we engage in it, reason can be valid, but how, if it is universally valid, we can engage in it" (p. 75).

Whatever the answer to this question, it will clearly have a form that "accounts for our capacity to think these things [reason] in a way that presupposes their independent validity" (p. 75). Beyond that, it's challenging to imagine what a satisfactory answer would look like. Since no description of unconscious and non-rational complexity is sufficient to account for our capacity to reason, that leaves few other options. It leaves either some theological explanation, or, as Nagel prefers (*The Last Word*, pp. 127–143; *Mind and Cosmos*), some naturalistic explanation involving biological evolution (perhaps Darwinian or some teleological variant) plus a fundamental law of nature that whenever an organism of sufficiently high neurobiological complexity develops it 'acquires' a faculty of reason and consciousness.

My own preference is Nagel's, but I cannot delve further into details here. Suffice to say these issues are extremely interesting, and surely also at the center-of-the-bull's-eye of Harris's interests.

How Doesn't He Know All This?

You may get the impression from *Waking Up* and subsequent podcasts on the issue of consciousness ("The Light of the Mind") that Harris simply isn't aware of these philosophical issues arising from reason. However, in a 2015 podcast with Tim Ferris ("Sam Harris on Daily Routines"), Harris named Nagel's *The Last Word* as one of the five books he recommends everyone should read, saying that it "champions rationality in a very compelling way." Yet, to the best of my knowledge, he has never mentioned or analyzed the issues Nagel raises concerning reason. Maybe that's because Harris doesn't agree with Nagel's take, but if so, that doesn't come across in his unqualified recommendation of *The Last Word*.

The closest Harris has come to touching on these issues, so far as I'm aware, is in recapping his first discussion with Jordan Peterson ("Speaking of 'Truth'"). There he says, "I have always said that the scientific worldview presupposes the validity of certain values—logical consistency (up to a point)" and subsequently denies Peterson's claim that "all scientific truth claims can be judged on the basis of the single (Darwinian) criterion of whether the claimants survive long enough to breed." The combination of these two views implies rejection of the claim that "logical consistency (up to a point)" can be judged "on the basis of the single (Darwinian) criterion"; but Harris doesn't say this explicitly, nor does he refer to any of Nagel's arguments.

So it's a puzzle why, in *Waking Up*, Harris overemphasizes the novelty of consciousness and downplays the novelty of human minds, insofar as human minds have a faculty of reason. And it remains puzzling why he has (apparently) never commented on the philosophical issues raised by reason, since the publication of *Waking Up*.

Wrapping Up

Consciousness cannot be an illusion, but it is *not* "the one thing" in this universe that cannot be an illusion. Reason is another thing in this universe, distinct from consciousness, that cannot be an illusion, and this has profound implications for our understanding of how human minds emerge from the unconscious and non-rational complexity of brain function. It implies that it is impossible to explain the existence and development of reason—an aspect of human minds—purely in terms of the unconscious and non-rational complexity of brain function, and it is a mystery how we are able to engage in it at all. A mystery at least as significant as the mystery of how consciousness emerges from brain function. It is also a mystery why Harris doesn't seem to recognize all this, given his level of familiarity with Nagel's work. If he ever does, he will have to become more radically antireductionist about the mind-body relation than he professes in *Waking Up* and elsewhere.[1]

Bibliography

Ferris, Tim. 2015. Sam Harris on Daily Routines, The Trolley Scenario, and 5 Books Everyone Should Read (#87). July 8th, 2015. *The Tim Ferris Show*. Podcast, MP3 audio, 1:00:42. <https://tim.blog/2015/07/08/sam-harris-on-daily-routines-the-trolley-scenario-and-5-books-everyone-should-read>.

Harris, Sam. 2014. The Mystery of Consciousness. In *Waking Up: A Guide to Spirituality Without Religion*. Simon and Schuster.

———. 2016. The Light of the Mind: A Conversation with David Chalmers. April 16th. *Making Sense*. Podcast, YouTube. 1:45:00. <www.samharris.org/podcasts/making-sense-episodes/the-light-of-the-mind>.

———. 2017. Speaking of 'Truth' with Jordan B. Peterson. *Making Sense* (blog), January 23rd. <www.samharris.org/blog/speaking-of-truth-with-jordan-b-peterson>.

Nagel, Thomas. 1974. What Is It Like to Be a Bat? *Philosophical Review* 83 (October).

———. 1997. *The Last Word*. Oxford University Press.

———. 2012. *Mind and Cosmos: Why the Materialist Neo-Darwinian Conception of Nature Is Almost Certainly False*. Oxford University Press.

---

[1] I am grateful to Marc Andelman, Mike Laster, Dax Oliver, and Rick Sint for helpful feedback. Special thanks to Marc Andelman for excellent stylistic suggestions, most of which I have incorporated.

[16]
Intimations of the Numinous

REG NAULTY

The Buddha, Harris tells us, woke up from the dream of being a separate self which has thoughts, dreams, and feelings. Upon awakening from the dream, what did he find that he was instead? Harris's answer is consciousness and its contents, and that is all. There is a succession of conscious states, one after the other. That seems to leave me out, which is exactly Buddha's and Harris's intention. There is no enduring self.

In the best tradition of Buddhist mind-watchers, Harris informs us that he has spent years observing his own mind in meditation. And when he looks inwards, he never finds any sign of an inner self. Why is it then, that most people are convinced that it exists? Harris believes that most people don't have the skill and acumen to observe properly (*Waking Up*). However, the position that there is just consciousness and its contents generates paradoxes, one of which is that such consciousness does not seem to be anyone's. But we look into our own mind, not someone else's, and as for the self not persisting through time, hasn't Harris persisted through those many years of meditation? There is, though, a genuine question about the elusiveness of the self. Why is it so difficult to focus on it and inspect it? An answer is that it is transparent, so that it sees through itself to whatever is before it.

Harris writes that we suppose that we are unified subjects—the unchanging thinkers of thoughts and experience.

That is both correct and incorrect. There is a self which endures, but it does change—it has different moods, different stages of maturity, different trains of thought. But on Harris's showing, there is just a succession of conscious states which are not states of anything.

The Demolition of the Self in the East

The Westerner is astonished to find that the demolition of the everyday self, which seems such a bizarre undertaking to us, is something of an industry in the Indian philosophical and religious tradition. The motivation for such demolition varies. For Harris and his school, it is to show that there is no such thing as the self, but others wish to lay it aside in order to reveal something superior beneath it. Hand in hand with this tendency is a disagreement between Eastern and Western philosophy about the correct method to discover ultimate reality. On this point, I recall a Korean student who, when we were studying ancient Greek philosophy, remarked, with an amused smile, that the Greeks believed that ultimate reality could be found by thinking.

Well, how does the Indian tradition find it? The answer is meditation. And that consists precisely in stilling the thought stream. Enter S.N. Dasgupta, guru and philosopher, author of a celebrated five-volume history of Indian Philosophy. Should someone like him who does not believe that yoga meditation consists of thought, be writing books about it, when such books give expression to thought? The answer is that there is a difference between using the method itself and thinking about it later, which is where the books come from.

Stilling the thought stream is difficult, but with practice and guidance it can be managed. If it is engaged in for long periods of time over an extended period, that will, writes Dasgupta, weaken the constitution of the mind, so much so that it will be disintegrated and the new model self will shine forth in its own light, free, in the loneliness of self-illumination. Dasgupta insists that sense perception and logical thought—modern science—are incapable of comprehending the ultimate truth about the purity and unattached character of our true self, but meditation does. It reveals that the self has a self-shining, which is unique (*Hindu Mysticism*, p. 82).

Dasgupta is a Hindu, and Harris is sympathetic to aspects of Buddhism. Yet, that eminent Tibetan Buddhist, the Dalai Lama, agrees with Dasgupta. The Dalai Lama reports that as a result of long and continued meditation we become used to a kind of absence and vacuity, and when we get used to it, we notice an underlying clarity, a luminosity, and they are characteristics of the self. And in Japan, where the Buddhism is different from that of Sam Harris, they transcend the ego, the small self (in Japanese, *shoga*) to identify with the big self (in Japanese, *taiga*). Harris meditates a lot. He may find the big self one day.

Harris, the Empirical, and Scientific Rectitude

Like the British skeptic Richard Dawkins, Harris frequently reminds the reader of her duty to be scientific. And he proudly claims that Buddhism uses the method of science that is "empirical." Well, not quite. Empirical means use of the senses: seeing, hearing, touching, and smelling. Science makes great use of our sense of sight—seeing digital displays, observing the night skies, watching the course of an experiment, but it also uses our other senses. For example, hearing as when we hear electronic beeps, and the sense of touch is important in ascertaining degrees of hardness.

The main 'method' of Buddhism, however, is meditation, which is a form of introspection. Now that, as a scientific method, has drawbacks. Its object is not in public space which is accessible to all observers equally. Its object is part of the private inner world of the person doing the introspection, which diminishes its objectivity. So as a method it is not ideal from a scientific point of view. Despite that, meditation techniques can be replicated by different people, which is something meditation shares with science. And introspection more generally is an essential part of life. We use it when we are trying to locate a pain at the dentist, winemakers and chefs use it when they are trying to improve a flavor, and the careers of confectioners depend on it, and, as we shall see, it figures prominently in religion.

Conscience and Second Thoughts

The phrase "the still, small voice" is one of the great clichés of religion, and is a standing challenge to atheism. Of course, it is found within, as an object of introspection. The most ambitious and elaborate exposition and defense of conscience at an intellectual level in comparatively recent times was given by Cardinal Newman in his opaquely named, *An Essay in Aid of a Grammar of Assent*. The book is, among other things, a classification of the kinds of belief and the way in which rational belief is justified, but above all, it aims to show how the feelings of good and bad conscience enable us "to believe as if we saw" (1955, p. 96). Unfortunately, the book is not easy to read, which may be because Newman re-wrote it eight times, and did not do a great job in putting it back together.

It is the feelings of conscience, according to Newman, from which we learn of the existence and nature of God. These are feelings of good conscience and bad conscience which come to us after our actions. Newman described the former as deep peace, a sense of security, a resignation and a hope, the latter as confusion, foreboding, and self-condemnation. Newman's argument is that the alarmed recoil of bad conscience and the elation of good conscience are caused by judgments, inwardly received, of guilt and innocence, and consequently, what conscience reveals to us of God is that he is our judge. Moreover, Newman, maintains, the judge is holy, just, all-seeing, and retributive. Evidently, these are very precise characteristics to infer from what, in the case of bad conscience, would have been an essentially disturbed and confused reaction. George Fox, for example, interpreted the feelings of bad conscience as a reproof, rather than as a sentence of guilty. Such disagreement seems inevitable, but is compatible with conscience functioning as a signal that something has gone wrong or right.

After the heavy certainties of *The Grammar*, it is astonishing to read in a letter Newman wrote to the Duke of Norfolk, just five years later, that though conscience is the highest of teachers, it is the least luminous, because the sense of right and wrong is so easily puzzled and perverted by pride and passion. Newman was then seventy-five. He probably couldn`t bring himself to revisit the subject again. As it happens, similar terrain had been covered by Wordsworth before him. The poem was one of his greatest, *Intimations of Immortality from Recollections of early Childhood*:

> Heaven lies about us in our infancy!
> Shades of the prison house close
> Upon the growing Boy,
> But he beholds the light, and whence it flows,
> He sees it in his joy;
> . . . And by the vision splendid
> Is on his way attended;
> At length the man perceives it die away,
> And fade into the light of common day.

Unlike Newman, Wordsworth does not focus "the vision splendid" on conscience, but both have a similar regret, the loss, in Wordsworth's case, and the damage in Newman's case, to our sense of the sacred.

Society Makes a Claim

About a generation after Newman, Freud made an objection to the religious interpretation of conscience which had never occurred to Newman. In a passage in which Newman is elucidating the experience of good conscience, he wrote that it is like the soothing, satisfactory delight which follows reception of praise from a father. That is because, according to Freud, the praise to which we are responding is the praise of our actual father which we have internalized. More generally, we internalize the approvals and disapprovals of our own fathers.

However, children were found in the homes of widowed and abandoned mothers who had never been influenced by a father, yet whose conscience was quite normal. The internalization view of conscience was retained, but its origin was shifted to our "significant others." In two sentences which deserved to make him famous, the Harvard sociologist Daniel Bell wrote in the Sixties that the idea of reality, sociologically, is fairly simple. It is confirmation by significant others. These are the people who matter to us, those whom we take seriously. They may be our most important caregivers, teachers, sporting heroes, politicians, peers. They may even be great figures from the past. If we find an idea attractive, and there is nothing notable against it, and we learn that one of our significant others believes it, we believe as they do. There seems no doubt that our significant others play a role in the acquisition of beliefs and values.

A Confucian Contribution and an Advanced Warning.

Given the effects that blemishes of character can have on Newman's conscience, and the haphazard effect of our socially acquired values, does conscience survive in any useful form? Perhaps it does. Consider the following imaginary case of a Chinese woman living in the far western province of China. Let us suppose that she accepts what the government says about its achievements: that it has given the Chinese people the best life they have ever had—the best accommodation, the best food, the best health care, the best education, the best defense from external enemies, and that it deserves gratitude. She agrees that those who undermine it any way require corrective action. Despite that, she was disturbed by the way the Uyghur women were browbeaten and badgered by local authorities, and she had a mind to help them. No one she had known, she reflected, would have helped these women, but she did, though hesitatingly. And when she did, she felt only joy, exactly according to Newman`s scenario. At forty, said Confucius, I no longer suffered from perplexities, at fifty, I knew what were the biddings of Heaven. Perhaps such a learning curve is not an uncommon experience.

Newman's account of conscience has it that we learn about the moral quality of our action after we have done it. Wouldn't it have been more useful if we had known that before we did it? If there were something like a sense of inner restraint before an action, that would suggest a model like Wordsworth's, although less extravagant—that we bring something of God into the world with us. The metaphor of the seed is employed by some churches—it needs to be protected in its early life and nourished with the wisdom the church has to offer, until it is able to stand strong and alone.

Wonders in Public Space

Conspicuous sanctity is more common than most people imagine. There is the case of a saintly nun mentioned by the philosopher Raymond Gaita, who happens to be an atheist. He was working as a ward assistant in a ward where there were patients with advanced dementia, and he noticed that the specialists there condescended to the patients, as he himself did. But the nun did not. She worked on a different roster, so he did not see more of her, but he saw enough to notice that her sanctity was conspicuous. There are different paths to this condition. One consists in gradually coming to know and love God over time. For example, someone may have experienced severe misfortune and called on God for help, without even believing that God exists, just as someone who has fallen into a river on a dark night may call out for help without knowing whether anyone is there. Were that to happen on several occasions, the person might well come to love God for his own sake, not just as a source of benefactions. He might then address God lovingly. That may flower into an experience of God`s presence within him. Thus, Marmaduke Stephenson in Colonial America was "filled with the love and presence of the living God," and Thomas R. Kelly, an academic in America in 1938, said that he had been literally melted down by the love of God (*Quaker Faith and Practice*).

Such a spiritual condition may become visible to other people. Thus Montaigne, who often gets into history books as a skeptic, writes of the divine supernatural and extraordinary beauty that we see sometimes shine in a person like stars under a corporeal veil. Sometimes the veil is removed. Thus George Fox (1624–1691), as he was riding through a crowd of noisy undergraduates in Cambridge, kept on horseback, and as he rode through them, they exclaimed "he shines, he glisters!" (*Quaker Spirituality*, p. 91).

And there is the great Russian mystic, Saint Seraphim of Sarov (1759–1833) during his memorable meeting with the nobleman Nikolay Motovilov, who had visited his monastery as a pilgrim. In a record of their meeting, Motovilov wrote that he could not look at Father Seraphim because lightning streamed from his eyes and his face had become more brilliant than the sun. Seraphim told him not to be afraid, because he was shining just as brightly himself. Such divine beauty is also known in Islam. Tradition has it that Hasan ibn Ali, the prophet's grandson, was once asked why those people were most beautiful who prayed at night, and he replied that it was because they were alone with the All-Merciful who covered them with light from His light. Religion needs manifestations of the supernatural in public space. Christianity should stop being coy about the divine beauty.

It is noteworthy that the pathway to God presented above is that of devotion. Broadly speaking, the novelist Leo Tolstoy fits in here. After he wrote his great novels, *War and Peace* and *Anna Karenin*, he had a religious conversion, after which he stopped writing fiction for a time, but later took it up again in short stories. Religious themes, which were largely absent in his great novels, were very much in evidence in these, but the way of devotion is not mentioned. Tolstoy doesn't seem to have believed in prayer.

What he did believe in were good works and non-violence. Although his pathway is different, the outcome is strikingly similar. There is an inward revelation of God. In the story "Father Sergius," "little by little, God began to reveal Himself within him" (*Great Short Works*, p. 545), significantly, after he left his monastery, and in the stories "What Men Live By" and "Two Old Men," there is a transfiguration. It was as though traditional, holy Russia were sowing its seeds into the future before the long, bitter persecutions of the Soviet period.

A House of Many Mansions

In *Waking Up*, Harris gives severe and extended criticism to the neurosurgeon Eben Alexander's book *Proof of Heaven: A Neurosurgeon's Journey into the Afterlife*. Harris argues that we shouldn't take it seriously. People on drugs have trips like Alexander's Near-Death Experience (NDE). More generally, Harris writes that the deepest problem with drawing sweeping conclusions from the NDE is that those who have had one and subsequently talked about it did not die.

Well, there is an account of what the afterlife is like from someone who had been dead for twenty years. That person was Frederic Myers, a classicist at Cambridge University, who died in 1901. What recommends him was that he took evidential considerations seriously. He was a member of a group of psychical researchers at Cambridge to whom he gave an undertaking that when he died, he would come back through a medium with information about what the afterlife was like. He came through with his account in 1920, but before that, in 1915, he aided Raymond Lodge who had been killed in action on the Western Front, to communicate with his father, Sir Oliver Lodge, who was a famous scientist. The one claiming to be Raymond, proved that he was indeed Sir Oliver's son, by providing details of family arrangements, pets, habits, and properties. He referred to Myers, who was known to his audience, as "FM," which gave him something of an introduction to his communications in 1920.

Very often, the account sent by Myers to a medium did not make sense by itself. That was deliberate, to prevent the mediums from improvising once they had got the general idea. The sense was made by an additional account sent to a different medium later. Arrangements were made to facilitate this. Myers peppered his deliverances with classical allusions to confirm his identity to his audience. In all, between the years 1924 and 1931, Myers transmitted an average sized book.

Immediately after death, according to Myers, we are usually met by friends, work mates, and relatives who died before. The normal transition is a simple and peaceful going into a pleasant, sometimes blissful sleep, though, if we pass over in a disturbed state, as in suicide, it may take time to orient ourselves. In this stage of the after-life, we retain bodies which look like earth bodies, but lack the mechanical properties of mass and weight, like an image in a mirror. Communication is by direct image telepathy, hence there are no language barriers.

There follows a brief, unstable stage, which gives way to a later stage which is more stable and seems to be rather like life on earth. Very large numbers of souls, transmitted Myers, remain comfortably in this stage for long periods, even centuries, without making any effort to move on. An unexpected feature of this stage is that there is an option of re - incarnation. If it were felt that life on earth was better, there is freedom to go back.

The next stage, Myers calls the "plane of eidos", since it features sounds and colors outside the range of our earthly experience. As it happens, the richness and beauty of these colors are now matched by those induced by some drug experiments. Another respect in which technology is catching up with this stage is that, according to Myers, we can build up a likeness of ourselves and project it across the world to someone. That can now be done as a hologram, although it requires physical equipment.

In this stage, sleep is no longer necessary. Also, there seems to be something rather like purgatory. The intense experience of "profound despair and inconceivable bliss" (*The Life Beyond Death*, p. 110), continues Myers, burns away the pettiness and animosities of Earth, and frees us at last from its domination.

Myers was on the plane of eidos when he delivered his descriptions of the next life. What he knew of later planes he learned from others. On the next plane, so he was informed, we acquire a body of flame, which enables us to tour the stellar universe without being harmed by its temperatures and turbulence. There is corroboration of the body of flame from the life of one of the saints, St Vincent de Paul (1581–1660). He tells us that when St. Jeanne de Chantal died, he saw her soul rise like a globe of fire, and, coming down from above, another and larger globe in which the first was lost. St Vincent recognized the globe of fire coming down as St. Francis de Sales, with whom St Jeanne had worked in establishing an order of nuns, the Visitandines, whose mission it was to visit the poor and the aged in isolated farm houses. Perhaps it's worth mentioning that there is nothing in Catholic teaching which supports the existence of this plane.

There is a further plane, about which Myers knew little, but which he called "The Plane of White Light." Souls at this stage, are capable of living without form, of existing as white light in the pure thought of the creator.

Someone once said that humanity has been incapable of conceiving an interesting heaven. Myers shows that not to be true. The next life has long aroused skepticism, fear and even terror. Frederic Myers's account shows that these are misplaced. Life after death comes across as congenial, interestingly different from life on Earth, affording opportunities for friendship and love, and a continuation of our divine adventure. We may look forward to the future with good hope.

Subjecting these issues to close examination can have the effect of making them seem less important than they are. However, the existence of an inner self remains up for debate even within the Eastern tradition, so Harris should not be so quick to jettison it. Moreover, it establishes our capacity to survive death, if such a capacity exists, and conscience is about God helping us to do the best we can, both of which are momentous issues.

References

Alexander, Eben. 2012. *Proof of Heaven: A Neurosurgeon's Journey into the Afterlife*. Simon and Schuster.

Bell, Daniel. 1965. The Disjunction of Culture and Social Structure: Some Notes on the Meaning of Social Reality. *Daedalus* 94:1.

Bennett, H.S., ed. 1941. *Fifteen Poets: From Chaucer to Arnold*. Clarendon.

Britain Yearly Meeting (Society of Friends). 2009. *Quaker Faith and Practice: The Book of Christian Discipline of the Yearly Meeting of the Religious Society of Friends (Quakers) in Britain*. 4th ed. London, England: Quaker Books.

Dasgupta, S.N. 1973. *Hindu Mysticism*. New York: Frederick Ungar Publishing Company.

Ellison, Jerome, and Arthur Ford. 1974. *The Life beyond Death*. Sphere.

Harris, Sam. 2015. *Waking Up: A Guide to Spirituality without Religion*. Simon and Schuster.

Naulty, Reg. 2015. Review of Sam Harris, *Waking Up*. *Sophia* 54:1.

Newman, John Henry. 1955. *An Essay in Aid of a Grammar of Assent*. Doubleday.

Steere, Douglas V., ed. 1990. *Quaker Spirituality: Selected Writings*. Paulist Press International.

Tolstoy, Leo. 1967. *Great Short Works*. Harper Perennial.

Part VII

No End to Faith

[17]
A Rational Proposal

BETHEL MCGREW

I believe that the Bible is the word of God, that Jesus is the
Son of God, and that only those who place their faith in Jesus
will find salvation after death. As a Christian, I believe these
propositions not because they make me feel good, but
because I think they're true.

Readers may recognize this little *credo* as a first-person
adaptation of Sam Harris's opening paragraph in his 2006
Letter to a Christian Nation. This work was addressed, in
some sense, to people like me. This opening paragraph, with
"You" replacing "I," was intended as a fair and accurate char-
acterization of Harris's opponents, however (in)consistently
that fairness and accuracy were maintained in the rest of
the work. So, I own the soft impeachment. I am a Christian.
I accept the tenets of the Christian faith. My problem with
Sam Harris is that I do not think the word "faith" means
what Sam Harris thinks it means.

When asked to define "faith," Christians often point to the
book of Hebrews, Chapter 11. In the King James version,
"Faith is the substance of things hoped for, the evidence of
things not seen." Elaborating further, some might make the
word synonymous with "trust." I have "faith" in God in the
same sense that I have faith in the pilot of my next trans-
Atlantic flight. All of my senses, reasoning faculties, and
prior experience lead me to conclude that the pilot is reliable,
so I trust him. I have "faith" in him.

But notice what faith is *not*, according to this definition: It is *not* an alternative to reason. It is *not* a belief formed without evidence. And while embracing faith in the Christian God certainly involves a deeper decision-making process than the decision to buy a sensible used car, it is also not a decision to be made lightly or irrationally. If we are asked why we think it is true, then we are compelled to answer that question in a way that will be accessible to any good-faith inquirer of any religious or non-religious persuasion. We are compelled to explain why, in our judgment, Christianity gives the truest account of reality at all levels of existence, even if we face questions where we must admit our knowledge is incomplete. We reach this conclusion not only by studying the books of the Bible, but by studying the book of Nature, which the Bible itself points to as a source of truthful revelation (see Romans 1).

Suffice it to say, once I read past Sam's opening lines, I find it progressively more difficult to recognize my own perspective, which is the perspective of many of my fellow Christians past and present. It is this perspective that I intend to present in this essay.

Faith versus Reason?

In Harris's taxonomy of Christianity, there are apparently two and only two kinds of Christians: fundamentalists and liberals. Harris has never regarded the latter as serious opposition for his purposes, because they tend to reject almost as much of the Bible as he does. By contrast, he argues that there's a certain strength in the fundamentalist position, a certain integrity. Of course, he is notoriously unhesitant to heap scorn upon it. But in some curious sense, he respects it.

I may not identify as a fundamentalist myself, but I have no desire to follow Harris's example and pile on yet more scorn. In secular and Christian circles alike, the very label "fundamentalist" frequently serves as little more than a rhetorical conversation-stopper, a way of signaling one's cleverness while avoiding real substantive engagement. Alvin Plantinga's tongue-in-cheek definition remains the most memorable: "a stupid sumbitch whose theological opinions are considerably to the right of mine" (*Warranted Christian Belief*, p. 245).

Nevertheless, there are elements of fundamentalism that are vulnerable to some of Harris's critiques. Passages like this may be grating in tone, but they contain the seed of a legitimate argument:

> Along with most Christians, you believe that mortals like ourselves cannot reject the morality of the Bible. We cannot say, for instance, that God was wrong to drown most of humanity in the flood of Genesis, because this is merely the way it seems from our limited point of view. And yet, you feel that you are in a position to judge that Jesus is the Son of God, that the Golden Rule is the height of moral wisdom, and that the Bible is not itself brimming with lies. You are using your own moral intuitions to authenticate the wisdom of the Bible—and then, in the next moment, you assert that we human beings cannot possibly rely upon our own intuitions to rightly guide us in the world; rather, we must depend upon the prescriptions of the Bible. You are using your own moral intuitions to decide that the Bible is the appropriate guarantor of your moral intuitions. Your own intuitions are still primary, and your reasoning is circular. (*Letter to a Christian Nation*, pp. 48–49)

Harris is correct that some strains of Christianity can tend towards this circular trap when they issue blanket condemnations of "fallible human intuition," including moral intuition. This is a tenuous epistemological foundation for a framework that also makes frequent intuitive moral appeals on topics like abortion. Pro-life Christians will reasonably argue that our moral sense should signal the intrinsic wrongness of doing violence to an unborn infant's body, whether or not we adhere to any particular religious framework. Yet when it comes to "hard passages" in the Bible where God is said to mandate the human slaughter of infants (which, incidentally, are in intra-biblical tension with various other passages on innocent bloodshed), they argue that our fallen human intuition cannot be placed above Scripture. I believe this is a tension that needs to be honestly addressed among conservative Christians.

This deep skepticism of human intuition informs fideism, the belief that faith truly is in tension with reason and that to seek evidential justification is to disrespect "the gift." Earnest Christians, seeking to resolve concrete questions in areas such as scriptural reliability, have too often done so in communities that were predisposed not to assist them in that search. The injunction to "just have faith" is of little encouragement when the very grounding for one's faith is in flux.

However, it is one thing to observe that this is the sociocultural expression of "faith" in some particular sub-strains of conservative Christianity. It is another thing to conflate "faith" with "belief *sans* evidence" on behalf of all conservative Christians everywhere. Harris does this freely throughout his work. "The core of science," he writes in *Letter to a Christian Nation*, "is not controlled experiment or mathematical modeling; it is intellectual honesty. It is time we acknowledged a basic feature of human discourse: when considering the truth of a proposition, one is either engaged in an honest appraisal of the evidence and logical arguments, or one isn't. Religion is the one area of our lives where people imagine that some other standard of intellectual integrity applies" (*Letter to a Christian Nation*, pp. 64–65).

In context, he is lambasting a statement from the National Academy of Sciences that science and religion embody two different "ways of knowing." As Stephen J. Gould would put it, they are "separate magisteria," treating separate kinds of questions. Harris, quite understandably, is not impressed. His litany of religious truth claims may be a bit crude (including the shallow assertion that if you "don't believe the right things about God," you will suffer eternally—thus implying that you might earnestly send yourself to Hell by the equivalent of forgetting to check the right box on a divine list). But he is not wrong to point out that religious truth claims are still truth claims, purporting to be factual statements about the nature of reality. As such, they should be as honestly appraised as any other statements about reality.

So far, so reasonable. But Harris doesn't stop there. A little further on, he concludes:

> The conflict between science and religion is reducible to a simple fact of human cognition and discourse: either a person has good reasons for what he believes, or he does not. If there were good

reasons to believe that Jesus was born of a virgin, or that Muhammad flew to heaven on a winged horse, these beliefs would necessarily form part of our rational description of the universe. Everyone recognizes that to rely upon "faith" to decide specific questions of historical fact is ridiculous—that is, until the conversation turns to the origin of books like the Bible and the Koran, to the resurrection of Jesus, to Muhammad's conversation with the archangel Gabriel, or to any other religious dogma. It is time that we admitted that faith is nothing more than the license religious people give one another to keep believing when reasons fail. (p. 66)

Here once again, we see the automatic conflation of "faith" with "anti-reason," Harris is, of course, entitled to his belief that religious truth claims are in fact poorly evidenced. But many serious Christians have historically begged to differ.

The Silenced Majority

Harris is not alone in this conflation among popular critics of religion. In their long essay "Postmodern Religion and the Faith of Social Justice," James Lindsay and Mike Nayna explicitly define "faith" in such a way as to contradict the "TJB" (true, justified belief) definition of knowledge:

There is a bright, clear line between faith-based beliefs and knowledge, and that's epistemological justification. The lack thereof is unambiguously what the author of Hebrews meant by "things not seen," and faith can be understood as the proxy for justification, which makes the 'special knowledge' of revealed wisdom special. ("Postmodern Religion and the Faith of Social Justice")

This is not a compelling piece of exegesis. To "see" a thing is but one of many ways to be justifiably hopeful about its reality. Even for those Christians who do embrace a fideist epistemology, their hope is likely built on many subconscious justifying clues that they just haven't brought out and articulated in full. As C.S. Lewis famously wrote, "I believe in Christianity as I believe that the sun has risen: not only because I see it, but because by it I see everything else" (*The Weight of Glory*, p. 140).

Lewis further elaborates on the interplay between faith and reason in a passage from *Mere Christianity*. He first notes that man is not a strictly rational creature, as evidenced by our instinctive panic when surgeons arrive to put us under anesthetic on a hospital table. But this is not a tension between faith and reason, because our faith in the surgeons, like my faith in the airline pilot, is *grounded* in reason. Rather than faith versus reason, this is an instance of faith *and* reason against "emotion and imagination"—specifically, irrational emotion and unrealistic imagination. So with Christianity. Lewis is explicitly "not asking anyone to accept Christianity if his best reasoning tells him that the weight of the evidence is against it." Faith is not the art of suppressing reason, but rather "the art of holding onto things your reason has once accepted, in spite of your changing moods." Otherwise, he submits, "you can never be either a sound Christian or even a sound atheist" (*Mere Christianity*, pp. 123–24).

I could go century by century and call up many similar quotations. "Now it is not required nor can be exacted at our hands, that we should yield unto any thing other assent than such as doth answer the evidence which is to be had of that we assent unto." Thus Richard Hooker, writing in the sixteenth century (*Ecclesiastical Polity*, p. 157). "Whatsoever is against right reason, that no faith can oblige us to believe." Thus Bishop Jeremy Taylor, writing in the seventeenth century (*Works*, p. 104). "Let Reason be kept to; and, if any part of the Scripture account of the redemption of the world by Christ can be shown to be really contrary to it, let the Scripture, in the name of God, be given up." Thus the eighteenth-century Anglican bishop, Joseph Butler, in his magisterial *Analogy of Religion* (p. 159). "If Christianity is shown by reason to be irrational or anti-rational, it is your duty and mine to abandon it tomorrow or perhaps tonight." Thus the late nineteenth-century Catholic priest Matthew A. Power ("The True Rationalism," p. 241). And so on, and so forth.

This is the inconvenient truth with which Sam Harris and his ilk must contend if they are to offer a truly comprehensive assessment of the Christian religion: Many of the Enlightenment's brightest minds were also devout Christians. Like their secular counterparts, they understood the epistemological heart of the Enlightenment as a commitment to the pursuit of true, justified belief, with the difference that they were not constrained in that pursuit by scientism—not to be confused with science. So, while the Enlightenment gave us David Hume, whose verdict on the probability of miracles Harris accepts uncritically, it also gave us Hume's rivals, scholars like William Paley, George Campbell, and Thomas Bayes. It is to Bayes that we owe Bayes's Theorem, which can be used to assess the potential cumulative weight of witness testimony against the low prior probability of an extraordinary event. Bayes's intuitions, though still developing, would be vindicated centuries later in the contemporary literature on miracles and probability. Incidentally, Bayes was a Presbyterian minister. Yet another cleric who believed, like Bishop Butler, that "probability is the very guide of life" (*Analogy*, p. 40).

Even mere theism gets only a cursory treatment from Harris, for whom the retort "But who made God?" seems to carry some significant philosophical heft. He labors under the belief that it "begs the question" to explain that "God," by definition, is uncreated (*Letter*, p. 73). By contrast, consider this rather striking quotation: "If God did not exist, he would have to be invented. But all nature cries aloud that he does exist: that there is a supreme intelligence, an immense power, an admirable order, and everything teaches us our own dependence on it." To which cleric or apologist do we owe this assertion? To none, as it happens, for it comes from none other than Voltaire.

Whence, What, Whither?

When the agnostic Swiss playwright and novelist Max Frisch died, he asked that his funeral be conducted in St Peter's Church in Zurich. But he wanted the service to be stripped of any religious trappings. A couple of friends would speak, with no Amen. There would be no priest to bless the mourners. There would be no prayers offered. There would be no passages read aloud from the Bible or the Book of Common Prayer.

One of the guests was the philosopher Jürgen Habermas, who used this unceremonious ceremony to open his now famous essay "The Awareness of What Is Missing." The essay suggests that rational post-Christians should not be content to rest on the triumph of reason over religion. Rather, they should admit honestly that their hardest work still lies before them. The funeral of Max Frisch brought this home to Habermas in unsettling fashion. Reason may be regnant, but on that day, he found it uncomfortably quiet in the face of death. Thus, he proposes it is incumbent on reasonable men to come together and fill the hole that religion left behind.

Sam Harris has expressed a similar sentiment. "Clearly," he writes, "it is time we learned to meet our emotional needs without embracing the preposterous. We must find ways to invoke the power of ritual and to mark those transitions in every human life that demand profundity—birth, marriage, death—without lying to ourselves about the nature of reality" (*Letter*, p. 88).

But this assertion contains the seeds of its own contradiction. It is "clear" to Harris by the natural light that we have "emotional needs" and that births, marriages, and deaths "demand profundity." But it might sincerely be asked: Why? "Well, they just do," Sam might say. I agree. But why? I might further ask, given that Harris recognizes the existence of these "emotional needs," why does he find it so ludicrous that Christian missionary doctors might be concerned for more than just their patients' physical needs? Harris lambastes such doctors while simultaneously praising those doctors who "are moved simply to alleviate human suffering, without any thought of God" (*Letter*, p. 33). It is unclear whether he has ever encountered someone whose human suffering was alleviated by thoughts of a God who preordained their existence, loved them to the point of sacrificial death, prepared a path to life beyond death, and offers forgiveness of their sins.

All of this is "preposterous" within Harris's frame, of course. It's preposterous to imagine that God came down from Heaven, was incarnate by the Holy Ghost of the Virgin Mary and was made man, then suffered under Pontius Pilate, was crucified, dead, and buried, and rose again on the third day, in the fulfillment of his words "I am the Resurrection and the Life. He that believeth in me, though he were dead, shall never die." We are all reasonable modern men, here. We now understand that, in the ordinary course of events, virgins do not get pregnant and dead men stay dead.

You may ask, "But just how stupid *was* a first-century Jew?" We aren't sure, but we are quite sure we are less stupid.

But if not that "preposterous" notion, what, then? Where does the significance of the birth, the marriage, the death come from? Where do *we* come from? What *are* we? And where are we going?

Sam Harris is, of course, full of his own ways of answering these questions. And still, they remain unsatisfactory for many people, for whom the value of a birth, a marriage, or a death does not seem to be adequately explained by a secular modernist narrative of everything. To quote Douglas Murray, responding to Richard Dawkins's bold claim that all human mysteries have been "solved" by science, "the fact is that we do not feel solved. We do not live our lives and experience our lives as solved beings" (*The Strange Death of Europe*, p. 266). Like Dawkins, Murray believes "no intelligent person" could deny that we are, in Darwin's words, "created from animals." This is something we "know." But, paradoxically, he believes we also "know" that we degrade ourselves when we behave like animals. We "know that we are something else, even if we don't know what that else is."

This in and of itself does not constitute proof that Richard Dawkins or Sam Harris are wrong. But it does appear to be an apt application of A.J. Balfour's observation that "for a creed to be truly consistent, there must exist a correspondence between the account it gives of the origin of its beliefs and the estimate it entertains of their value; in other words, there must be a harmony between the accepted value of results and the accepted theory of causes" (*The Foundations of Belief*, p. xviii). Perhaps Harris and his New Atheist colleagues would chafe at the word "creed." If they prefer, they can call it an anti-creed. The principle—and the puzzle—is the same.

While we are dwelling on those things we can't not know about the human person, whether or not we have a fully adequate narrative to frame them, we could mention a few others. We could note, for example, that promiscuous sex tends to leave men and women unhappily unfulfilled. We could note that however we choose to explain the origins of male and female genitalia, they have the appearance of complementary design. We could note that by eight weeks of development, a human fetus begins to react to harmful stimuli, and by ten weeks, the whole body is sensitive to touch—facts of which Harris seems unaware when he writes that "one can reasonably wonder whether most aborted fetuses suffer their destruction on any level" (*Letter*, pp. 36–37).

For readers questioning my left turn from philosophy of religion into anthropology here, I am only following Sam Harris's example. Indeed, he toggles quite freely from one to the other as he accuses Christians of being disconnected from Reality, writ large. But what's sauce for the atheist goose is sauce for the Christian gander.

Conclusion

In his memoir *The Great Good Thing*, the writer Andrew Klavan describes the precise moment when he realized he was on the threshold of becoming a Christian:

> G.K. Chesterton said that in stumbling onto his Christian faith he was like an English yachtsman who had gone off course: he thought that he had discovered a new island when, in fact, he had landed back in England. I saw now that I was like an archaeologist who, after a lifetime of digging, had unearthed the lost foundations of a civilization that turned out, in fact, to be his own. I had spent fifty years of reading and contemplation and seeking and prayer and I had managed to do nothing more than reinvent the Christian wheel. (*The Great Good Thing*, p. 244)

In this moment, Klavan looked back over defining "epiphanies" in his life—moments when he had profoundly grasped suffering, joy, love, moral clarity, or the essential comedy at the center of tragedy. Each of these things found its natural end in tenets of the Christian faith. Suffering naturally tended towards the cross of Christ. Love naturally tended towards the love of Christ. Moral clarity naturally tended towards the conclusion that man is uniquely valuable and made in the image of an ultimate moral lawgiver. And the enduring comedy of life, the "laughter at the heart of mourning," what could this be if not "the realization that this life is not what we were meant for, that death is not what we were meant for, that who we are is not who we're supposed to be"?

He felt this even in the most low-brow humor, or perhaps *especially* in the most low-brow humor. The man who slips on a banana peel laughs because he knows he has dignity to lose, a height to fall from. "So it is with us when we sin. So it is with us even when we die. We are meant for something better, and we know it, and even as we suffer and mourn, we also laugh" (p. 245).

This did not mark the end of all Klavan's doubts. He still had to examine his motives honestly. He still had to consider the sum total of all these epiphanies while his inner David Hume protested that "There are no miracles. There can be no resurrection. The clockwork world is all in all" (p. 247). Still, the incarnation had an attraction, a consonance with his epiphany that man was made in a divine image. If this was true, the notion that God himself might become man was not so preposterous as all that.

Curiously, it was the abrupt ending of Mark that sealed the deal. With his professional writer's eye, Klavan sensed instantly that the original ending had been lost, leaving a "jagged edge" behind. The empty tomb confronted him, compelled him, and called to him. From that point on, even as he continued cross-examining himself, he found that he could not go back. He could not return to his old "irrational prejudice" that "the symbols of reality are more real than the reality they symbolize" (p. 247). In the end, he concluded that the Christian narrative made sense, in the way that C.S. Lewis's rising sun made sense—by also making sense *of*: "The story of Christ's life, death, and resurrection not only made sense in itself, it made sense of everything I had experienced and everything I had come to know. It made sense of the world" (p. 248).

None of this is especially likely to persuade Sam Harris, who has always wondered how obviously intelligent men could be swayed by such an obviously irrational fantasy. He might note that Klavan wasn't necessarily converted to my own precise view of Scripture. Or he might press that Klavan's case for the resurrection wants more justification to be truly convincing, which justification Harris maintains the Christian cannot supply. I would be happy to expand on Klavan's arguments in that respect. But I don't present Klavan as a case study because he is precisely like me. I present his testimony simply because if there is one thing one could *not* say of his conversion with any seriousness, it is that he approached it with a lowered standard of intellectual integrity. Rather, he was persuaded, through various converging lines of evidence, that it was more reasonable to believe than not to believe. He was persuaded that faith and reason were not enemies, but dancing partners.

Near the conclusion of *Letter to a Christian Nation*, Harris writes, "We desperately need a public discourse that encourages critical thinking and intellectual honesty" (p. 87). I couldn't agree more. Such a discourse is the discourse I have always attempted to model, and always shall. I invite Sam Harris to join me.

Bibliography

Balfour, Arthur James. 1901. *The Foundations of Belief*. Eighth edition. Longmans, Green.

Butler, Joseph. 1819. *Analogy of Religion*. Hartford: Samuel G. Goodrich.

Harris, Sam. 2006. *Letter to a Christian Nation*. Knopf.

Hooker, Richard. 1888. *The Laws of Ecclesiastical Polity*, Book II. Routledge.

Klavan, Andrew. 2016. *The Great Good Thing*. Nelson Books.

Lewis, C.S. 1952. *Mere Christianity*. Macmillan.

———. 2001. *The Weight of Glory and Other Addresses*. HarperOne.

Lindsay, James, and Mike Nayna. 2018. Postmodern Religion and the Faith of Social Justice. *Areo* (December 18th) <https://areomagazine.com/2018/12/18/postmodern-religion-and-the-faith-of-social-justice>.

Murray, Douglas. 2018. *The Strange Death of Europe*. Bloomsbury.

Plantinga, Alvin. 2000. *Warranted Christian Belief*. Oxford University Press.

Power, Fr. Matthew A. 1908. The True Rationalism. In *Religion and the Modern Mind: Lectures Delivered Before the Glasgow University Society of St. Ninian*. Hodder and Stoughton.

Taylor, Jeremy. 1854. *The Whole Works of the Right Rev. Jeremy Taylor*, Volume 8. Longman, Brown, Green, and Longmans.

[18]
Is Sam Harris Right about the Miracles of Jesus?

MICHAEL BARROS AND BETHEL MCGREW

In *The Moral Landscape*, Sam Harris argues against the credibility of Christian beliefs in miracles by attacking the reliability of the New Testament texts and the uniqueness of the miracles themselves. He describes the New Testament texts as "discrepant and fragmentary copies of copies of copies of ancient Greek manuscripts" (p. 168). Then, in the style of David Hume, he lists miracle claims from other religions in an attempt to demonstrate that Jesus's miracles are not unique. Some find these arguments compelling, but just how damning are they? On a more careful examination of the biblical texts' integrity and historical context, Harris proves to be no more persuasive than his skeptical predecessors.

The Textual Reliability

While discussing the Gospel miracles in *The Moral Landscape*, Harris states that miracles of that sort "do not even merit an hour on cable television." He dismisses their credibility because they come from a "prescientific religious context of the first-century Roman Empire, decades *after* their supposed occurrence, as evidenced by discrepant and fragmentary copies of copies of copies of ancient Greek manuscripts" (p. 168). This is a dense statement that may make some Christian readers uncomfortable. And parts of it are true, as far as they go—which isn't very far.

Early Christianity was indeed prescientific (though it's not clear which law of modern science is necessary to determine whether a man is dead or alive). It did develop in the first-century Roman Empire, and the earliest manuscripts were indeed copies of copies dated decades after the events they reported. But if a text's development in the "prescientific religious context of the first-century Roman Empire" shakes someone's faith, that faith rests on a shaky foundation indeed. As for discrepancies in the text, these have been known by theologians and Bible scholars for a long time, yet many still retain their Christian faith. Some examine the same facts and walk away with even more confidence.

When commenting on the historicity of the biblical text, Harris relies almost exclusively on the work of Dr. Bart Ehrman, a New Testament scholar specializing in textual criticism who has written several books, including six *New York Times* bestsellers. Much of his work, indeed much of what he is famous for, is his skepticism about the reliability of the New Testament. He believes that the text was corrupted over time, which he details in his book, *The Orthodox Corruption of Scripture*. Dr. Ehrman is an effective communicator, but he's not unchallenged in his field. One of his most outspoken critics is another textual critic named Dr. Daniel Wallace. Wallace says of Ehrman, "The *text* is not the basic area of our disagreement; the *interpretation* of the text is. And even here, it's not so much the interpretation of the text as it is the interpretation of how the textual variants arose and how significant those variants are. That's where our differences lie" ("Textual Reliability," p. 29).

Harris expands on his concerns about the New Testament in the notes section of his book, where he writes, "Bible scholars agree that the earliest Gospels were written decades after the life of Jesus" (*The Moral Landscape*, pp. 252–53). Right off the bat, it's subtly misleading to refer to "the earliest Gospels" here, as if anything besides Matthew, Mark, Luke, and John was ever a serious candidate for inclusion in the canon. (We'll return to this common, yet false trope later.) Further, though some scholars do favor late dates for the four canonical Gospels, the texts' precise dating is in fact underdetermined. Other scholars leave room for the hypothesis that at least the Synoptic Gospels (Matthew, Mark, and

Luke) could have been written and circulated much closer to the events they report. In debate with Bart Ehrman, Dr. Peter J. Williams has taken an agnostic stance, saying he doesn't "have a view" (Williams-Ehrman, Premier Unbelievable?). One known line of argument for earlier dating begins with the observation that the Book of Acts ends abruptly before the Apostle Paul's Roman execution in 67 A.D., and its prologue asserts that the same writer had already composed the Gospel of Luke. So the Synoptics could potentially be placed within about thirty-five years of Jesus's death, perhaps even earlier.

Turning now to the manuscript record, our earliest extant Gospel manuscript is P52, a fragment of John dated to the early second century. John's composition is commonly dated around 90 A.D. Mark has a gap of roughly 60–85 years between its conjectured composition and its earliest manuscript, P137. This gap may seem significant, but it's very small compared to most classical literature. Wallace, contrasting the New Testament with other historical and biographical works from the ancient world, notes that Plutarch's *Lives* had about an 800-year gap and Herodotus's *Histories* had about a 500-year gap before its earliest manuscript but 1,500 before its first substantial copy (SMU Debate). This doesn't mean that historians conclude that everything must be wildly unreliable, so most things we think we know about ancient history are nonsense. If, for example, someone asked, "Who were the Essenes?" very few historians would say, "I wish I could tell you, but the earliest manuscript of Josephus is from almost a millennium after his life, so there's simply nothing we can reliably say about them."

This leaves the question of how much it should bother us that there's some gap between the Gospels' composition and the events they relate. As already noted, we don't in fact have enough evidence to assert unequivocally that this gap is many decades wide for all four Gospels. But even for the latest Gospel, John, we note that the gap is still much smaller than for other ancient historical texts. One could also point to the strong oral tradition of ancient Jewish culture, which could have reliably preserved the accounts until they were written down. And even in our own time and culture, we have many examples of vivid eyewitness testimony reliably conveyed decades after the fact, such as oral history interviews with World War II veterans. So, in the end, how problematic is such a gap? Not very, unless one applies a double standard to New Testament history and the rest of ancient or modern history.

Just a Game of Telephone?

It's true that we don't have the original texts of any of the gospels, and this idea of "copies of copies of copies" sounds damning, like a religion based on a two-thousand-year-old game of telephone. In Greek, there are over 5,800 manuscripts, with the overwhelming majority coming from after the eighth century ("Textual Reliability," p. 19). This means that most of the manuscripts are indeed copies of copies of copies. However, Dan Wallace rejects the comparison to a game of telephone, providing multiple counterarguments (pp. 35–36):

- The message is passed on in writing, not orally.
- There are multiple streams of transmission, not one.
- Textual critics don't rely on the last person in each transmission line but have access to earlier ones.
- Patristic writers comment on the text throughout history, often filling in chronological gaps between manuscripts.
- New Testament books were most likely copied multiple times and may have been used even after a few generations of copies had been produced.
- There was at least one very carefully produced transmission stream, and there is sufficient evidence to show that even a fourth-century manuscript from this line is more reliable than just about any second-century manuscript.

More compelling than the "copies of copies of copies" argument is the statement about the variants between manuscripts. There are about 500,000 variants between the Greek manuscripts, excluding misspellings and nonsense readings. (Gurry, "The Number of Variants"). But does this mean, as is implied by Harris, that we can't know what the original texts would have said?

Making Sense of the Variants

To understand the implications of the variants, Wallace breaks them into categories ("Textual Reliability," pp. 39–40). The largest category is simple spelling changes that don't change the meaning of the text. For example, the most common variant is using the Greek letter ν (nu), which normally occurs at the end of words that precede words that start with a vowel but in some places might appear before a word beginning with a consonant. This is similar to me saying, "Grab me an drink" in one text versus "Grab me a drink" in another. Several variants are obviously nonsense, showing the scribe to be either tired or unfamiliar with Greek.

The next largest category of variants is synonyms or changes which don't affect the translation, like the use of definite articles when writing names. Some manuscripts read "the Mary" or "the Joseph," while others read "Mary" or "Joseph." There are also many variants that change the word order. In Greek, word order is more for emphasis than meaning, so again, the meaning is unaffected. Wallace provides the example, "Jesus loves John," which can be written in Greek in a total of sixteen different ways, all of which would be properly translated to "Jesus loves John" because the word order does not affect subject and object.

Finally, we have the category of meaningful but non-viable changes in the text. These would be significant changes, but they're found in only a single manuscript or group of manuscripts and are unlikely to reflect the text's original meaning. For example, one scribe changed 1 Thessalonians 2:9 from "the Gospel of God" to "the Gospel of Christ," while nearly all other manuscripts have the former. This is dismissed, because it's unlikely that one medieval scribe captured something everyone else missed.

Hopefully, it can be seen that nearly all variants do not influence our understanding of the content of the New Testament. Most do not affect the meaning of the text at all, while most of those that do are non-viable. There are so many variants compared to most classical texts because there are so many manuscripts compared to most classical texts. Wallace asserts that because of the large number of manuscripts, the *number* of variants is meaningless; what matters is the *nature* of the variants (Veritas Forum). The only variants worth any attention are both meaningful and viable, changing the meaning of the text and having a good chance of being authentic.

These meaningful and viable variants make up the smallest category, representing only one-fifth of one percent of all textual variants. This includes anything that changes our reading of the passage, even if the change is not theologically significant. For example, Mark 9:29 discusses demons that can only be exorcised by prayer and fasting, but it's likely that the passage originally ended without mentioning fasting. This passage does affect orthopraxy, with practical effects for exorcists, but not theology.

Seven variants in this category are selected by Ehrman at the end of *Misquoting Jesus* (2007), as the major problematic passages he considers most meaningful and viable:

- Mark 16:9–20
- John 7:53, 8:11
- 1 John 5:7–8
- Mark 1:41
- Hebrews 2:9
- John 1:18
- Matthew 24:36

The first three are the most significant, but they have been known by New Testament scholars for over a century. In fact, many translations of the Bible include a note stating something to the effect of "the earliest manuscripts do not have this passage (or passages) in them."

Mark 16:9–20 is the resurrection narrative in Mark. The earliest manuscripts end on a cliffhanger, with the young man in white at the tomb of Jesus telling Salome and the two Marys that Jesus has been resurrected, but without confirmation by Jesus's resurrection appearances. This is somewhat surprising, but it's a weak argument from silence that the earliest Christians simply did not believe in the resurrection. In fact, the original Greek has the look of interrupted text, and it is plausibly conjectured that the Gospel's original ending was simply lost.

John 7:53–58:11 is the story of the woman caught in adultery. Its loss would admittedly be disheartening to many Christians, especially considering the emotional weight and strong cultural imprint of the phrase "Let him who is without sin cast the first stone." It might encourage them to know the story still has a very old provenance, despite its agreed-upon status as a later addition to John's text, so it may still be based on fact. Regardless, no theological systems would collapse in its absence.

1 John 5:7–8 includes the infamous *Comma Johanneum* (Johannine Comma), a confirmation of the Trinity that states that the Father, the Word, and the Holy Spirit are one (Wallace, *The Textual Problem*). This reads as "in heaven, the Father, the Word, and the Holy Spirit, and these three are one. And there are three that testify on Earth." The shorter version reads, "For there are three that testify, the Spirit and the water and the blood, and these three are in agreement." The latter is the version that scholars agree is most reliable and is notably less explicit about the Trinity. Although this is no secret, the Revised Standard Version excluded it in 1885 (Wallace, "The Gospel According to Bart") and it has been amended in modern translations such as the New International and New Revised Standard Version.

Of the seven passages Ehrman mentioned, none affects our understanding of the miracle claims of the Gospels. Only Mark 1:41 has anything to do with a miracle, but the discrepancy doesn't concern whether or how a miracle was done, only whether Jesus felt compassion or anger when he did it. Here, Wallace agrees with Ehrman that it was anger ("Lost in Transmission," p. 21).

Thus, when Harris writes that "many" passages "show signs of later interpolation . . . and these passages have found their way into the canon" (*The Moral Landscape*, p. 252), his claim is partially true, but mostly overstated. People have added passages over the centuries, but very few have made their way into the canon. Of those few, even fewer have any theological significance, and none of those affect our understanding of the texts' miracle claims.

The Canon

Next, Harris aims at the formation of the canon, suggesting that the selection of books makes them unreliable.

> In fact, there are whole sections of the New Testament, like the Book of Revelation, that were long considered spurious, that were included in the Bible only after many centuries of neglect; and there are other books, like the Shepherd of Hermas, that were venerated as part of the Bible for hundreds of years only to be rejected finally as false scripture. (*The Moral Landscape*, pp. 252–53)

It's true that Eusebius cast a dubious eye on Revelation's eschatology, writing in the early fourth century. But the book's authoritative status and attribution to John the Apostle were strongly affirmed by a who's who of earlier church fathers east and west, including Papias, Irenaeus, Justin Martyr, Melito, Clement of Alexandria, Origen, and Tertullian. As for *The Shepherd of Hermas*, this book was never seriously close to being canonized. In chapters 10 and 20 of *De Pudicitia*, Tertullian, a church father who lived between the second and third centuries, rejected it as apocryphal. He claimed that the councils of churches had regularly judged it not to be canon and that the Epistle to the Hebrews was more widely accepted. So, Harris's specifics are off or at least overstated. To describe the assembly of the Bible as a "haphazard . . . cobbling together" (*The Moral Landscape*, p. 253) is to caricature the canonization process.

So, if Harris's overall point is that we can't know what the Gospels originally had to say, he's only correct in rare, usually theologically minor instances. These don't affect our ability to build a robust case for the Gospels' integrity as reliable source documents, even though there might be small discrepancies that would trouble a committed biblical inerrantist. But it's one thing to question biblical inerrancy. It's another thing to question biblical reliability. Harris offers no compelling reason to abandon the latter.

How Unique Should Miracles Be?

The first point that Harris makes in his polemic against the miracles of Jesus is about their lack of uniqueness. He claims that "miracle stories are as common as house dust" and "All of Jesus's otherworldly powers have been attributed to the South Indian guru Sathya Sai Baba by vast numbers of living eyewitnesses" (*The Moral Landscape*, p. 167). Sathya Sai Baba is the center of a great deal of controversy regarding authenticity and ethics. Still, even if he weren't, he placed himself alongside Jesus in a shared mission rather than in competition. But Harris is making the point that Sai Baba is but one among many incarnations of this miracle-dealing, virgin-born spiritual leader, none of which are believable. This argument seems to leave Christians with one of only two options:

1. Dismiss miraculous figures from other religions as frauds, exclusively acknowledging miracles done by Judeo-Christian figures like Jesus, the Prophets, and the Apostles.

2. Acknowledge that there is as much evidence for the miracles of other religions and therefore deny the uniqueness of the Bible.

However, biblical tradition has long rejected this as a false dichotomy, both acknowledging the existence of other miracles and maintaining that those done with the power of the true God are set apart. When Moses and Aaron confront the Pharaoh, and Aaron's staff transforms into a snake, the Egyptian magicians follow suit, transforming their staves into snakes as well (Exodus 7:10–12). Prophetic dreams were given to an Egyptian cupbearer and baker (Genesis 40: 5–19), a Pharaoh (Genesis 41:1–8), and the king of Babylon (Daniel 2:1–45). When the Gospel was being preached in Samaria, a man named Simon performed magic and had many convinced that he was "the power of God" (Acts 8:10). We encounter individuals with access to supernatural abilities throughout the Bible, many of whom are neither Jewish nor Christian. The Bible has never denied their existence but has instead chosen to contextualize them.

In the Moses and Aaron story, Aaron's transformed staff consumes both those which belonged to the Egyptian magicians (Exodus 7:12), demonstrating that the God of Israel was more powerful than the gods of Egypt. The dreams given to the pagans (Genesis 40–41; Daniel 2) indeed bore truths about future events, but the interpretation of those truths was only accessible through an intermediary, such as Joseph or Daniel, who remained loyal to the God of Israel. The magician Simon may have had magic, but he was still wildly impressed with the miracles performed by Philip (Acts 8:14). When he offered the Apostles money in exchange for the Holy Spirit, Peter chastised him for thinking that it could be bought (Acts 8:18–20), demonstrating that God's gifts are wholly different from the magic Simon learned.

These examples demonstrate one of the essential characteristics of the Bible: it both engages with and sets itself apart from other religions. John H. Walton's great work *The Lost World of Genesis One* places the creation story of the Bible within its Ancient Near Eastern context, arguing that it was written as a reply to rival creation stories. Does their Enuma Elish say the primordial waters mingled to create life? Well, we say that the Spirit of God was above the waters at the beginning (Genesis 1:2). This theme continues throughout the Bible. They've got a flood because the gods can't get any rest; we've got a flood because human hearts were evil (Genesis 6:5). The book of Proverbs seems to borrow from the Egyptian *Instruction of Amenemope*, as if to say, "Sure, Egyptians have some wisdom, but it's incomplete without our God." The Bible and its believers have never claimed that it holds no similarities with other religions, but for every similarity, there is something that sets it apart. So, Harris's claim that miracles have been attested across the world is in concert with, rather than contention with, Christianity.

At the same time, Christians aren't compelled to concede that it is special pleading to claim stronger attestation for the Gospel miracles than for various other religious miracles. Objective criteria can be brought to bear on all of the above, and the case can be made that the Gospels pass muster where many other services simply fail. This isn't intellectually dishonest. It's just good historical praxis.

How Unique Are the Miracles?

Harris explicitly points out a few miracles he believes to violate scientific laws (Harris, 2010, p. 168): the virgin birth, the resurrection, the ascent to Heaven, and God's inconsistent intervention in our world. Of these, the virgin birth is the one he expands on the most, citing cases like Genghis Khan and Alexander the Great. But even a cursory look at the primary sources reveals that these and many other popularly cited "virgin births" are not "virgin" at all. Quite the contrary. We don't even have a virgin birth story for Genghis Khan himself, only an ancestor of his, who, according to *The Secret History of the Mongols*, was conceived when a glowing deity impregnated the mythical Alan Gua. Plutarch's *Life of Alexander* describes an account where Alexander's mother is impregnated by Zeus, who took the form of a serpent. Many other cases could be cited that involve a physically incarnated deity impregnating a human. So, what's left? Not much. There are a few disputed accounts of Lao Tzu being born of a virgin, a disputed Native American account, and probably a few others which bear some cultural significance that we've overlooked. However, it is not true on any substantial level that the Christian template for virgin birth is cross-cultural and widespread.

The resurrection wasn't greatly emphasized by Harris but is worth addressing because of its centrality to Christianity. Within its cultural context, the Christian resurrection story is novel. In fact, its novelty is of central importance to New Testament scholar N.T. Wright's great defense of the resurrection, *The Resurrection of the Son of God* (2003). In this work, Wright asserts that any scholar who concludes that the early Christians came to believe in the bodily resurrection and were wrong about it must explain how that happened (pp. 6–7). The ancient people were not under the impression that rising from the dead was a common occurrence, and the Romans and Greeks would have thought they sounded ridiculous. It would have been much less conspicuous if the New Testament authors had chosen to describe it as a spiritual resurrection. Instead, they go out of their way to express the physicality of the resurrection, with the resurrected Jesus eating fish (Luke 24:40–43; John 21:9–14) or telling Thomas to touch his wounds (Luke 24:39). Worse yet, the resurrection of Jesus didn't even fit in with the beliefs of his own people! The resurrection which they expected would have involved everyone at once at the end of the ages, none of this "first fruits" nonsense where a single guy gets resurrected without anyone else. The idea of a dying and rising Messiah was not part of Jewish theology at the time and would have been an extremely odd thing to make up if the Jesus movement was looking to gain any traction. Finally, and significantly, the polymodal (multi-sensory) physicality of Jesus's resurrection appearances leaves no plausible room for honest error, provided the Gospels are a true reflection of the apostles' earliest reports. This itself can be debated, but scholars such as Dr. Peter J. Williams and Dr. Lydia McGrew, along with many older scholars, have made the conservative case rigorously, using arguments from incidental interlocking, intimate familiarity with local culture and geography, and many other internal and external confirmations of reliability.

The Historical Account of Miracles

It seems that Harris's core issue with the miracles of Jesus is revealed by his invocation of Hume (*The Moral Landscape*, p. 253), who said: "No testimony is sufficient to establish a miracle, unless the testimony be of such a kind, that its falsehood would be more miraculous, than the fact, which it endeavors to establish . . ." (*Philosophical Works*, p. 131). If Harris accepts this, it wouldn't matter if we had one hundred percent confidence that all the Gospels' content had been present since the earliest manuscripts, if they'd been written immediately after the life of Jesus, and if they bore no similarities whatever to any other religion. Testimony of that sort would still be insufficient. C.S. Lewis, responding to Hume's view of miracles, wrote:

> Now the regularity of Nature's course, says Hume, is supported by something better than the majority vote of past experiences: it is supported by their unanimous vote, or, as Hume says, by "firm and unalterable experience." There is, in fact, "uniform experience" against Miracle; otherwise, says Hume, it would not be a Miracle. A miracle is therefore the most improbable of all events. It is always more probable that the witnesses were lying or mistaken than that a miracle occurred. (*Miracles*)

Lewis opens *Miracles* by pointing out how the philosophical views we have prior to looking at evidence of miracles can dictate the way we interpret the evidence. He gives three types of views which we might hold (*Miracles*, p. 9):

1. They are impossible, in which case no evidence can convince us.

2. They are possible, but improbable, so only mathematically demonstrative evidence will convince us.

3. They are not intrinsically improbable, so existing evidence ought to be enough to convince us that they've occurred several times.

Lewis places Hume in the second category, requiring a mathematically compelling argument to weight the probability in favor of the miracle. He states that "history never provides that degree of evidence for any event," and so, if we think like Hume, "history can never convince us that a miracle occurred" (*Miracles*, p. 9). The agnostic philosopher John Earman would agree with Lewis's assessment of Hume, even provocatively titling an entire book *Hume's Abject Failure*. And more can even be said beyond Lewis, as contemporary work like McGrew and McGrew's "The Argument from Miracles: A Cumulative Case for the Resurrection of Jesus of Nazareth" shows how a compelling probabilistic argument could, in fact, be plausibly mounted and modeled.

To conclude, the contents and history of the Gospels are not so mysterious that we can have little to no confidence in them. In fact, "we have sufficient data to . . . construct the original New Testament in virtually every place" according to Wallace ("Inerrancy and the Text"). We can further have confidence that the Gospel writers were up close to the facts and giving a reliable report of the events related. And even if other traditions had some plausibly similar miracle claims, this wouldn't be grounds to dismiss Christian claims, because neither Christians nor Jews have made the claim that other cultures cannot have miracles, only that their miracles are reliably attested and set apart. In the final analysis, there is no reason for a Christian historian to check his faith at the door while doing history. Of course, if Harris thinks like Hume, then history could never change his mind anyway.

Works Cited

CNSTM. 2011. SMU Debate. Retrieved from The Center for the
    Study of New Testament Manuscripts (October 1st)
    <www.csntm.org/videos>.
Earman, John. 2000. *Hume's Abject Failure: The Argument
    Against Miracles*. Oxford University Press.
Ehrman, Bart D. 2007. *Misquoting Jesus*. New York: HarperOne.
———. 2011. *The Orthodox Corruption of Scripture*. Oxford
    University Press.
Ehrman, Bart D., and Daniel B. Wallace. 2011. The Textual
    Reliability of the New Testament: A Dialogue. In R.B. Stewart,
    ed., *The Reliability of the New Testament*. Fortress Press.
Gurry, P.J. 2016. The Number of Variants in the Greek New
    Testament: A Proposed Estimate. *New Testament Studies*.
Harris, Sam. 2011 [2010]. *The Moral Landscape*. Free Press.
Hume, David. 1996. *The Philosophical Works of David Hume*.
    Thoemmes.
Leoni, T. 2009. The Text of Josephus's Works: An Overview.
    Journal for the Study of Judaism.
Lewis, C.S. (2015). *Miracles*. HarperOne.
———. 2017. The Efficacy of Prayer. In C.S. Lewis, *The World's
    Last Night* (pp. 1–10). HarperOne.
McGrew, Timothy, and Lydia McGrew. 2009. The Argument from
    Miracles: A Cumulative Case for the Resurrection of Jesus
    of Nazareth. In William Lane Craig and J.P. Moreland, eds.
    The Blackwell Companion to Natural Theology. Wiley
    Blackwell.
Thucydides. 1954. *The History of the Peloponnesian War*. Penguin.
The Veritas Forum. 2018. *How Badly Was the New Testament
    Corrupted?* Veritas at SDSU [video]
    <www.youtube.com/watch?v=zZ5cgQUJnrI&t=4291s>.
Wallace, Daniel B. 2004, June 25). *The Textual Problem in 1 John
    5:7–8*. Retrieved from Bible: <https://bible.org/article/textual-
    problem-1-john-57-8>.
———. 2006. The Gospel According to Bart: A Review Article
    of *Misquoting Jesus* by Bart Ehrman. *The Journal of the
    Evangelical Theological Society*, 327–349.
———. 2009. Challenges in New Testament Textual Criticism
    for the Twenty-First Century. *Journal of the Evangelical
    Theological Society*, 79–100.
———. 2010. Inerrancy and the Text of the New Testament:
    Assessing the Logic of the Agnostic View. In M.R. Licona and
    W.A. Dembski, *Evidence for God: 50 Arguments for Faith
    from the Bible, History, Philosophy, and Science*. Baker Books.

————. 2011. Lost in Transmission: How Badly Did the Scribes Corrupt the New Testament Text? In Wallace, *Revisiting the Corruption of the New Testament: Manuscript, Patristic, and Apocryphal Evidence*. Kregel.

Walton, John H. 2009. *The Lost World of Genesis One: Ancient Cosmology and the Origins Debate*. InterVarsity Press.

Williams, Peter J., and Bart Ehrman. 2019. The Story of Jesus: Are the Gospels Historically Reliable? Premier Unbelievable? (video) <www.youtube.com/watch?v=ZuZPPGvF_2I&t=1778s>.

Wright, N.T. 2003. *The Resurrection of the Son of God*. Fortress Press.

Zeichmann, C.B. 2017. The Date of Mark's Gospel apart from the Temple and Rumors of War: The Taxation Episode (12:13–17) as Evidence. *The Catholic Biblical Quarterly*.

[19]
Scientism as Religion and Religion as Wisdom

RON DART

The publication by Sam Harris of *The Four Horsemen: The Conversation that Sparked an Atheist Revolution* (2019) did a splendid job of summarizing the science contra religion drama that emerged as the most recent act of the centuries-long debate.

Three distinct positions can be taken in this intellectual melodrama of sorts. There is science as the enlightened and rational way forward, religion dated, backward, and superstitious. Such an approach idealizes a certain type of science (the scientific family is a layered and complex one) and demonizes religion.

The reaction to such an approach, often by various types of religious fundamentalists, is to demonize science and a certain type of rationalism and idealize a form of reactionary religion (or alternate yet questionable views of science). This either-or approach has a long history that rarely leads to serious or substantive thoughtful conclusions—scientism and religiosity rarely birth healthy children.

There is, though, a third way that is more conducive to meaningful dialogue between good science and thoughtful religion. The third way is more mature, and is more dialogical and wary of simplistic polarizing tendencies that yield little significant intellectual fruit.

When I lived in Switzerland in the high Alps in the early 1970s, I was quite taken by Michael Polanyi's *Personal Knowledge: Towards a Post-Critical Philosophy. Personal*

Knowledge is a demanding read by a gifted scientist, but it is much more philosophically sophisticated and nuanced in its understanding of the varied methods of science and how different methods both reveal and conceal what can be known. As Polanyi rightly noted, the personal does much to predetermine insights, conclusions, and various notions of objectivity. A more historic and comprehensive approach to the science-religion dialogue can also be found in such serious scholars as Elaine Howard Ecklund, Robert Russell, Paul Davies, Keith Ward, and John Hedley Brooke, to name but a few thinkers who have grappled with the science-religion issue and go to places Harris simply lacks the ability, interest, or skill to do. The "warfare thesis" between science and religion that some jousters chose to enter and remain in creates the "conflict myth" that has many an acolyte and disciple but rarely ventures into a more dialogical approach. Opposition, polarization, and conflict are lucrative.

Harris emerged with energy and a loyal following post-9/11 with his bumper crop book *The End of Faith* (2004). It was, perhaps, understandable that Islam was the target but a skewed version of Islam was described. Danger is ever present and afoot, when a thinker from one discipline enters the turf and territory of another discipline. Harris's understanding of religion tends to be meager, and the conclusions he reaches tend to reflect such a limited understanding.

I have been fortunate to teach Comparative Religions for decades and as part of such a teaching bent, the religion-science topic is regularly on the table. Of course, certain forms of religions are toxic and unhealthy, and Harris (along with many others, both religious and secular) have rightly so exposed such follies. There is nothing new about this. A read of Erasmus's sixteenth-century *In Praise of Folly* is but one portal into such critiques from within religion itself. But, Galileo's children have, equally so, a questionable history. Science has often been a docile and passive servant of state or corporate power and the consequences have been tragic for many. So, to trash the worst features of religion and offer science as the antidote is somewhat naive and cyclopean. It is much more honest, therefore, to recognize there is good, mediocre, and bad religion, just as there is good, mediocre, and bad science.

The religion-science dialogue will move to a higher and more qualitative level when the best of both heritages heed and listen to one another. But, after Harris turned on Islam in *The End of Faith*, he then turned on Christianity in *Letter to a Christian Nation* (2006). The method remained much the same. Religion is the problem—science, reason, and objectivity the antidote and solution. Should the religious and scientific dynamic in the area of intellectual, social, and political thought be reduced to such polarized either-or categories? This is typical of a fundamentalist way of thinking, for life is often more layered and subtle. Yet, there are always some who seem to have a desperate need for certainty, clarity, solid and sure answers to the troubling questions and challenges of life. There is, in short, fundamentalist thinking in the political right and left just as there is in the science-religious tensions and clashes—uncritical and uncriticized positions within the scientific clan or religious tribes are equally problematic. Alas, I fear, Harris is often uncritical of his notions of science and excessively critical of much he does not understand about religion—such is always the danger of the amateur and dilettante.

Mystery Minds versus Puzzle Minds

The French thinker Gabriel Marcel suggested that there are two types of thinkers: puzzle mind types and mystery mind types. The puzzle mind types are driven by the need to fit the pieces of the puzzle together into a solid, clear, and distinct answer. The mystery mind types realize there is much that can be known, but there is much we only know in part, crumbs on the trail that are not definite or conclusive yet evoke within fuller and finer vistas that can only be momentarily seen in and on the journey. Harris, it seems, is a committed devotee of the puzzle mind—such a thinker reveals much good but equally so, much is concealed in such an addictive need.

Next, let's turn to Jordan Peterson who is more of a mystery mind type. Peterson and Harris have had a variety of dialogues on science and religion. Peterson has attempted to hold together, in a way Harris does not, the complex and layered mythic way of both science and religion. In fact, many of Peterson's dialogical partners are keen on such questions.

In 2020, I edited a book on Jordan Peterson, *Myth and Meaning in Jordan Peterson*. In it, there is a thoughtful article by Esgrid Sikahall, "Professor Peterson, Professor Peterson: What Is Your View on . . . Science and Religion?"

Sikahall, in his article, probes, in a way Harris does not, a much more complex understanding of science and religion. He also nudges Peterson to go yet further and deeper with his mythic approach to religion and the relationship between religion and an existential approach to reading—applying sacred texts to life. This approach yields a richer discussion than a sort of questionable version of science with its monological messaging and polarization. The latter path has limited possibilities and breeds a closed-mindedness to a larger range of questions and the human thirst and hunger for meaning, purpose, and depth. I might also add, in the first book of this series, *Jordan Peterson: Critical Responses* (2022) three of the chapters (11, 12, and 19) deal with the Peterson-Harris exchanges and positions on science-religion, truth claims, and the facts-values distinction.

Hermann Hesse and *The Glass Bead Game*

Hermann Hesse was one of the most significant European writers in the mid-twentieth century, and he was a rite of passage thinker for the North American counter-culture of that era. Hesse's final summa and tome was *The Glass Bead Game* (it took more than a decade to write in the turbulent European context of the 1930s). Hesse won the Nobel Prize for Literature in 1946 for a lifetime of political, literary, artistic, religious, and scientific probes, his insights on folk-fairy tales and myth of the highest quality. But it was *The Glass Bead Game* that summarized many of the larger issues at the time and its timeless quality makes it a classic worthy of multiple meditative reads. The historic context of *The Glass Bead Game* is one in which cultural fragmentation, dis-integration, wars, and low level and pop intellectual life dominates. It is in this midst of such deterioration that the emergence of a higher level of intellectual life emerges.

In the book, the Castalian class transcends such petty and tribal tendencies—its vision and goal are to synthesize that best and noblest that has been thought and said both across time and civilization. It took many a decade for a Castalian to be trained in the art, science, and skill of historic synthesis allowing for the application for a renewal of culture and civilization moved forward into the future from its backward and reactive tendencies. A significant analogy for the Castalians was music and the way many instruments (what seemed to be different colliding, competing, and contesting sounds) could be brought together into a harmonious and convincing unity of goodness, beauty and truth.

The shorter book by Hesse that anticipated *The Glass Bead Game* was *Journey to the East* and Hesse dedicated his larger tome to "the Journeyers to the East." The East for Hesse is not the literal East. There is, yet again, as in the religion-science polarization, a tendency for the less thoughtful, to demean and denigrate Western thought and culture, including religion and Christianity and idealize the Orient and various types of Eastern religions, Buddhism being quite trendy for disaffected westerners. Such an either-or approach, I might add, we find in Harris's appeal for a certain type of Buddhism. The point to note, though, is the approach to Hesse which attempts to transcend the polarization of West versus East into a higher unity and synthesis in which Occident and Orient engage in a deeper and more meaningful form of dialogue. The East, for Hesse, was not, as mentioned above, the literal and often romanticized and idealized East by westerners in search of inner and spiritual depth. The East was, in a more metaphorical and literary manner, where the sun arises, where light emerges, where the new day begins. Such a birthing of the new day was a meeting of East and West, a meeting that synthesized contemplation, wisdom and insights that could be mined from such classical religious and cultural heritages across time and the best of civilizations. Hesse's vision of a meditative approach and immersion in such ways of being opened the portal into a grander synthesis and unity.

This vision of a higher unity that Hesse pointed to ran counter to the polarizing tendencies of certain approaches to the science-religion and orient-occident opposites that Hesse attempted to overcome. But, Hesse was also wary of such a legitimate longing for a nuanced unity and the attempt by the Castalians to embody it both in thought and deed. In *The Glass Bead Game*, the Elder Brother, a Chinese sage, says

> Anyone can create a pretty little bamboo garden in the world. But I doubt that the gardener would succeed in incorporating the world into his bamboo grove. (p. 114)

It is this attempt by the Castalians, as Hesse understood, as a German, only too well, to "incorporate the world into his bamboo grove" that was the danger, in thought and deed, in selectively choosing facts, information, statistics that fit nicely into a small intellectual grove that seems to offer clear, distinct and sure answers about the uncertainties, mysteries and ambiguities of our all too human journey (as Nietzsche rightly saw, Hesse ever engaging Nietzsche in most of his novels). Such is the tension between the perennial puzzle mind and the mystery mind, the dominance of the former often silencing or marginalizing the suggestive probes of the latter.

I have lingered on Hesse and *The Glass Bead Game* to situate Harris in a larger and longer dialogue on how science-religion and religion-spirituality (West and East) can be viewed in a confrontational and polarizing manner (many only seem to think in such a simplistic and fundamentalist manner). It should be noted, though, that Hesse was acutely aware of the limitations, in the world of thought, word, deed, and power politics that can undermine such an approach—such is the ending of *The Glass Bead Game*, future unclear and unsure. But, there can be no doubt that Hesse's approach to thought, word and deed in the religion-science and religion-spirituality dialogue is, in principle, more about unity and synthesis than polarization and antithesis. It is in this sense that Hesse can come as a kindly dialogical partner to Harris in his more either-or rather than both-and approach to these larger and more meaningful dialogues that have been with us from the beginning of time and will continue to be with us as time and the human quest and questioning ever unfolds and continues.

Socrates and Diotima

Nietzsche and Heidegger suggested that the beginning of the end of Western philosophy began with Socrates's more rational, logical, analytical approach to thinking. This approach stood in opposition to both Greek tragic thought (Aeschylus, Sophocles, Euripides) and the more speculative and contemplative Pre-Socratic way of doing philosophy.

The dialogue is a perennial one regarding whose version of Socrates Plato is embodying in his many Platonic dialogues in which Socrates is often the main protagonist, but there can be no doubt that most versions of the dialogues portray Socrates as a thinker who understands the role of authentic philosophy that approaches timeless issues in a rational, inductive, empirical, logical, and deductive manner. Those who could not withstand or justify their conclusions before such an approach were dismissed as being traditionalists, superstitious, irrational or foolishly religious. It was this methodological approach that placed reason on the throne, set such a monarch as the imperial and judicious discerner of truth and colonized and subordinated other ways of knowing and being.

Nietzsche and Heidegger, although not negating this Apollonian way of knowing, suggested there were other ways that unconcealed that which the rational way concealed. There is, though, much more to Socrates-Plato than Nietzsche-Heidegger dare and care to recognize. Yes, indeed, there is the analytical-empirical-rational Socrates, this being a lower-level way of knowing that both reveals and conceals insights and wisdom. The higher way of knowing as articulated and dramatically unfolded in Plato's *Symposium* and *Phaedrus* is about growing wings on the soul and a being led into the deeper mysteries of wisdom and love that a certain notion of reason lacks the ability, skill and method to understand. Such is the way of *"nous"* and the guidance of Diotima, the priestess mentioned in Plato's Symposium who was so important to Socrates's understanding of life. It is Diotima who respects and honors both the lower-level way of knowing but also a higher way of knowing the reason is often blind to, reason doing the puzzle mind approach. Diotima walks the receptive Socrates into the more contemplative, mystical, and meditative way of a fuller and more comprehensive unity of wisdom and love. In short, the method and approach of intuition-reason and wisdom-knowledge make for enlightened dancing partners. Such was the more complex and complicated way of classical Greek philosophy. The one-dimensional cyclopean understanding layers of knowing has been, to some degree, co-opted, in the Western enlightenment by the *logos*, the goods delivered by such an approach necessary but not sufficient for a fuller understanding that *mythos* delivers.

The ongoing dialogue, certainly worth the heeding and hearing, between Jordan Peterson and Sam Harris hovers, lingers, and returns to this tension again and again, Peterson living the complex tension in a way Harris lacks the ability to do. Yet, again, we see polarization in Harris that Peterson deftly avoids. In short, there is more subtle and nuanced thinking in Peterson than Harris. As mentioned above, Harris has a tendency to slip into a polarized approach to being and knowing: science versus religion, Buddhist meditative practices (Orient-East) versus irrational Muslim-Christian religions (Occident-West).

There is a structural pattern in how Harris interprets complex theological, philosophical, and political realities that reveal as much as they conceal. His reductionist approach is more indebted to a period of Western intellectual history he constantly recycles and is somewhat addicted to while the fuller Western ethos is much more comprehensive and open-minded. Peterson, however, points in such a direction, but he lacks the historic religious, philosophical, and political background to more maturely articulate.

William Blake and the Four Zoas

I was quite fortunate a few decades ago to correspond with some of the leading scholars and thoughtful activists on William Blake (Northrop Frye, Allen Ginsberg and Kathleen Raine). Each approached Blake from different paths and each, in their unique way, illuminated much about Blake's fourfold vision and its contemporary relevance, such a relevance having affinities with the classical Greek and the fuller Christian synthesis. Blake lived at a time in which a form of Enlightenment science and reason had come to sit on the throne, judge and jury of what is acceptable and what not. Such a tendency certainly continues within a tribe in the larger enlightenment family, the rationalist approach at odds with the romantic opposition. Blake's fourfold synthesis attempted to honor how each faculty within the human perceptual way of knowing needed to be integrated in an organic manner so all levels of reality (obvious and subtler) would be included, so the doors of perception would generously open.

Blake suggested, in his unique language, that there were four Zoas (faculties within the human perceptual lens) that needed to be united. The five senses or the bodily way of knowing was called "Tharmas." Such a purely physical and sensual way of knowing revealed much that was necessary to make sense of the material world. The next level and faculty of knowing was the emotions and intuition which Blake called "Luvah."

Those who had a stunted emotional life missed much in a basic understanding of the self, inter-relational dialogue, and intuitive insights. The third faculty of knowing was the imagination that Blake called "Urthona." Myth and imagination walked the curious and interested to places, when teamed up with "Tharmas" and "Luvah," that pointed to many perennial truths on the human journey into wisdom and insight. The final faculty of knowing was reason or "Urizen." Blake was rightly concerned that "Urizen" had usurped, imprisoned or silenced the other faculties, hence a single vision dominated by a form of rationalist scientism sat on the throne, muting the other legitimate faculties. Blake was certainly not opposed to the necessary role of "Urizen" but there was a worrisome imbalance in the force when "Urizen" commanded and demanded obedience. Blake suggested that when "Tharmas," "Luvah," "Urthana," and "Urizen" respected and legitimated the revealing-concealing role of one another, a more peaceful, just, and unitive vision would create "Albion" in England's green and pleasant land. This meant that Blake would not "cease from mental fight" until such a battle was fought to restore a deeper level of innocent on the far side of rational realism.

Harris: Hesse, Diotima and Blake

I have lightly touched on Harris's tendency to, often, slip into a polarizing approach in the religion-science and in Western-Eastern tensions in which science is understood as a variation of Buddhist meditation and a rational way of knowing that colonizes myth, imagination, and much else. Such a way of knowing and being fits snuggly and comfortably into the procrustean bed of the puzzle mind and a more one-eyed cyclopean way of seeing—such an approach both reveals much and conceals much of the better and best, the wily Odysseus ever eluding Cyclops and his kith and kin.

There is also a more subtle and nuanced way of thinking that suggests that how we see will determine what we see. In short, we need different seeing eyes to see different levels of reality. There are obvious affinities between Blake and Diotima and, in conclusion, I will turn yet again to Hesse, a dialogue between Harris and Hesse offering much to feast on and pleasantly enjoy.

Anyone can create a pretty little bamboo garden in the world. But, I doubt that the gardener would succeed in incorporating the world in his bamboo grove.

Such is always the temptation of the puzzle mind—an intellectual shrinking of the world into a small, secure, predictable bamboo garden and grove.

References

Blake, William. 1963 [1809]. *Vala, or The Four Zoas*. Clarendon.

Harris, Sam. 2004. *The End of Faith: Religion, Terror, and the Future of Reason*. Free Press.

———. 2006. *Letter to a Christian Nation*. Vintage.

Hesse, Hermann. 1957. *Journey to the East*. Noonday.

———. 1969. *The Glass Bead Game (Magister Ludi)*. Bantam.

Hitchens, Christopher, Sam Harris, Richard Dawkins, and Daniel Dennett. 2019. *The Four Horsemen: The Conversation that Sparked an Atheist Revolution*. Random House.

Marcel, Gabriel. 1973. *Tragic Wisdom and Beyond: Including Conversations Between Paul Ricoeur and Gabriel Marcel*. Northwestern University Press.

———. 2021. *The Mystery of Being, Volume I: Reflection and Mystery*. St. Augustine's Press.

Polanyi, Michael. 1958. *Personal Knowledge: Towards a Post-Critical Philosophy*. Harper and Row.

Sikahall, Esgrid. 2020. Professor Peterson, Professor Peterson: What Is Your View on . . . Science and Religion? In Ron Dart, ed. *Myth and Meaning in Jordan Peterson*. Lexham.

Woien, Sandra, ed. 2022. *Jordan Peterson: Critical Responses*. Open Universe.

About the Authors

MICHAEL BARROS is a teacher in the Humanities Department at Boise Classical Academy in Boise, Idaho. He received his MA in Biblical and Theological Studies from Trevecca Nazarene University and is a PhD student in the Department of Psychology at Northcentral University. His research interests include theories of perception and narrative transportation. He enjoys the integration of psychology and theology and hopes to study the transportation effects of biblical narratives.
E-mail: m.barros@boiseclassicalacademy.com

LISA BELLANTONI is an Associate Professor of Philosophy at Albright College. She received her doctorate from Vanderbilt University. Her books include *The Triple Helix: The Soul of Bioethics* (2012) and *Moral Progress: A Process Critique of MacIntyre* (2000). Her current research focuses on the social and political impact of emerging technologies, particularly artificial intelligence, and on our responsibilities to future persons. She is also interested in how science fiction influences our ethical attitudes towards space exploration, human enhancement, and other future engineering technologies.
Email: lbellantoni@albright.edu

ERIK BOORNAZIAN is a graduate of Eastern Connecticut State University and a professional poker player based in Florida. He has a wide variety of interests, including behavior analysis, game theory, and comedy. He published a paper on altruism in *The*

Behavior Analyst and has presented at the Berkshire Association for Behavior Analysis and Therapy.
Email: boornaziane@gmail.com

MARC CHAMPAGNE is an award-winning philosopher and regular faculty member in the Department of Philosophy at Kwantlen Polytechnic University. He is the author of *Consciousness and the Philosophy of Signs: How Peircean Semiotics Combines Phenomenal Qualia and Practical Effects* (2018) and *Myth, Meaning, and Antifragile Individualism: On the Ideas of Jordan Peterson* (2020). His work has appeared in journals such as *Cybernetics and Human Knowing*, *Synthese*, *Phenomenology and the Cognitive Sciences*, *Philosophical Psychology*, *Cognitive Semiotics*, *History and Philosophy of Logic*, and many more. He holds a PhD in Philosophy from York University and a PhD in Semiotics from the University of Quebec in Montreal, and he did his post-doctoral studies at the University of Helsinki. Email: marc.champagne@kpu.ca

RON DART has taught in the Department of Political Science, Philosophy, and Religious Studies at the University of the Fraser Valley (British Columbia) since 1990. Ron has published more than forty books, the most recent being *The Gospel According to Hermes: Intimations of Christianity in Greek Myth, Poetry, and Philosophy* (2021), *Myth and Meaning in Jordan Peterson: A Christian Perspective* (2020) and *Hermann Hesse: Phoenix Arising* (2019). He is on the National Executive of The Thomas Merton Society of Canada and is the Canadian contact for the Evelyn Underhill Society and Bede Griffith Sangha.

MAANELI "MAX" DERAKHSHANI is a postdoctoral researcher currently based in the Department of Mathematics at Rutgers University, New Brunswick. He completed his PhD in the Foundations of Physics at Universiteit Utrecht under Professor Guido Bacciagaluppi, and continues to work on the Foundations of Physics as his primary area of research. Dr. Derakhshani has published his research in journals such as *Physics Letters A, Journal of Physics, Pure and Applied Mathematics Quarterly, Physics of Life Reviews*, and the series Boston Studies in the Philosophy of Science: his work has also been discussed in *New Scientist, Science Magazine, EurekAlert!*, and the Foundational Questions Institute blog. Dr. Derakhshani has been awarded grants from the Foundational Questions Institute and John

Templeton Foundation, and is currently a member of the Foundational Questions Institute and Fellow of the John Bell Institute for the Foundations of Physics.
Email: maanelid@yahoo.com.

JAMES DILLER is a professor in the Department of Psychological Science at Eastern Connecticut State University. He earned his doctoral degree from the behavior analysis training program at West Virginia University. His research interests include the philosophy of radical behaviorism, issues around pedagogy and training of behavior analysts, and maladaptive choice.
Email: dillerj@easternct.edu

MEGAN DRURY is a Midlands4Cities funded PhD Researcher at The University of Nottingham in the UK. Megan has focused her doctoral thesis on the ontology of sex, the metaphysics of gender, and the phenomenology of transgender experiences. She is particularly interested in the underlying motivations of the anti-trans ideological production of 'sex' as a valuable 'objective' category and explores the connections between bodies, identities, discipline, and politics in her work.
Email: Megan.Drury@nottingham.ac.uk

DAVID GORDON is a Senior Fellow of the Ludwig von Mises Institute in Auburn, Alabama, and Editor of *The Journal of Libertarian Studies*. He is author of *The Philosophical Origins of Austrian Economics (2020), An Introduction to Economic Reasoning* (2016), *The Essential Rothbard* (2007), *Resurrecting Marx: The Analytical Marxists on Exploitation, Freedom, and Justice (1991),* and *Critics of Marx (1986).* A three-volume anthology of Dr. Gordon's articles and reviews was published in 2017 as *An Austro-Libertarian View.* He is editor of *Secession, State, and Liberty* (1998) and co-editor of H.B. Acton's *Morals of Markets and Other Essays* (1993). He has contributed to *Analysis, Mind, Ethics,* and many other journals.
Email: dgordon@mises.com

STEPHEN R.C. HICKS, PhD, is a Professor of Philosophy at Rockford University, USA, and has had visiting positions at Georgetown University in Washington DC, University of Kasimir the Great in Poland, Oxford University's Harris Manchester College in England, and Jagiellonian University in Poland. He is the author of *Explaining Postmodernism: Skepticism and Socialism from Rousseau to Foucault* (2004) and *Nietzsche and the Nazis: A Personal View* (2010), as well as articles in *Review of Metaphysics, Business Ethics Quarterly*, and *The Wall Street Journal*.

LEONARD KAHN is Associate Dean of the College of Arts and Sciences and an Associate Professor in the Department of Philosophy at Loyola University New Orleans. He is also the 2021–2022 Donald and Beverly Freeman Fellow at the US Naval Academy's Stockdale Center for Ethical Leadership. His main areas of scholarship are moral theory and applied ethics. He edited John Stuart Mill's *On Liberty* (2004) and *Mill on Justice* (2012), and co-edited *Consequentialism and Environmental Ethics* (2013). He is the author of articles in *Philosophical Studies*, *The Journal of Moral Philosophy*, *Ethical Theory and Practice*, *Ethics, Policy, and Environment*, *Essays in Philosophy*, and *Southwest Philosophical Studies* as well as of chapters in many books, including, most recently, *Autonomous Vehicle Ethics: The Trolley Problem and Beyond* (2022) and *Applying Nonideal Theory to Bioethics: Living and Dying in a Nonideal World* (2022). Email: lakahn@loyno.edu

JOBST LANDGREBE is a scientist and entrepreneur with a background in philosophy, mathematics, neuroscience, and bioinformatics. Landgrebe is also the founder of Cognotekt, a German AI company which has since 2013 provided working systems used by companies in areas such as insurance claims management, real estate management, and medical billing. After more than ten years in the AI industry, he has developed an exceptional understanding of the limits and potential of AI. Dr. Landgrebe is co-author, with Barry Smith, of *Why Machines Will Never Rule the World: Artificial Intelligence without Fear* (2022). Email: jobst.landgrebe@cognotekt.com

JOHN LEMOS is the McCabe Professor of Philosophy at Coe College in Cedar Rapids, Iowa. His philosophical interests lie primarily in the areas of free will and moral responsibility, evolutionary biology and philosophy, and ethics. He has published three books: *Commonsense Darwinism: Evolution, Morality, and the Human Condition* (2008), *Freedom, Responsibility, and Determinism: A Philosophical Dialogue* (2013), and *A Pragmatic Approach to Libertarian Free Will* (2018). In addition, he has published numerous articles in a variety of

journals, such as *Dialectica, Law and Philosophy, Metaphilosophy, Philosophia, Philosophy of the Social Sciences*, as well as others.
Email: jlemos@coe.edu

BETHEL MCGREW holds a double bachelor's in philosophy and mathematics and a PhD in mathematics from Western Michigan University. Her work has appeared in *First Things, National Review, The Spectator, The Critic,* and *Plough*, among other outlets, and her Substack is one of the top twenty Faith newsletters on the platform. Under her former pen name, she contributed to Ron Dart's edited anthology *Myth and Meaning in Jordan Peterson: A Christian Perspective* (2020) and to Sandra Woien's *Jordan Peterson: Critical Responses* (2022).

REG NAULTY holds a BA in Philosophy from the University of Adelaide and an MA and PhD from Australian National University. He has worked as a lecturer in philosophy and senior lecturer in philosophy and religion at Charles Sturt University in Riverina in New South Wales. He has published over two hundred articles, reviews, and poems in seven countries; he mainly writes about philosophy of religion, religion, and social philosophy. He is a member of the Society of Friends (Quakers), leans to the universal church, and is married with four children and eleven grandchildren.
Email: mardi.reg@bigpond.com

RAY SCOTT PERCIVAL is a philosopher specializing in philosophy of science and philosophy of mind. He wrote *The Myth of the Closed Mind: Understanding Why and How People Are Rational* (2012), and the documentary *Liberty Loves Reason* (2018). He has taught at the University of Lancaster and the United Arab Emirates University. He co-founded and edited (with Barry McMullin) one of the first academic websites, The Karl Popper Web, and the peer-reviewed journal *The Critical Rationalist*, and organized the Annual Conference on the Philosophy of Sir Karl Popper. Dr. Percival is the founder of Enlightenment Defended (2020), an online discussion community. He has published articles and reviews for *Nature, The New Scientist, Science Spectrum, The Times Higher Educational Supplement, National Review*, and *Quillette*.
Email: profpercival@yahoo.com

LUCAS RIJANA is a political scientist completing his Master's in Political and Social Theory at the University of Buenos Aires. He has taught at the University of San Isidro as Assistant Professor. His research focuses on freedom and domination in contemporary republican theory. He argues against systemic conceptions of domination. He currently resides in Mannheim, Germany.
Email: lucasrijana@gmail.com

ANTONY SAMMEROFF is a psychotherapist based in Glasgow, Scotland, a podcaster and economics journalist, published with the Mises Institute, The Foundation for Economic Education, and The Future of Freedom Foundation. He is the author of *Universal Basic Income: For and Against* (2019). Representing a libertarian point of view, he has debated prominent leftists, including Richard Wolfe, Martin Ford, and Ben Burgis, and he had a whole week devoted to him on the Tom Woods Show.
Email: frequency528@hotmail.co.uk

BARRY SMITH is one of the most widely cited contemporary philosophers. He is the author of *Austrian Philosophy: The Legacy of Franz Brentano* (1995), co-author of *Building Ontologies with Basic Formal Ontology* (2015), editor of *Structure and Gestalt* (1981) and co-author (with Jobst Landgrebe) of *Why Machines Will Never Rule the World: Artificial Intelligence without Fear* (2022). Professor Smith has made influential contributions to the foundations of ontology and data science, especially in the biomedical domain. Most recently, his work has led to the creation of an international standard in the ontology field (ISO/IEC 21838), which is the first example of a piece of philosophy that has been subjected to the ISO standardization process.
Email: ifomis@gmail.com

DAVID RAMSAY STEELE is the author of *The Mystery of Fascism: David Ramsay Steele's Greatest Hits* (2019), *Orwell Your Orwell: A Worldview on the Slab* (2017), *Atheism Explained: From Folly to Philosophy* (2008), and *From Marx to Mises: Post-Capitalist Society and the Challenge of Economic Calculation* (1992). He is co-author, with Michael R. Edelstein, of *Three Minute Therapy: Change Your Thinking, Change Your Life* (1997; second edition 2019) and *Therapy Breakthrough: Why Some Psychotherapies Work Better than Others* (2013). Dr. Steele received

the 2017 Thomas S. Szasz Award for Outstanding Contributions to the Cause of Civil Liberties.
Email: dramsaysteele@gmail.com

MARK WARREN is an Associate Professor of philosophy at Daemen University. He received his doctorate of philosophy at the University of Miami in 2014. His areas of studies include metaethics and metaphysics.
Email: mwarren@daemen.edu

SANDRA WOIEN is a Senior Lecturer in the School of Historical, Philosophical, and Religious Studies at Arizona State University. Her research interests primarily comprise theoretical concepts of well-being and their practical application to pivotal life decisions such as end-of-life dilemmas. She is the editor of *Jordan Peterson: Critical Responses* (2022), and her work has appeared in *The Conversation, American Journal of Bioethics,* and *BMC Medical Ethics*.
Email: sandra.woien@asu.edu

Index